SHROUDED MEMORIES

True Stories from the White Mountains of New Hampshire

Written by Floyd W. Ramsey

Shrouded Memories

Copyright © 1994 by Floyd W. Ramsey
Originally published by the author in January 1995
First Bondcliff Books paperback edition 2002
Third Bondcliff Books paperback edition 2005
Fourth Bondcliff Books paperback edition 2010

Library of Congress Control Number: 2002106629
ISBN 1-931271-05-4

All rights reserved. No part of this book may be reproduced in any form or by any electronic or mechanical means including storage and retrieval systems without permission in writing from the publisher and/or author, except by a reviewer who may quote brief passages.

Text and composition by Glen Press, Lincoln, N.H.

Printed in the United States by Sherwin Dodge Printers, Littleton, N.H.

Additional copies of this book may be obtained directly from:
Bondcliff Books
P.O. Box 385
Littleton, NH 03561

To The Reader

It is my fervent wish that you will enjoy reading this book as much as I have enjoyed writing it. In it you will meet many different families and individuals who began their lives with the same dreams and aspirations that we all have. However, in some instances fate had plans for them that were different from their own. As a consequence, something strange and dreadful happened to them. This fact is all too clearly illustrated in the story of the Willey family who lived in Crawford Notch in the 1820's, and also in the case of the Bugbee-Towne families who lived in Lancaster in the 1880's.

Though much of what I wrote about occurred long before I was born, I actually knew a few of the people whose lives I chronicled. For example, for a brief period in my life I worked with Elie Gendron at the paper mill in Lincoln. He was a rotary cutter operator and I was a sweeper. By chance we happened to be the last two men to leave our department on that last Saturday of his life. Just before punching out he jokingly asked me, "Do you know why I never leave any beer in my refrigerator when I go away for the weekend?" Laughing, I confessed that I didn't. With a chuckle, he said, "Because in case anything happens to me, I don't want my relatives drinking it all up before I get back."

He was murdered the next day near the Cog Railroad!

Though I never met Drs. Miller and Quinn personally, their particular tragedy was to have an unforgettable impact on my life. I relate the extremely unusual manner in which I became involved with them in the story entitled, "The Missing Doctors." In preserving their memory through this story, I hope that in some small measure this helps to atone for my failure to act on their behalf at the time that their drama was first unfolding.

On a more positive note, by writing the story "The Night the Bomber Crashed," a segment of our local World War II history has been preserved in ways that I never dreamed possible at the time I wrote it. Following its initial publication in the popular quarterly magazine entitled *"Magnetic North,"* it was subsequently reprinted in our state-wide newspaper, *"The New Hampshire Sunday News."* Later it was dramatized on public television on the highly acclaimed program, *"New Hampshire Crossroads."* The host, Fritz Wetherbee, has termed it one of the best episodes he has narrated over the past five years. As a consequence, the incident has aired repeatedly since its first showing over the Labor Day weekend in 1992. Finally, it reached another wide audience when it was serialized in the excellent advertising medium, *"The White Mountain Shopper."*

In conclusion, I want to state that the writing of this book has enabled me to continue my role in life as a teacher. When I left the classroom for the last time on January 27, 1984, due to health problems, for seven years afterwards I awoke every morning dreaming that I was still in the classroom. Through that period of time, while earning my living as a medical courier, I was able to research and write the majority of stories that comprise this book. Now that the task is completed, if there was one last lesson that I could teach it would be this: Love Jesus with all of your heart every waking moment of every day for the rest of your life. I do. That is what has made this book possible. Without Him I couldn't have done it.

*This book is dedicated to my wife, Laura-Beth;
my mother, Catherine;
my daughter, Bonnie;
and to all of the Religious
who have been so special
in my life.*

Acknowledgments

This book would not have been possible without the patient understanding, encouragement and assistance given by my wife, Laura-Beth; nor without the interest shown in my writings by my mother, Catherine; my daughter, Bonnie; my brother, Bill; my sisters, Franny Fowler, Pat Bennett, Betty Dauphine, and Kathryn Moyer; my mother-in-law, Sadie Barry; and my brother-in-law Charles Barry, and his wife, Rebecca, an excellent writer who is a constant source of inspiration to me.

I owe a special debt of gratitude to my first editor, James McIntosh of Franconia, who published my early articles in the excellent quarterly magazine, "Magnetic North." I am also equally indebted to Glen Parker, publisher of "The White Mountain Shopper," who not only popularized my articles but also made it possible for them to be published in book form. This completes a dream that I have had ever since early childhood. I also want to extend a special thanks to his wonderful staff which is comprised of Judy Boyle, Sue Whitman, Minda M. Black, Fred Campbell and Gregory Nault.

I also wish to acknowledge my sincere gratitude to the following for the many ways in which they kindly and patiently assisted me throughout my years of research: Kenneth Cramer, Archivist, and Sue Cox, Reference Section, Baker Library, Hanover, NH; Richard J. Wolfe, Curator, Rare Books, Countway Library of Medicine, Boston, MA; Constance Carter, Library of Congress, Washington, DC; Lisabeth Holloway, Director, History of Footcare and Footwear, Pennsylvania College, Pennsylvania, PA; Gabor S. Boritt, Civil War Studies, Gettysburg College, Gettysburg, PA; Ann Shumard, Curatorial Assistant, Office of Photographs, The National Portrait Gallery, Washington, DC; Connie McBirney, Curator of Manuscripts, Indianapolis Historical Society, Indianapolis, IN; Dr. Roderick J. Bachmann, D.P.M., and his wife, Brenda, Warren, NH; Kathryn E. Bulchis, District Ranger, and Forester Connie Chaney, Androscoggin Ranger District, Gorham, NH; Richard Hamilton, President, White Mountain Attractions, North Woodstock, NH; the State Library, Concord, NH; The Bureau of Vital Statistics, Concord, NH; The New York Genealogical and Biographical Society, New York City, NY; The Registry of Deeds for Oxford

County, Fryeburg, ME; The Public Library, Oberlin, OH; The Lorraine County Health Dept, Oberlin, OH; The Bureau of Vital Statistics, Augusta, ME; the Selectmen's Office, Gloucester, ME.

Without the help of the following librarians none of my stories would have been possible: Barbara Emery, Kennebunk Public Library, Kennebunk, ME; Carol Govoni and Thelma Branscombe, Lincoln Public Library, Lincoln, NH; Barbara Robarts, Weeks Memorial Library, Lancaster, NH; Virginia Walsh, White Mountain School Library, Littleton, NH; Jean Palm, Randolph Public Library, Randolph, NH; Kathryn Taylor, Ellen Morrow, and Jean Dodge, Littleton Public Library, Littleton, NH; Muriel Brown and Ruth Miller, Bethlehem Public Library, Bethlehem, NH; Ann Cullinan, Conway Public Library, Conway, NH; Nancy Taylor, Auburn Public Library, Auburn, ME; Dorothy Cook, Fryeburg Public Library, Fryeburg, ME; Barbara Eastman, Chatham Public Library, Chatham, ME; Selena Cate, Lisbon Public Library, Lisbon, NH; Carolyn Garner, Pasadena Public Library, Pasadena, CA; Brenda Gross, Jefferson Public Library, Jefferson, NH; Dolores Schueler, Social Studies Dept., Boston Public Library, Boston, MA.

I wish to thank the members of our invaluable historical societies for the information they provided which I could not have obtained from any other source: Frances Heald, The Littleton Historical Society; Ann Croto, the Albany Historical Society, Albany, NH; Helen Merrill, Wilma Corrigan and Rupert Corrigan of the Jefferson Historical Society, Jefferson, NH; Mary Clough, the Lisbon Historical Society, Lisbon, NH; Lillian Burns, the Whitefield Historical Society, Whitefield, NH; Faith Kent and Bart Sheridan of the Lancaster Historical Society, Lancaster, NH; Francis Peabody of the Gorham Historical Society, Gorham, NH; Jean Hallagher, Leslie Sargent, and Charles Harrington of the Upper Pemigewasset Historical Society, Lincoln, NH; Mrs. Harold Wyatt, the Meredith Historical Society, Meredith, NH, and William Copeley of the New Hampshire Historical Society, Concord, NH.

Without the assistance of various law enforcement personnel, my stories dealing with criminal mischief such as the murders of Orville Gibson in Newbury, Vt., Eli Gendron of North Woodstock, and George Maxwell in Franconia would not have been possible. To that end I am grateful to: Charles E. Barry, Sheriff of Grafton County; the late Sheriff Herbert Ash, Campton, NH; Allyson Robie, State Police Headquarters, Concord, NH; Howard Sanborn, Chief of Police, Bethlehem, NH; Lt. Leo Jellison, Commander, F Troop, State Police, Twin Mountain, NH; Warden Everett Perrin and his secretary, Judy Palmer, the New Hampshire State Prison, Concord, NH; Ernest Kennedy, County Clerk's Office, Chelsea, Vt.; Attorney Harvey Otterman, East Orange, Vt.; and Attorney Edward Reichert, Gorham, NH.

Among the special classroom teachers to whom I am especially grateful for the important roles they have assigned my stories in their classrooms, and also for important research assistance from time to time, are: Sue Hawkins, Lynn Emery, and Bonnie Hicks, the Jefferson Elementary School, Jefferson, NH; Ruby Houlihan, the North Country Alternative School, Littleton; NH, Richard F. Alberini, Robert O'Connor, and Patricia Tucker, Littleton High School, Littleton, NH; Richard Massimilla, Lin-Wood High School, Lincoln, NH; and Marilyn Andrews, the Pine Tree School, Center Conway, NH.

I owe a debt of gratitude to author Thomas W. Murphy, Jr., of Kennebunk, ME, for his assistance in the preparation of the Lizzie Bourne story; also to author Robert E. Pike of Eatontown, NJ, who assisted me with the Orville Gibson research, and to author Richard Pinette of Errol, NH, for the information he shared concerning the missing doctors in the Pemigewasset wilderness.

Finally, I wish to thank the following people for all of the assistance they gave me in so many different ways: President George Bush, the White House, Washington, D.C.; Governor Judd Gregg, the State House, Concord, NH; Executive Councilor Ray Burton, Bath, NH; Elizabeth Hastings, the Governor's Office, Concord, NH; Dr. Robert Averill, Dartmouth '72, of Shelburne, MA; J. Willcox Brown, Dartmouth '37, Concord, NH; Betty Hill, Portsmouth, NH; Woodrow Kantner, Stuart, Fl.; Paul Dovholuk, Littleton, NH; Dr. Allan Handy, Pagosa Lakes, CO; Richard Chubb, Lake Havasu City, AZ; Murray Clark, Lincoln, NH; Barbara Kimball, Littleton, NH; Nina Clark, Franconia, NH; Ralph Martin, No. Woodstock, NH; Mr. and Mrs. William Martin, Lincoln, NH;

Ethel Smith, Jefferson, NH; Herbert Willey, North Conway, NH; Robert and Barbara Descoteaux, Vina Gorham, and Douglas Philbrook, Gorham, NH; Dr. Ernest Cross, Randolph, NH; Rodney Crouse, Stowe, ME; Maurice Clark, Sr., Lincoln, NH; Gary Remal, Augusta, ME; Marsha Cousineau, No. Woodstock, NH; Robert and Elizabeth Sweet, Sugar Hill, NH; Roland, Ellen, and Dorothy Dorr, Whitefield, NH; And last, but not least, John Govoni, Plymouth, NH, and all my friends at the Mount Washington Observatory.

Table of Contents

The Missing Doctors 13
J.E. Henry, *Profile of a Logging Legend* 25
The Famous Cherry Mountain Slide 39
Dolly Copp and Family, *Beyond the Legend* 51
Murder at the Cog Railway 65
A Hero Remembers 75
A Chronicle of the Willey Family Tragedy 77
The Haunting of Hannah Nute, *The Final Word* 91
A Melancholy Occurrence on Mount Washington 99
The Light in the Window,
    An Unusual Passaconaway Love Story 107
The Bugbee-Towne Mystery 113
New Hampshire's Famous UFO Kidnapping 127
The Taft Visit
    A Tender Moment for an Unhappy President 139
The Unsolved Murder of Orville Gibson 151
Farr Memories
    Shattered Glory and Unfinished Dreams 165
The Kahlers of Bethlehem
    A Family Footnote to History 187
Franconia's Famous Murder
    The Hanging of Samuel Mills 203
The Night the Bomber Crashed 225
War Hero Remembered 247
The Short Adventurous Life of Dr. Benjamin Ball 249

The Missing Doctors

Doctor Ralph E. Miller

TRAPPED in a remote wilderness valley which was surrounded on three sides by high mountains, the hour-long, erratic flight of Piper Comanche N5324P ended when it lost the engine and the right wing sheared off the tops of three white birches. At the moment of impact, the plane flipped over and landed on its back in saplings and deep snow.

As a wintery silence settled over the stricken plane, it would be only a matter of hours before the grueling seventy-three-day-long search would begin for its two prominent occupants.

Despite moderately bad weather that day, which was Saturday, February 21, 1959, Doctor Ralph E. Miller, 60, and Doctor Robert E. Quinn, 32, made an emergency flight from West Lebanon Airport to Berlin, N.H., in Doctor Miller's cream and red Piper Comanche. Prior to take-off, Doctor Miller filed a six-hour round-robin flight plan that would bring them back by way of Gorham and Littleton. Though the flight originated from an urgent call by Berlin Hospital for a heart specialist, while Doctor Quinn was treating that case Doctor Miller planned to visit some of his own patients in the Whitefield area.

At the time of the tragedy, both men were on the staffs at Dartmouth Medical College, Mary Hitchcock Memorial Hospital and the Hitchcock Clinic. Doctor Miller was a noted professor of pathology. He was also a twenty-year pilot and charter member of the Lebanon Civil Air Patrol, as well as a veteran of two Arctic research flights for Dartmouth College. Doctor Quinn was a specialist in cardiology and pulmonary diseases.

After dropping Doctor Quinn off at the Berlin Airport in Milan, Doctor Miller flew back to Whitefield. Consequently, three times that day dozens of people either saw or heard the plane as it flew in and out of the area.

Doctor Robert E. Quinn

That afternoon, with the weather worsening, at 2:41 Doctor Miller cancelled his original flight plan by telephone from Berlin. Immediately afterwards he and Doctor Quinn drove to a Milan restaurant for a quick lunch.

A short time later, when the weather appeared to be improving, the doctors returned to the airport. At approximately 3:30, Captain Warren MacKenzie of the Civil Air Patrol saw the plane lift into the air. It was presumed that Doctor Miller had gone aloft simply to check the weather, and to file an updated flight plan to Whitefield and Lebanon by radio.

Unfortunately, the plane was headed out of the area.

Richard Pinette, a local school teacher, and also a captain in the Civil Air Patrol, glimpsed the plane passing overhead as he left the Berlin hockey arena. He remarked to Lawrence Dwyer, Superintendent of Schools, "We'll be looking for that plane tomorrow."

Tragically, he proved to be correct.

Seconds later the plane was lost to sight in a violent snow flurry.

Unexpectedly snarled in "instrument" weather, Doctor Miller was forced to fly low in order to maintain visual contact with the highway since he had only eight hours of instrument flight training.

His plane was definitely identified at 3:35 flying south of Berlin 1000 feet over Route 2 by an Army pilot staying at the old Tower Inn in Jefferson. No one west of that point, however, either heard or saw it according to a subsequent investigation conducted by Conservation Officer Paul Doherty.

Mrs. Geoffrey Elliot of the Cascade-section of Berlin may have actually been the last person to see the plane in the air. After returning home through Franconia Notch, shortly after she learned of its disappearance, she reported spotting it heading south over Twin Mountain.

Inadvertently, her report was smothered by the more than 350 similar reports that poured in from all over northern New

Hampshire and parts of Vermont and Maine.

As a matter of record, only minutes after takeoff Doctor Miller twice made the attempt to reach Whitefield Airport by radio. Though both efforts were unsuccessful, the calls were picked up by an Army pilot on an instrument flight over Concord, N.H. They were entered into his log book. And the fact that Whitefield Airport failed to respond.

That evening, at around 9:00, the Civil Aeronautics Authority was first alerted to the plane's disappearance by Doctor Modestino G. Criscitiello, a friend of the Quinn family, when the doctors' wives, Ruth Quinn and Betty Miller, became alarmed over their husbands' failure to return home.

The initial search preparations were delayed when it was learned that the original flight plan had been cancelled. To eliminate the confusion, a state trooper was sent to Berlin Airport. Immediately he reported back that the plane was not there.

Over the next eight days one of the largest concentrated air and ground searches in New Hampshire's history took place. Air Force, Army National Guard and Civil Air Patrol planes, as well as private planes and military helicopters from four New England states searched a vast area of the New Hampshire wilderness, along the Connecticut River Valley, the Lebanon, Claremont, and Keene regions, and parts of Vermont and Maine whenever the weather permitted.

Ground forces were made up of volunteers from the Dartmouth Outing Club, National Guard, state police, conservation officers, and civilian personnel. Professional colleagues of the doctors joined the search teams on both the ground and in the air.

Doctor Philip Nice, a Hitchcock pathologist and former paratrooper, led the Dartmouth Outing Club in many of the ground search efforts while Doctor Miller's son, Ralph, Jr., a second-year Dartmouth medical student and a member of the Olympic Ski Team, was active throughout the Outing Club's efforts.

Early in the search some officials felt if the doctors had survived the crash that they had a 50-50 chance of survival despite the extremely cold temperatures, continuing snow storms, and the

(Photo courtesy of New Hampshire Fish and Game Department)

Into the first month of the search, Doctor Philip Nice, left, a Hitchcock pathologist and a colleague of Doctors Miller and Quinn, is seen conferring with Conservation Officer Charles E. Barry just outside the temporary search headquarters located at the Tramway in Franconia Notch.

rugged New Hampshire terrain. Their conclusion was based on the facts that both doctors were equipped with medical bags, that Doctor Miller was familiar with survival techniques, and that both men would be carrying matches for starting a fire since both were heavy smokers.

By the fifth day of the search top officials admitted that they were baffled by the complete lack of clues or any traces of the lost plane. More openly, they admitted that hope was all but gone that the doctors could still be alive.

On Sunday night, March 1, Governor Wesley Powell officially halted the search efforts after conferring by telephone with Aeronautics Director Russell Hilliard and Colonel Harry M. Rodd, commanding officer of the Civil Air Patrol.

Then on Wednesday, March 4, the Governor made the surprise announcement that the search would be continued by the 14th Rescue Squadron from Fort Ethan Allen, Vermont. He said the

THE MISSING DOCTORS   17

Squadron's services were obtained through U.S. Senator Styles Bridges, and were also requested by Doctor John Sloan Dickey, President of Dartmouth College, and Representative Robert Monahan of Hanover.

Despite the discontinuation of the main search, many of the military and private planes continued searching constantly. Some of them were aircraft financed by Dartmouth College and Mary Hitchcock Hospital. Fish and Game Department personnel often flew along as observers.

Finally on Tuesday, May 5, near 4:00 p.m., the search ended.

Pilot Richard Stone of Newport, N.H., flying under contract with Dartmouth College, and accompanied by Conservation Officer Ernest Melendy of Franklin, a District Chief, looked down into the valley of the East Branch of the Pemigewasset River and saw the plane laying upside down across the Thoreau Falls Trail.

Found in the midst of the Pemigewasset wilderness, the plane was only fifteen air miles from Whitefield and twelve miles north of the papermill town of Lincoln.

In order to protect the location, Stone maintained radio silence and reported the find directly to John Rand, Executive Director of the Dartmouth Outing Club.

The next morning, at 4:00, a hurriedly mobilized ground party began the difficult trek into the area to find the wreckage and to retrieve the bodies. Their progress was hampered by pockets of deep, melting snow and flood-like conditions caused by the run-off.

The party, headed by Doctor Nice, included Ralph Miller, Jr., Rand, Stone, Melendy, and Conservation Officers Everett and Charles Barry, a father and son team from Franconia.

A mile from the plane Officer Everett Barry discovered a knife-like instrument laying in the snow. His first thought was that it had been dropped by a trapper. Young Miller excitedly recognized it as a surgical knife of the type used by his father.

It was now known that the doctors had survived the crash!

Upon arrival at the crash site the ground party immediately found Doctor Miller's body under the left wing, which was hanging over the trail. He was wearing a winter parka and boots, and it was

(Photo courtesy of Dartmouth Outing Club)

At last, the search for the missing doctors has ended! This is what pilot Richard Stone saw when he looked down into the valley of the East Branch of the Pemigewasset River late in the afternoon of Tuesday, May 5, 1959.

evident that his jaw had been broken and that he had suffered facial lacerations prior to death.

An intricately woven pair of snowshoes, made from birch saplings and tied together with surgical tape, were hanging from a nearby branch. The bindings were made from Ace bandages and adhesive plaster.

About two hundred feet north of the aircraft, Officer Charles Barry happened upon Doctor Quinn's body lying on the trail. He was clad only in street clothes, and his shoes were missing.

They were never found.

His own homemade snowshoes were also picked up on the trail near his body.

With both doctors now accounted for, radio silence was finally broken. The party radioed out for a helicopter, to remove both bodies and themselves.

THE MISSING DOCTORS 19

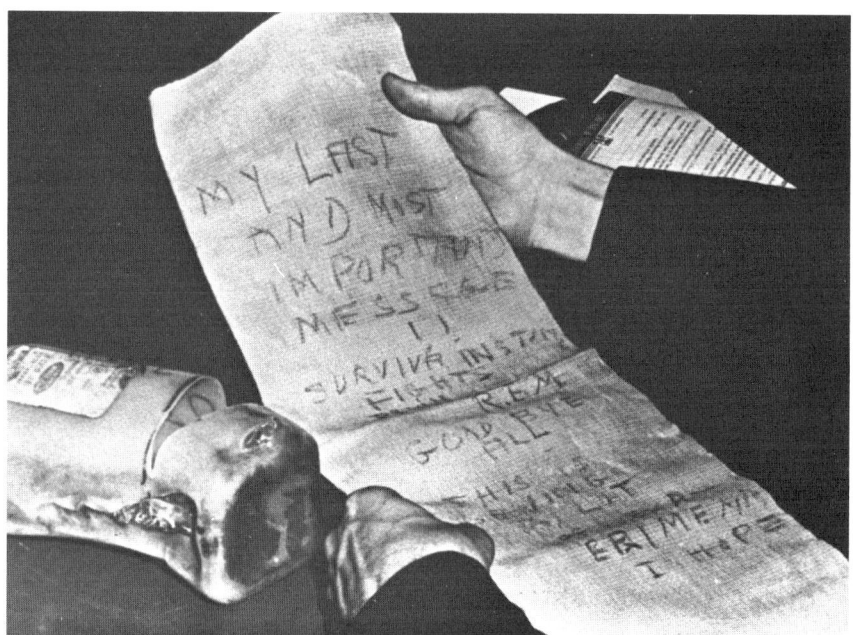

(Photo courtesy of Dartmouth Outing Club)

Doctors Miller and Quinn left notes to both the searchers and to their families. This message was scrawled on the back of the plane's upholstery on Doctor Miller's last day. Beside it is the plastic container which held other messages written on notebook paper.

After returning to their investigation of the tragedy, they saw that a fire had been built under the left wing and that one of the plane's doors had been torn off on which to build it. About the door there were entire medical journals charred only at the edges. There were also two to three foot lengths of yellow birch which had refused to burn. They had been cut with a hacksaw and a surgical saw, and still remained piled at the site.

Inside the plane a plastic bottle was found on which Doctor Miller had drawn a line and had written, "Cut here." It contained notes kept during the four days that the doctors had lived. Those addressed to the doctors' families remained confidential. Others were made public.

Beginning on Monday, February 23, Doctor Miller wrote: "Decided against any snowshoeing (sic). All energy used for wood cutting—"

"I have little hope—good bye Betty—it has been wonderful."

"No regrets except for Bob. Have fun."

That same day, Doctor Quinn wrote: "Up until today we were hopeful of being found, but no signs of rescue ship."

"Tried to walk out yesterday. No luck. I have become particularly weak. Fighting cold is hard."

The next day Doctor Miller wrote: "Tuesday noon—Still trying—though tools broken. Snow—No hope left."

On Wednesday, Doctor Miller wrote in crayon on the plane's seat fabric: "My last and most important message!! Survival instinct fights pain. R.E.M. Goodbye to all. This is saving a lot of experiments I hope."

Another "Goodbye" was found scrawled on the underside of the left wing.

Later that day, after the ground party had finished clearing a landing site three-quarters of a mile south of the plane, at 2:00 p.m. a small bubble-topped helicopter landed with Doctor Reginald DeWitt, Grafton County Medical Referee, aboard. Officially, he had to view the bodies before they could be removed.

Following his examination, the doctors were placed in body bags. The ground party then struggled through the snow to get them to the helicopter. However, after they were lashed to it on stretchers, the aircraft experienced difficulty achieving lift-off. At the last minute it cleared the trees.

Now realizing that his helicopter was too small to chance lifting out the ground party, the pilot refused to return. With no other choice, the exhausted crew then widened the landing site. When it was completed, a larger helicopter from Plattsburgh Air Force Base, New York, made three trips in and out removing them two at a time.

Just prior to the final lift-off, Lincoln Police Chief Fred Johnson arrived on the scene. He had hiked in nine miles from the Kancamagus Highway. He was about to spend an uncomfortable night alone by the plane acting as a security guard.

The next day Civil Aeronautics Administration officials were

The Missing Doctors

(Photo courtesy of New Hampshire Fish and Game Department)

Toward mid-May of 1959 the final curtain dropped on the tragedy when Sam Hall of Plymouth pulled the dismantled plane out of the woods. Ironically, the plane is reputed to be still flying today after being restored to its original condition.

helicoptered in to determine the cause of the crash. With them was Captain Richard Pinette of the Berlin Civil Air Patrol. He was invited along in recognition of the role he had played as a search coordinator and relief pilot.

In his recently published best selling book, Northwoods Echoes, Captain Pinette revealed that the Piper Comanche crashed because it had run out of gas, and not because of carburetor icing as Doctor Miller indicated in his notes. Pinette said that there were only two quarts of gas found in each of the plane's two tanks. He observed that this was not enough gas to reach the plane's engine.

Once the investigation was completed, the drama moved to a swift conclusion.

On the afternoon of May 9, a public memorial service was held for both doctors in Dartmouth College's Rollins Chapel. College President Dickey delivered the eulogy.

A few days later an insurance adjuster named Barney O'Keefe arrived from New Jersey and began the plane's salvage operation. On the recommendation of Edward and Murray Clark of Lincoln, he hired Sam Hall of Plymouth to pull it out of the woods. Hall's son, Steven, 19, owned a J-5 Bombardier equipped with a fully integrated trailer that proved to be almost custom-made for the difficult task.

After the wings were detached, as a test run they were taken to the roadbed below Camp 24. The next day the Halls returned for the fuselage. Once the wings and fuselage arrived at the Kancamagus Highway, they were loaded on a truck driven by Madison Sears. Sears then drove the disassembled airplane to Plymouth where it was temporarily stored in Hall's garage at 8 Garland Street. Here it awaited delivery to Teterboro Airport in New Jersey.

Following the plane's removal, the curtain dropped on the tragedy. But, it did so with an all-too-familiar irony. When the two men attempted to walk out of the wilderness on their homemade snowshoes that last Sunday afternoon of their lives, they died never knowing that where the trail appeared to "peter out" it opened up again just a hundred yards beyond that point. But, even worse, that they were only eight-tenths of a mile from the U.S. Forest Service's North Fork cabin when they turned back. Inside the cabin they would have found a stove, blankets, and a supply of badly needed food.

In essence, this was truly the fatal moment when their mission of mercy became their flight of no return.

The Rest of the Story

Briefly told, I had an unusual and unforgettable encounter with Doctor Ralph E. Miller shortly after he and Doctor Robert E. Quinn disappeared while on their return flight from Berlin, NH. Because of the way everything eventually turned out, I wish that it had never occurred. But, it did, and I am relating it now only to add to what is already known about the tragedy.

At the time that the encounter happened I was working the night shift at Franconia Paper Corporation in Lincoln to support my young family, and commuting to Plymouth Teachers College daily where I was juggling a full academic schedule.

The author, Floyd W. Ramsey, was 28 at the time he received the telepathic communication from Doctor Ralph E. Miller.

On Sunday, February 22, 1959, I became aware of the doctors' plight through the news media. That night, just before going to bed, I checked the outside temperature. It was ten below zero. Concerned, I wondered if the doctors could survive such cold if they were still alive.

Somehow, that night I was awakened from a sound sleep by Doctor Miller. Sitting bolt upright in bed, I found myself staring into his face. His features were clearly seen, as was his thatch of white hair. Telepathically he said to me, "Look toward Crawford Notch." That was all. He then abruptly disappeared. Exhausted, I fell back asleep.

The next morning, affected by the experience, I walked a short distance from my house to Pollard Road. Standing in the street, I pointed north toward the Pemigewasset wilderness. Despite the direction given in the message, I intuitively felt that that was where the doctors would be found.

In the days that followed I grew more troubled as the search progressed without producing any results. For my part, I simply did not know what to do about Doctor Miller's message. From the outset I had been assailed by strong doubts that anyone would attach any importance to it. Particularly because of the manner in which it had been received. Finally I developed a paralysis of will to act and did nothing.

When the plane was discovered in the Pemigewasset wilderness ten weeks after its disappearance, and the bodies were brought out, I was left emotionally scarred.

Then in the early 1960's, while I was a teacher at Lincoln High School, I learned about a pioneering telepathic experiment that took place between author Harold Sherman and famous Australian explorer Sir Hubert Wilkins. It was conducted from the fall of 1937, and lasted into the spring of 1938, while Sir Hubert was on a secret mission in the Arctic wastes for the Soviet government.

As pre-arranged, Sherman acted as the receiver in his New York City home. Three nights a week, from 11:30 to midnight, Sir Hubert transmitted his thoughts to him from the Arctic. Later, when the experiment ended, it was found that of the hundreds of impressions Sherman recorded, seventy percent were correct.

As for Doctor Miller, why wasn't his message more precise? The answer was found in part of his notes dated Monday, February 23, that read: "My charts do not give enough details to be sure where we are."

At the time of his thought projection he was merely indicating the direction he felt the search planes should look.

I wish I had known about the Sherman-Wilkins experiment while he and Doctor Quinn were alive. It was partly as a result of ignorance that I did nothing.

And that is what it all boils down to now. I did nothing. And for that I have always been sorry.

— FWR

J.E. Henry...
Profile of a Logging Legend

The Henry Family sitting on the porch at the Henry homestead on Pollard Road, Lincoln. From the top, left to right, are J.E. and his wife Lide, and their children – Ida, John, Charles, George, and Harriet.

JAMES EVERELL HENRY, more commonly referred to as "J.E.," was one of the most colorful and controversial personalities ever born and raised in northern New Hampshire. A railroad logger by profession, he played a unique role in the history of the White Mountains. Toward the end of his life, working with his three sons, he literally carved the town of Lincoln out of the Pemigewasset wilderness and brought it into the Twentieth Century. Yet, despite this extraordinary accomplishment, there does not exist in Lincoln today a single statue, monument, or plaque testifying to what he did there. Why?

To find the answer, let's turn to an article written by Ernest Russell based on an interview he had with the Henrys in February,

1909. Russell was sent to Lincoln by Collier's magazine to specifically investigate the "scandalous" logging practices being carried out there by J.E. Henry & Sons Co. (By 1890 there was a strong movement afoot to save the forests, and the Henrys were one of the enemies of that movement.)

Prior to his departure for Lincoln, well-intentioned friends warned Russell, "They're bulldogs—those Henrys. You'll be kicked out of Lincoln in short order." He expected to be. But he wasn't. During his stay he was handed the workings of the entire Henry operation on a silver platter. After he left the area, he went for the Henry jugular.

In part, this is what he wrote for the May 8, 1909, issue of Collier's:

"Somewhat apart from the closely clustered village, in a little white-painted house which overlooks the valley and faces...Loon Pond Mountain, lives—if you can call it that—Jim Henry. Sightless, feeble with his...years, relinquishing to his sons, because he must, an industry that has been the very core of his existence, he frets away his few remaining years."

At the time of his investigation, Russell found J.E. in declining health. He was approaching 79, and it's possible that he may have suffered more than one debilitating stroke prior to Russell's arrival. (Before he died, he suffered seven in all.) He was feeble, but he wasn't fretting away his remaining years quite the way Russell thought. The writer somehow failed to note the dominant hold that J.E. still exercised over his sons. The oldest, George, was responsible to him for all the logging operations; the second oldest, John, ran the office and the financial end, and Charles was superintendent of the papermill. Evenings they were expected to report that day's business to him. Afterwards they were given their orders for the next day.

Also, he wasn't really "sightless," but his eyesight had been failing for a number of years. The daily paper was read to him, and he particularly enjoyed listening to "blood and thunder" type stories from old Argosy magazines. And, possibly due to poor circulation, he always felt cold so he spent much of his last five years sitting next to a radiator. When the weather permitted, he occasionally went for automobile rides.

Recounting J.E.'s early years, Russell wrote:

"He looks back on a boyhood of bitter poverty, of scanty meals, and the hardest labor. He remembers yet the taunts of other lads who stepped on his bare toes, blue and cracked with the cold. "I fought an' licked 'em when I could," he says, 'an' when I couldn't, I set my teeth an' said, "you ain't agoin' to step on my toes always an' by God, they hain't."

Adding to this, J. E. was born in Lyman, New Hampshire on April 21, 1831. He was the eldest of six children born to Joseph Henry and Mary Calhoun. When he was six, the family settled on a farm on Mann's Hill in Littleton. It was here that J.E.'s bitter boyhood poverty molded the stern, domineering-type personality by which he was later known. When J.E. was 15, his father was kicked by a horse and lost the sight in one eye. With the family's struggle for existence already precarious, J. E. took over his father's work of driving freight with a four-horse team. Working long, cruel hours, he made trips to Franklin and Concord, New Hampshire, Portland, Maine, and Montpelier, Vermont. In 1849 Joseph Henry bought the Peabody Place in West Littleton where he died two years later.

These were Ernest Russell's observations on this aspect of J.E.'s life:

"When Jim Henry's father died in 1851 the chief item in the little estate was a timber lot in Littleton. The boy Jim—he was only nineteen then—promptly bought out the shares of the other children—on credit of course—and "logged" it himself. He cleared fifteen hundred dollars in this first operation of his life..."The bark had got into his hair," as they say in the lumber camps...

If any proof be needed of Jim Henry's genius for his calling it may be found in the rare instances when he deserted it. Whenever he is found scheming in oil or in horses, disaster lies just ahead; he turns to timber and everything comes his way. Moreover he fares best when unrestrained by partnerships or agents. His shrewd, intriguing mind and tight-closed lips permitted no confidences, delegated nothing of importance to subordinates. All his life he has dominated everything and everybody that touched his own activities — and the ledgers tell the story."

Overall, this is what Russell is talking about. While living at the Peabody Place, J.E. met Eliza Ann Ide. She lived in Upper

Waterford, Vermont, and was nicknamed "Lide." The daughter of Deacon Joseph Ide, the local tanner, she was often called "Deacon Ide's Devil" because of her mischievous nature.

Anyway, she and J.E. were married on April 5, 1854, and a few months later he bought the family farm and it became known as the Henry Homestead. Here the first four of their five children were born. The first two were girls; Ida Mary in 1855 and Harriet Sarah in 1857. Then came George Everell in 1862, and John Higgins in 1863.

During the ten years they lived here, J. E. farmed and bought woodlots throughout the Littleton area. He sold the logs to local sawmills and accumulated a working capital. He then sold the homestead, moved his family to Cambridge, Massachusetts, invested his money in Ontario oil and lost everything.

With his fighting instincts aroused, he moved his family to Newbury, Vermont, bought a woodlot, removed the timber, and made back what he had lost.

In the early seventies he formed a partnership with Charles Joy of Haverhill, New Hampshire, and Alvi T. Baldwin of Newbury, Vermont. Together they made multiple land purchases in the Bath, Haverhill, and Woodsville areas.

During the twelve years that the Henrys lived in Woodsville, their fifth child, Charles Buck, was born in 1875.

At this time J.E. was a happy man. He had the family that he wanted, and he was getting a foothold on the financial ladder of success. As soon as his sons were old enough, he wanted to show them how to make a dollar "tick."

Now, remember what Russell said: "Whenever he is found scheming in oil or in horses, disaster lies just ahead." He had tried oil. Now comes the horses.

During the 1870's wheat farming was booming so J. E. bought a large ranch at Tintah, Minnesota. Traveling there with Lide, he soon had a small village going on the property. And, like himself, most of his help was from New Hampshire. One day, in a moment of anger, he decided to show his crew who was boss by not paying them. It was a bad decision. Quickly he was seized and strung up. With his future flashing before his eyes, he promised to pay them if he was let down. Not one to leave well enough alone, once back on

J. E. HENRY

Among J. E.'s great walking and camp bosses were, from left to right, Louis Morrison, Billy Curtis, and Abe Boyle. Back row, Billy "the Bear," Boyle, Joe Morrison, Joe Boyle and Newt Rogers.

his feet he got feisty and reneged. Up he went again. This time he stayed there until he recognized the virtue of honesty. When he came down, he paid.

But he had pushed the help too far. They threatened to kill him if he ever came back. He never did. He gave the ranch to his two daughters, Ida and Harriet.

He returned to logging a wiser man.

A year after J.E. and Lide celebrated their silver wedding anniversary in Woodsville, he and his partners bought large tracts of virgin spruce near the base of Mount Washington at a place called Fabyans. The deal was signed on April 20, 1880, and the purchases cost the firm $33,000. Less than a year later, J. E. and Baldwin bought out Joy for $25,000. Several months elapsed and then J. E. bought out Baldwin for $35,000.

As Russell said, "He fares best when unrestrained by partnerships or agents." To be more precise, he meant partnerships outside of the family. Nine years down the road it will be J. E. Henry & Sons Co.

After the timber at Fabyans was exhausted, J. E. moved his family and business to the Zealand Valley. He had started logging here in 1881, but now he was ready to give the area his full attention.

As his lumber and charcoal operations prospered, so did the village of Zealand. Until it was totally wiped out by fire in May, 1904, it was always looked down on as the ill-reputed east end of Carroll. Actually, this Zealand Valley operation was J.E.'s first experience in "big lumbering." And he made the most of it. Though he built here one of the steepest and most crooked logging railroads ever found in all of New England, he was learning efficient logging methods and putting together a hard core of loyal workers. In 1885 lumber baron George Van Dyke of Lancaster, head of the Connecticut Valley Lumber Company, leased the Zealand lumber mill from him for five years. J. E. then concentrated on supplying logs to the mill while Van Dyke turned out lumber, laths, and box boards. Thirty teams of horses drew the logs to the mill, and they also produced enough manure so that it was profitably sold by the carload for fertilizer.

It was not until July 8, 1886, that disaster struck. The "Fire Rape of Zealand" had begun, and it may have been started by sparks from one of J. E.'s logging locomotives. Whatever its cause, it burned down three of his logging camps, killed several horses, destroyed a good part of his railroad, and wiped out 12,000 acres of stumpage valued at $50,000.

In the autumn of 1908, prior to going to Lincoln, Ernest Russell went to the Zealand Valley to see firsthand what the Henrys had done there prior to their departure in 1902.

Appalled by what he found, this is what he wrote:

Jim Henry flung himself upon the Zealand forest, the finest in the valley of the Ammonoosuc. For eleven years he ravaged it, building his mills and his railways, creeping up the valley, scaling the steep slopes and tearing from their foothold the giant spruce. Little he heeded the slash that marked his course and invited that crowning destruction of all—a big "burn." Money was all he saw, all he labored for. "Nature, unaided," says Dr. Thomas E. Wills of the

J. E. HENRY

(Floyd W. Ramsey Photo)

This mural, originally installed in the Lincoln Post Office on May 30, 1960, symbolically depicts two woodsmen, Doctor E.D. Burtt making his rounds, Jim Carey, the Company cop, and J.E. driving by with his team of fast horses.

American Forestry Association, "must work and wait a thousand years to repair the wreck wrought in this landslide region by one man and his sons in the quest for gold."

Following the slow death of the Zealand Valley, J. E. turned his sights toward the timber of the Pemigewasset wilderness which lay twenty-five miles to the south. Through a purchase and sale agreement signed with the New Hampshire Land Company on September 27, 1890, he and Van Dyke became the owners of over 70,000 acres of virgin timber encompassing the towns of Lincoln, Livermore, and Franconia. They paid $500,000 for it. Following the purchase, J. E. quietly hired Will Richardson, a Littleton surveyor, to do a timber study. When it was completed, he learned the tract had a potential value of $5,000,000. He wanted Van Dyke out of the picture.

The break between the two men came when J. E. said to Van Dyke, "Now, George, I'll make you a proposition. We bought in here together, but this ain't big enough for the two of us. And besides, you're busy on other big jobs. So, I'll leave it up to you. I'll give or take $100,000 for your share or mine. What do you want to do, buy or sell?" Knowing J. E.'s wiley ways, and how he was always ready to "sugar anything off" if he smelled a profit, Van Dyke sold.

J. E. now had to assume all of Van Dyke's financial obligations. Also, in order to raise the money for the premium, he sent his son John to Boston to make a substantial loan. The purchase that he had just made cost him a lot more than he had. This transaction illustrates what he often told others: "The only way to keep interested in making money is to buy something you want before you can pay for it. This way you have to struggle to make enough to pay for it."

At the age of 62, J. E. was ready to begin the greatest slaughter of forests in his career. But, before he left Zealand he had one final trick he was itching to pull off. He knew he was leaving behind several mountainsides covered with hardwood. And it was all facing the famous Bretton Woods Hotel. He approached the hotel company about buying it. They didn't like his price.

"All right," he warned them, "then I'll put up some charcoal kilns and burn every tree in sight!"

They didn't believe him.

When he sent in a crew carrying bricks and axes, and the maples began to fall, the hotel company dug deeply into its pockets.

Finally, in August of 1892, at two a.m., thirty horsemen, followed by a long line of heavily laden wagons trekked southward through Franconia Notch to the Lincoln wilderness. On their arrival, the party pitched tents in a clearing selected by the surveyor, Will Richardson.

As the Henrys pulled in, Lide had a grim look on her face. Since she had married J. E., she had moved twenty-seven times. She now swore to him that she would only leave Lincoln in her coffin.

Years later Jim Doherty, a former Henry worker, wrote of these first days: "When we got to Lincoln we found only four farmhouses: The Dearborn Place, the Parker Place, and the two Pollard farmhouses. They were located on the "Back Road" ... What is now the village of Lincoln was then all woods. Main Street, Church Street, Maple Street, and the mill site were all cleared out of the forest.

"Well, the day after we got here we all went to work clearing land, building houses, and putting in the railroad. Jim Ward was woods boss, and Jim Boyle was section boss on the railroad and 'Old J.E.' was boss of us all. We all went to work at six o'clock in the morning and we worked till six o'clock at night. When the night came, we knew we had been busy. Payday brought us from $22 to $24 a month, besides our board.

"During the fall we had 100 to 150 men working and by winter we had finished six houses, a store, a barn, a blacksmith shop and a harness shop. Besides that we had cleared a lot of land, and made a start on the railroad. By March two miles of track was finished and logs started rolling into Lincoln. Then a portable sawmill was set up and the lumber sawed for more houses which were built along Main Street...

"During those first months the women and children stayed in the farmhouses and the rest of us stayed in tents or any other place we could find. The 'Old Man' slept on a mattress on the floor of the harness shop. We had plenty to eat, much of the food being shipped in from the outside."

Though J.E. & Sons were quietly accepted by Lincoln's established inhabitants, as his settlement grew and the East Branch & Lincoln Railroad stretched north along the Pemigewasset River, an uproar arose in North Woodstock concerning unsightly alterations in the environment.

On August 11, 1894, the following statement appeared in the *White Mountain Echo*, a summer weekly published in Bethlehem: "The wealthy lumber king has been among us a year and has his work of devastation well under way. He is not a lumberman, but a wood-butcher, a mutilator of nature, a destroyer of the property of a thousand for the benefit of himself. The bare unsightly sides of Black Mountain, the dwindling streams and barren slopes of Coolidge, all testify against him."

J.E.'s rugged individualism, expressed through his relentless drive for power and profit, also left people with the impression that he was indifferent to human suffering. One such man was Charles Clark of Franconia who worked for him only one winter. In the logging camp where Clark stayed, he allegedly saw sick men go largely unattended. In disgust, he left the woods in March convinced that J.E. was simply unfit to work for. When Clark arrived home he told his family, "He not only worked us to death, but he treated us like he owned us and we were his possessions."

This was true. Having worked hard all his life for what he had, J.E. demanded a great deal from everyone that became a part of his payroll. For example, a girl hired to work in his Pollard Road home was expected to work every minute that she was there. In addition to house cleaning, she was required to braid rugs, mend clothes, feed the pigs, milk the cows, and split wood. In return, she was paid $3 a week.

Another bone of contention was J.E.'s payroll deduction system. Legend had it that he presided over paydays wearing a gun to ensure that everyone agreed with what they received. Needless to say, they often didn't. An example of why they didn't was the time J.E. encountered a woodsman searching the snow for something. Asked what he had lost, the man replied, "A chain, but I can't seem to find it." The next payday the cost of a logging chain had been deducted from his pay. What he had actually lost was the chain to his watch.

Under this system it was not unusual for men to sometimes find that they had no pay coming at all.

As he grew older, J.E. was heard to say that no one ever made a cent working for him. Since his control and administration of Lincoln was extremely rigid, and the townspeople were dependent on him for their needs, this was probably an accurate statement. After all, he owned the company store where they traded and the company houses that they rented. The money he paid them, one way or another, found its way back to him.

As the years passed, the physician that was so badly needed finally appeared in 1904. He was Doctor E.D. Burtt, and shortly after his arrival Lincoln suffered a typhoid fever outbreak. It was caused by a lack of sanitation facilities. Watering tubs lined the streets, and mothers dipped water from them as it was needed. Outdoor privies also added to the problem. Working together, Doctor Burtt and Charles Henry had community drinking water and sewage systems installed.

J.E. felt the pinch in his pocketbook.

On one of the water pipe installations being done just above his house, he tried to save money by having the workers lay the pipe through the middle of an old cemetery that had been there long before his arrival. When his neighbors got wind of it, they protested and stopped him. Annoyed by their outcry, he threw up his hands and asked, "Why? They're all gone in there, ain't they?"

The next year the small Lincoln Hospital was built across the

Looking from the west side of Main Street toward the sawmill, this is the ruin caused by "The Great Lincoln Fire" which occurred on May 13, 1907. Destroyed were the company barn, the ice house, the office and store building, the tenant houses on both sides of Main Street north of the store, and the homes of John and George Henry.

street from the Henry Papermill that went into operation on April 22, 1902. Hospital insurance was offered to all workers and their families for 50¢ a month, with the company making up the difference as needed.

Once, after assisting in the delivery of a family's eighth baby, Doctor Burtt remarked, "The first one was paid for. The rest belong to J.E. and Sons."

While an overworked Doctor Burtt tried to keep up with the town's medical demands, law and order was maintained by "Big Jim" Carey, the company cop. His two-cell lockup, located next to the hospital, was usually occupied by lumberjacks who got drunk and rowdy in the lower part of town known as "Pig's Ear." Following their arrest, these men often appeared before J.E. since he also sat on the judge's bench.

Before he retired at seventy-seven, J.E.'s last working year was made miserable by two major fires. The first occurred on May 11, 1907, while he was visiting friends in Littleton. Known as "The

Great Lincoln Fire," it started at 11:50 a.m. Its cause was attributed to a switching locomotive which may have belched some sparks on a hay supply at the company barn on Main Street. Fanned by a strong wind, the flames engulfed the barn and killed a number of work horses; also lost were the company store, nineteen company houses, and the homes of John and George Henry.

While Lincoln was still recovering from this disaster, on August 17 lightning set off a forest fire in the East Branch area called Owl's Head. The wide-spread devastation was partly attributed to the amount of slash left there by the Henrys while pursuing their clear-cutting practice involving the felling of small trees. Their papermill, which ran twenty-four hours a day, seven days a week, had a voracious appetite. And it was the suspicion of what was feeding that appetite that brought Ernest Russell to Lincoln in 1909. Following a visit to an East Branch logging operation with George Henry, Russell had this to report about the experience:

Here was indeed the tragic story of Zealand repeated. The snow-covered wilderness rang with the regular "chock, chock, chock," of the axes and the rasp of the big saws. Trees crashed down everywhere... It is desperately clean work that is going on in the East Branch wilderness. There was little talk—simply concentrated effort and energy, and through it all a perfectly apparent genius of direction.

I looked about me for some sign of the modern forestry idea of "culling" the reservation of young trees. There was no hint of it. Everything was coming down before those merciless axes, and the slash lay in great heaps, black against the snow.

Later I stood on the top of a car loaded high with spruce logs... going to the slaughter-pen in Lincoln.

Before leaving Lincoln, Russell was given a tour of the papermill by Charles Henry. Impressed with the efficiency he saw, as he and young Henry stood where three stokers were feeding seven furnaces with refuse chips, bark, and sawdust, he said, "I always imagined there was considerable waste in this papermaking business."

Giving a little snort of contempt, Charles Henry replied, "It's something like the stockyards pig here in this mill. You'll find there's nothing left but the squeal."

It was the kind of answer J.E. would have given. He had truly raised his sons in his image. And that's another reason why there is nothing in Lincoln today dedicated to his memory.

Following his seventh stroke, J.E. died quietly at home on April 18, 1912, only three days short of his eighty-first birthday. Just before the end, he called his wife to his bedside and said to her, "Lide, I wish you'd talk to the Lord for me. He's more used to listening to you."

And, knowing J.E., he made out all right on the deal.

The Famous Cherry Mountain Slide

THROUGH MOST OF JUNE OF 1885 New Hampshire residents grumbled about the wet and unseasonably cold weather. In early July they had more reason to complain. Violent thunderstorms had moved into the area. And, wherever these thunderstorms struck, tragedy followed. For example, on South Street in Littleton, lightning did considerable damage to the house of Theophilus Carbonneau. It also mangled the foot of his ten-year-old daughter, crippling her for life.

In Lancaster, Moses Kimball and his son-in-law were examining a sick cow in the pasture when lightning ended the animal's life. The impact threw Kimball violently backwards, and his son-in-law temporarily lost his eyesight.

At Jefferson Mills an errant ball of lightning entered the home of Charles Morse. As a consequence, two beds were set on fire and his wife was rendered insensible for a time.

Then on Wednesday, July 8, the weather took another unpredictable turn. Local thermometers shot past 90°. This heatwave, however, was shortlived. The next afternoon the thunderstorms returned accompanied by high winds. Trees were uprooted, bushes and shrubs blew away, and telephone and telegraph poles were extensively damaged.

That Friday morning damage by the storm reached its climax by unleashing one of the most destructive landslides that has ever occurred in the White Mountains. At the time of the catastrophe, the homes of John Boudreau and Oscar Stanley stood in the path of a million tons of debris that were traveling at express-train speed down 3600-foot Cherry Mountain in Jefferson.

The day before this dramatic occurrence, Oscar Stanley, 49, a hardworking, highly respected farmer who lived near Jefferson Meadows on the south side of the Cherry Mountain Road, was caught out in the storm. Shortly after lunch that day he had set off for Whitefield in his buggy to buy materials necessary to set up a cookstove in his nearly completed new home.

Following the destruction of his former home by fire on the night of June 4, for five long weeks his widowed mother Moranda, 74, his wife Ellen, 37, and his three daughters—Della, 18, Grace, 9, and Mora, 5, had been staying a half-mile north at his father-in-law's, John M. King. As for himself, he had been sleeping in his barn which sat on the opposite side of the road near the newly laid tracks of the Whitefield and Jefferson Railroad.

Initially he had worked on the rebuilding alone. However, after collecting what little house insurance he had, the money enabled him to hire two Whitefield brothers, Moses and Cleophas McDonald, to help with the carpenter work. His regular hired hand, Donald Walker, 23, who was engaged to his daughter Della, took care of the farm work. At the end of each exhausting day, the four men slept on beds set up in the barn. Every morning Della and Grace walked over to make the beds, and to sometimes serve dinners in the barn when the weather was disagreeable.

Now, with the haying season near and all but the ell completed, Stanley decided to move his family into the uncompleted house the next day. Preparing the meals there, he knew, would save valuable time. For the moment, though, his return from Whitefield was delayed. Finally, at 9:00 that night, he arrived back at the barn.

On Friday, July 10, when he awakened his men at daylight, he was disappointed to find that it was still raining. Despite this fact, he led the brothers across the road to the house following a quick breakfast while Don Walker remained behind to milk the cows.

Unknown to any of them, shortly before 6:00 a.m. lightning struck the bald spur known as Owl's Head which crowned the north side of Cherry Mountain. At nearly the same time two thunderclouds collided directly over the summit, releasing a deadly downpour. Minutes later giant boulders were dislodged forty feet from the top. When they landed on the saturated, clay-based covering of the steep north slope, the covering collapsed and began following rain-swollen Stanley Brook down the ravine.

Screaming and twisting its way for a mile and a half down the

The Famous Cherry Mountain Slide

Dramatically capturing the destruction wreaked by the Cherry Mountain landslide, this photo was a favorite of sightseers. It sold for 50 cents. Oscar Stanley is shown with his one-horned cow that was rescued from the mud.

mountain the slide grew in volume and velocity. Along the way it picked up nearly a million tons of earth and stone along with thousands of feet of fir, spruce birch, and ash. When it broke out into the open meadow just above Boudreau's shanty-like house, it swallowed a bridge that crossed the ravine. Its first victims were Silas Marshall's cattle that were pastured just below there.

Boudreau, asleep when the slide began, was awakened by the deep rumbling that it made. At first he thought it was distant thunder. However, as the deadly roar increased and his house began to shake, he ran to a window and saw a sight that paralyzed him with fear. All he could mutter was, "Mon Dieu! See him come!"

Miraculously, Boudreau and his family were spared only because a bend in the channel of Stanley Brook turned the slide toward the opposite side of the ravine. Though his house was left standing, the main body of the gigantic mass plowed down the middle of his land. As it flew by, some of the debris landed within twenty feet of his door and huge logs were hurled into his garden.

A quarter of a mile beyond, Oscar Stanley's attention was distracted by the same peculiar rumbling sound that awoke Boudreau.

"What is that?" he asked over the sounds of saw and hammer.

One of the McDonald brothers shrugged and replied, "Only a train on the road."

As the noise grew louder, a strange vibration could be felt in the house. Stanley now felt an inexpressible feeling of fear. "Boys," he said, "it is something terrible. Something awful is happening."

Going to the door, he looked toward the mountain. Through the gently falling rain he saw a forty-five foot high mass, which was at least a hundred feet wide, rushing toward the house. As rolling boulders banged against each other, flashes of fire shot out from the sides.

Stanley screamed, "I'm going to get out of this! The mountain is coming down!"

Propelled by the horror of the moment, the three men ran toward a wooden fence which stood on higher ground just west of the house. Momentarily looking back, they saw the monstrous mass engulf the house. Arriving at the fence, one of the McDonald brothers was literally thrown over it by the force of the wind given off by the slide.

Stanley himself had the narrowest escape. He came within eight feet of being drawn into the debris.

Hurtling across the road, the slide instantly destroyed the barn. Then, with its fury spent by the level ground, it slowed down and spread out over twenty acres of field. It finally stopped just short of the railroad tracks.

The road, now rendered impassable, was covered by fifteen feet of debris spread out over 495 feet. Trees, boulders, and the remains of the house were all a part of it. Where the barn stood, only the roof could be seen above the mud.

Trembling uncontrollably, the three men remained behind the fence watching waves of watery mud eight to ten feet high undulate past. Several minutes later they realized that the danger was over.

Stanley looked down at the barn roof and cried, "Don Walker is a dead man!" But Walker wasn't. Hearing Stanley's voice, he painfully cleared dirt and gravel from his mouth and hoarsely shouted, "Help!"

Reacting immediately, Stanley ran to the roof and crawled in

Daughters Della Stanley, 19, and Grace Stanley, 9, stand next to the rubble of the barn where Don, the hired man, was found fatally injured. To the left, a farmhand is pointing to a sign which reads, "This is where the HORSE was TAKEN OUT."

under an open corner. Working his way over the debris, he saw a hand pushed up through the mud. He also spotted Walker's head sticking out of the rubble.

Of that moment Stanley later said, "I found where he was buried in the ruins of the barn though he looked like a dirty log. I somehow lifted a stone from his back that weighed, I should think, four hundred pounds. Also another from his neck. His right leg was all twisted up in the roots of a tree, and his face was plastered with mud."

After Stanley was joined by the McDonald brothers, the three of them dug away the debris holding Walker down. Before he could be dragged out, his boots had to be cut off to free his feet. Once he was removed from under the roof, it was evident that his legs were severely damaged. He also had deep cuts about the face and head, and his body was extensively bruised.

Laying Walker gently on a bed of straw, the men put together a crude litter. When it was finished, he was carried to an open field. Here the decision was made to move him to John King's house while one of them rushed to Jefferson Depot to telephone Whitefield for emergency help.

Following the call, a special train immediately brought Doctors

In this photo, the Stanley family is posing near the remnants of their farm. From left to right: The one-horned cow, a farmhand, Mrs. Ellen Stanley, Grace, 9, Mora, 5, Della, 18, Mr. Oscar Stanley, and the horse, Jack. Boudreau's house can be seen off in the distance.

Patten, McGregor, and Morrison to the disaster area. When word of what happened finally caught up with Doctor Charles H. Burnham, the overworked local physician, he rushed by team down from the village. Doctor Gove later arrived from the Twin Mountain House.

While being examined, Walker told the doctors he heard and saw the slide coming. He said, "I rushed for the door, but the wind was blowing toward the mountain and had carried the sound from me. Otherwise I might have heard the noise in time to escape."

Wincing from the pain that racked his body, he continued, "When I got to the door, I had trouble pushing it open. I got out of the barn just as the avalanche struck. It threw me into the shed which opened from the barn. When it was over, I lay there buried up to my neck, having no idea how I would get out until I heard Mr. Stanley's voice."

As the doctors made a second examination of his injuries, Walker mumbled, "I never expected to get out alive. But, I'm all right, doctor, except for my legs."

To give him hope the doctors shook their heads in agreement. They knew his chances for recovery were doubtful at best. His left leg was found to be broken in several places below the knee, and his right leg was brutally crushed.

Knowing Walker was in good hands, Stanley took the opportunity to search for his missing livestock. At the same time the McDonald brothers looked for their tools. Though three cows, a calf, two hogs, a pig and the tools were never found, one cow was discovered alive where the stable once stood. Unfortunately she was buried up to her neck in mud, and she was missing a horn.

After being dug out and examined, she was also found to be suffering from a dislocated shoulder, several fractured ribs, and a broken neck. Despite these injuries, she survived for a time to be seen, pitied, and photographed by hundreds of visitors to the slide.

Before the morning was over, Stanley also unexpectedly found his horse Jack. Unlike the cow, he had only a minor head injury.

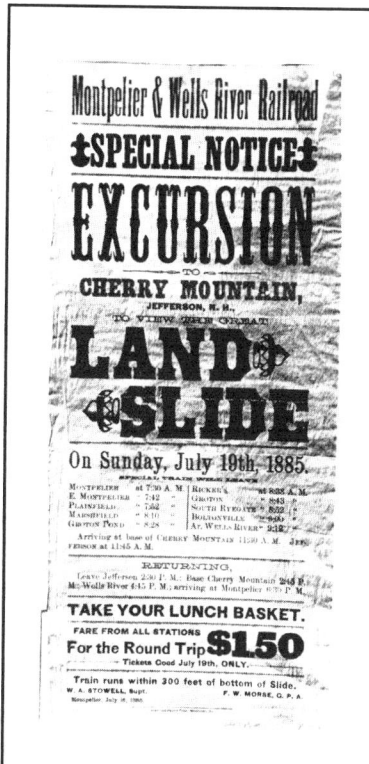

(Courtesy of Jefferson Historical Society)

On the Sunday that this broadbill refers to, twenty-six carloads of passengers rode to the slide by train. While the railroads profited from the tragedy, local innkeepers complained because the excursions were being sold on a round-trip basis.

While this was going on, telegraph wires were humming with news of the calamity. Jefferson, Whitefield, Lancaster, Twin Mountain, Bethlehem, and Littleton were gripped by excitement. People were soon on their way to the scene in droves. Those who knew that the Boudreau and Stanley houses were in the path of the slide were emotionally prepared to encounter a scene of devastation and death as tragic as the Willey Slide which occurred in Crawford Notch on August 28, 1826. At that time Samuel Willey, his wife, five children, and two hired men were buried by the avalanche.

Meanwhile, as the throng flocked to the scene, Ellen Stanley walked over the slide area. She was staggered by the desolation and confusion she found. Not only was their home gone, but so were the furniture and personal possessions they had stored in the barn since the night of the fire. And before her, forty acres of cultivated land lay buried under twenty feet of mud.

Oscar later told her that he estimated there were at least 400,000 feet of timber scattered over their property. He fixed their losses at between $3000 and $4000.

While the Stanleys were pondering how they were going to survive, the next morning several dozen tourists left Boston on the 9:30 Boston & Maine Railroad with the intent of visiting the slide. Neither the Stanleys nor the other 965 residents of Jefferson realized the impact that these summer visitors were going to have on their quiet life in the months just ahead.

By that Sunday alone, thousands of people had trampled over Stanley's and Boudreau's property on sun-hardened mud. Quickly taking advantage of the opportunities presented, enterprising locals set up makeshift tents and sold everything from full meals to cigars. To justify capitalizing on the disaster, part of the money they took in went to the Stanleys, part to suffering Donald Walker, and they pocketed what was left.

The following Tuesday, which was July 14, Walker not only turned twenty-four, but it was also the day that he was scheduled to marry Della Stanley. Instead, he died at 1:00 p.m. following the amputation of his right leg. His mother Mary was holding his hand when the end came.

The $25 he had received as his share of the proceeds made at the slide the previous weekend went toward his funeral expenses.

Then more tragedy followed. The Saturday following the funeral, Oscar Stanley's brother-in-law, Asa J. King, began to exhibit symptoms of insanity at his father's house. Emotionally distraught since the slide, Walker's death aggravated his condition. Before long he was driven to Lancaster where Doctors Mitchell and Stockwell officially declared him insane. By order of the Overseer of the Poor he was committed to the asylum at Concord, New Hampshire.

When Sunday, July 19, arrived, a young lady from Lancaster,

The Famous Cherry Mountain Slide 47

(Burnham Photo, Courtesy of Jefferson Historical Society)

Since the Stanley buildings were destroyed by the slide, the ones shown were put up to serve the needs of the hundreds of tourists who came to view the devastation. While Ellen Stanley poses with the horse, Jack, who was rescued uninjured, Oscar Stanley poses with the one-horned cow.

who admitted she was a "Sabbath breaker" was among the twenty-six carloads of passengers who rode to the slide by train. Describing what she saw, she wrote: "Just opposite where stood the Stanley house, is erected a stand for Mr. Stanley's benefit where everything eatable, from a twisted donut up to elaborate cakes and flaky pies are dispensed to the hungry crowd. Mr. and Mrs. Stanley made their headquarters here during the day, and both of them seemed polite unassuming people, answering any and all questions with the same patient air.

"A little below the stand is a placard marking the spot where Donald J. Walker met his death. The large stone is still lying there as found across his body. Many pieces were broken from it to be preserved as relics of the slide, and many a mother will point to these mementoes and tell her children of the sad fate of Donald J. Walker.

"A little distance along is another placard telling us where the cow was buried beneath huge timbers. Also the horse. They now stand in a tent curtained off, and a boy outside admits all whose curiosity is sufficient to invest ten cents.

"We missed seeing a hen that came out unscathed through this upheaval. The boy in charge told us, 'Three fellows came along, pushed me aside without paying, went in and threw the hen out.'

"A look under the barn reveals to sight broken bedsteads, remnants of chairs, broken dishes, a crushed table, and many other spoiled furnishings of household goods...."

Though the young lady hinted at the rowdyism there, she failed to mention that alcoholic beverages were also being sold. Littleton and Lisbon excursionists returned home that same day to report that many people there were intoxicated, and that "a disgraceful row had ensued among the lower classes."

Adding to this complaint, ministers and priests from Jefferson to Dalton were attributing poor church attendance "to the absence of those who went to the slide with the multitude to do evil."

Stung by the mounting criticism, the following Sunday the Jefferson selectmen and twenty police officers were at the slide. Before the day was out, arrests had been made. One party from Berlin was caught selling rum and fined $100. By the next Sunday, the police reported everything was quiet and under control.

In an attempt to recoup more of his losses, on July 22 Stanley sold a half interest in his farm to Frank P. Brown of Whitefield for $1500. In announcing the sale, Brown said, "The land is now to be enclosed, and to have erected upon it a restaurant and a stable for the accommodation of the horses of sightseers who will be charged ten cents admission to view so much of the slide as lays upon the farm."

At this time John Boudreau made it known that he was also enclosing his land, but was only charging "five cents a peep."

Following his announcement, he not only fenced in his land, but he also began charging ten cents to anyone who crossed his property to hike up the slide.

By the middle of August Stanley was still competing against Boudreau for the tourist trade. Running a daily coach to Jefferson Depot, he personally picked up sightseers. Boudreau attempted to

This is Jefferson's Main Street at the time of the slide, looking west from near the Waumbek Hotel. Since the townspeople were primarily engaged in the farming, lumbering, and hospitality industries, the tragedy proved to be a boost to the latter.

outmaneuver him by opening a toll road. Once it was operational, tourists coming from the Twin Mountain House could now reach his property without first driving to Stanley's.

By the end of August the railroads were running excursion trains to the slide seven days a week at reduced rates. This not only created more headaches for the Jefferson selectmen, but Oscar G. Barron, one of the most influential hotel men of this time, also warned them that he was going to make trouble for the town if the Cherry Mountain Road was not satisfactorily repaired. Particularly the section running from the Carroll line to the slide.

To meet his request, the town spent $500 just on the section he specified. However, their troubles were far from over. By year's end, due to the heavy expenditures required to maintain all of the Jefferson roads and bridges strained by the unusually heavy traffic to the slide, the town was shocked when it was discovered that it was heavily in debt.

That autumn, as the tourists finally headed home, Stanley got out of the slide business altogether. On October 29 he sold the remaining half of his farm to Frank Brown for $2000. For good measure, he threw in an additional twenty acres.

Following the completion of the sale he moved his family up to Jefferson Hill, which was then a long line of summer hotels and boarding houses. In the years ahead, he got involved with a number of land transactions there. For a short time he owned Cherry Cottage, and was later listed as the proprietor of the Waumbek Cottage.

Following his death at 79, his wife lived with their youngest daughter near the Jefferson Hill Library. When she died at 83, she was buried next to him in the lower section of the Forest Vale Cemetery on the Meadows Road.

All three daughters were tall, attractive women, even in their old age. Following their marriages to local boys, they lived out their lives close to one another on Jefferson Hill where they could see Cherry Mountain whenever they liked. Ironically, Della and Mora both died at 86 from bronchial pneumonia. Grace lived to the age of 92.

On close examination, Della has to be numbered among the victims of the slide. Subjected to the trauma of losing her fiance, Donald Walker, on their wedding day, she was further shocked by the profiteering her father participated in following Walker's funeral. He later disappointed her again when he became a "tavern operator," as she put it. To her dying day she would never talk about either the slide or her father with her grandchildren.

As for John Boudreau, like the slide, he just eventually faded from sight altogether.

Dolly Copp and Family
Beyond the Legend

THROUGH RUGGED INDIVIDUALISM, boundless resiliency, and a mutual sharing of soul-searing labor, Hayes and Dolly Copp lived out more than fifty years of their lives at the foot of Mount Madison in the wilds of Martin's Location. This remarkably enduring couple were among the last true pioneers of Nineteenth Century New Hampshire.

Oddly enough, the very characteristics that enabled them to survive their pioneer-styled life may have also been behind the later unraveling of their marriage. Whatever the reasons, their famous separation added a unique climax to their life together.

Going back to the beginning, Hayes was born in Wakefield, New Hampshire, on October 12, 1806. Christened Dodavah Hayes Copp, he was the son of Dodavah and Deborah Ann Copp. By preference he was known as Hayes D. Copp.

Raised on his father's farm, he spent his early years following a plow and performing the ceaseless toil that accompanies such an

(Photo courtesy of Mrs. Vina Gorham, Gorham, NH)

Boarded up, and in its final days, this was the home Hayes and Dolly Copp worked so hard to build in the wilderness area known as Glen Peabody in Martin's Location just south of Gorham.

existence. As a result, he developed a peculiar inward expression that stamped itself on his face. Later the expression developed into a stern, humorless look.

In 1827, as he approached his twenty-first year, he came to a crossroads in his life. He could either remain on his father's farm as an underpaid hireling, or he could strike off on his own and gamble that he would survive. Without hesitation he chose the latter path, left home, and traveled north seeking unsettled land.

After arriving at the farm of his cousin, Benjamin Copp, who was one of the original settlers of Jackson, New Hampshire, Hayes heard about the rich black soil waiting for the settler's plow seventeen miles north just beyond the notch then called "the Eastern Pass."

Upon receipt of this information, he left Benjamin's farm and set off for Martin's Location which was situated just before Shelburne Addition, a town that was renamed Gorham in 1836. Carrying only his pack, a long-barreled flintlock, and an ax, he came upon the remains of a road that had been obliterated by innumerable landslides. Later he learned that the deadly storm responsible for this damage had also wiped out the entire Samuel Willey family along with their two hired men in the valley to the west of Mount Washington.

Before the disaster occurred, in 1824 Daniel Pinkham had been commissioned by the State to build the twelve-mile-long road which would connect Jackson with the prospering lumbering town of Randolph. Given only three years to complete it, during the first two years of construction Pinkham lived through a road builder's nightmare. While working his way through the notch, he encountered endless boulders, thick growths of timber, steep and unyielding terrain, and more mountain streams than he ever believed possible. To his credit, he had the road nearly completed when the storm struck. Exhausted and anguished by the devastation, he temporarily abandoned the project.

Finding the debris too much to cope with, after a few miles Hayes left the ruined road and followed a trail that paralleled the Ellis River. Eventually crossing the Peabody River, he arrived at the site where he would begin homesteading at the foot of Mount

Madison. His claim was later designated as "Lot 7 in the 1st range."

To his credit, Hayes was the first person to settle in Martin's Location in Coos County, New Hampshire.

It is not really known how he acquired title to this land. The records are believed to have been lost in the Coos County Courthouse fire of 1886 in Lancaster. The possibility exists that he may have been just a squatter.

Working alone, for the next four years he felled trees, dug up roots, burned stumps, piled logs and managed to construct a one-room cabin and a small barn. During the initial phases of this clearing work, he "scratched in" turnip and pumpkin seeds and sowed small patches of oats. Whenever his fur cache allowed, he journeyed to Jackson to exchange pelts for badly needed supplies. While there, he occasionally attended Saturday night dances.

During one of these trips he met small, attractive Dolly Emery. She was born in Bartlett on April 25, 1807, and was the daughter of Nathaniel and Deborah Rogers Emery. Like Hayes she had light colored hair, blue eyes, and a tremendous store of energy and ambition.

By contrast, however, while Hayes was slow and deliberate in his speech and habits, she was high-spirited, quick-acting, and at times a little too sharp with her glib tongue. Also, while he preferred the solitude of the wilderness and the established routine of farm life, she was a highly creative person who enjoyed the theatre and visiting cities. And, while his manner and appearance were somewhat coarse, it was Dolly's nature to be attracted to the refined and the beautiful.

Despite their many differences they fell in love. On November 3, 1831, they were married in Jackson. He was twenty-five and she was twenty-four. When they departed for their wilderness home, Dolly's trunk contained her fine wedding china. These items would later play an important role in her life.

Though Hayes wasn't aware of it at the moment, the trunk also carried a pair of expensive, custom-made shoes from Portland, Maine. Dolly's small delicate feet were her particular vanity. And, of all her quirks, this one more than any other perplexed Hayes.

In the year ahead the couple quickly developed a spirit of working together that was necessary to their survival. Faced with pinching poverty, they both worked in the woods clearing the land. Before they could celebrate their first wedding anniversary, their son Jeremiah was born on September 7, 1832.

Following his birth, Dolly continued working in the woods with Hayes. Later, asked how she managed the situation, she replied, "I had to put the baby in the clothesbasket and carry it out in the field. I tended him there as I could find time."

(Photo courtesy of Jean Palm, Randolph librarian)

Because of his dour look, many people misunderstood Hayes Copp. One old-timer in Gorham once said, "Hayes Copp was the meanest man I ever knew in all my life." In reality, however, Hayes was a quiet, kindly man.

Testifying to this fact, Daniel Evans of Gorham stated, "I have seen Aunt Dolly piling logs in the clearing, and she would do as much work as any man."

That same year a relative became their first neighbor. Samuel Copp and his wife Betsy began farming just across the river.

On January 4, 1834, a doctress delivered Dolly's second son. Christened Nathaniel Emery Copp, he was named after Dolly's father. Dolly was definitely now living in a male-dominated household.

Later that year, as the Copps worked at replacing their log cabin with a long, two-story frame house, Daniel Pinkham finally extended the road past their farm. Bringing the road to completion a short time later, his years of backbreaking toil, continual discouragement, and niggardly poverty were finally at an end. The State awarded him his promised land grants which were a half-mile wide on both sides of the road from Jackson to Randolph. He was also given state land within the town of Jackson.

At the age of fifty-five his fame as a road builder was assured. More importantly, so was the preservation of his name. As early as

Dolly Copp and Family

(Photo courtesy of Jean Palm, Randolph librarian)

A warm, compassionate person, Dolly Copp loved being around people which made her farm life with Hayes that much more difficult. Her unusual decision to separate from him following their Fiftieth Wedding Anniversary eventually inspired the well-known expression, "Don't cop out on me now."

1851 the Eastern Pass had become known as Pinkham Notch.

Through this time period Hayes completed building the frame house and a large frame barn. These structures were soon followed by various outbuildings, and an ell which connected the house to the barn. Slowly the Copps were winning their struggle against the wilderness and their own poverty.

Nearly five years after Nathaniel's birth, happiness and light came into Dolly's life in the form of Hannah Sylvia Copp who was born on November 18, 1838. Dolly finally had the daughter that she wanted and needed so badly. And, as was the case with Hayes' first name, in time her first name was dropped and she became known only as Sylvia.

While Dolly raised her three youngsters, in addition to her regular household chores, she also continued to make the "tallow dips," the year's supply of soap, and to cleanse, card and spin the wool into yarn so she could make, mend, and darn the family's clothes. Nearly eleven years passed in this fashion before the birth of her fourth and final child.

When she was forty-two she gave birth to Daniel Stickney Copp on August 14, 1849. Following his arrival, instead of slowing down she worked all the harder. Unlike Hayes, she wanted more for her family than "just getting by."

Undeniably, she was an intelligent woman with a developing sense of direction. When time permitted, she often searched the woods for wild apple trees. After finding them, she selected the best ones and transplanted them in the backyard. Whenever she came across wild bees, she hived them for their honey. When she needed more linen, she raised flax in the narrow field by the river. At night, while rocking the cradle, she would spin and weave it into linen. When the weather permitted, she would lay it out on the grass near the orchard to be bleached by the sun.

Also possessed of an excellent business head, all of this activity was leading her towards becoming the first innkeeper in the Pinkham Notch area. Once she opened her doors to guests, not too many years passed before her culinary skills, warm hospitality, and quaint sayings made her almost legendary.

Adding to her stature as an innkeeper was the fact that she not only kept her prices minimal for her delicious meals and comfortable bedding, but also that her guests were unselfishly treated to the use of her precious heirloom silver and fine wedding china.

The year of 1849 was a pivotal one for the Copps. Hayes in particular. With the help of his two teenage sons, he had finally achieved his goal of having a successful farm. The census for that year showed that he had 50 acres of cleared land which produced ten bushels of wheat, twenty bushels of Indian corn, fifteen bushels of oats, four bushels of peas and beans, three hundred bushels of potatoes, fifteen bushels of buckwheat and ten tons of hay.

In addition, Dolly had made three hundred pounds of butter and forty dollars' worth of home-manufactured goods. As for livestock, they owned one horse, three milk cows, six other cattle, eleven sheep and one hog.

The hardship of these past seventeen years was particularly evident in Dolly's appearance. Not only were her shoulders noticeably bent, but her figure was stouter, her face seamed by worry wrinkles, and her thick, flaxen-colored hair was becoming quite thin. In time she would wear a wig to protect her head against the cold.

In the early 1850's the area stood at the threshold of the summer visitor business. As it did, Dolly was ready to reap her harvest. In 1852 the Atlantic & St. Lawrence Railroad connected Gorham with Portland, while the Boston, Concord & Montreal Railway steamed its way into Conway. With the appearance of both railroads, daily stagecoaches began carrying mail and passengers through Pinkham Notch.

That spring Colonel Joseph M. Thompson of Shelburne, New Hampshire, also bought seven hundred acres of land and a partially built house for $11,000 from John Bellows at the eastern base of Mount Washington. It was his intent to develop a first-class hotel there. After completing the ell, he immediately opened the building to the traveling public. This was the beginning of the famous Glen House.

Meeting Dolly, Colonel Thompson recognized the quality of her expertly crafted homespun, uniquely designed linen, and delicious homemade delicacies. Providing her a ready market for them at the Glen House, he enabled her to bring many comforts into the Copp house that the family would not have otherwise known.

Dolly's name also spread throughout New England, and beyond, in another fashion. Travelers who came into the region to admire the Presidential Range began hearing of a strange, satanic-appearing stone profile which stood out on the ridge of Imp Mountain. Many of them were told that it could be seen best from the dooryard of the Copp farm. As the six-horse stages rolled along the Glen Road, they often crossed the Peabody River and pulled up at the Copp doorway. Standing there nervously fidgeting with her old gold beads, Dolly would point out the profile and answer whatever questions were directed at her.

During the following summer of 1853, at the Alpine House in Gorham, a stock company was organized to plan the building of a carriage road from the Glen House to the summit of Mount Washington. Though construction of the eight-mile road did not begin until 1855, Jeremiah and Nathaniel left the farm when it did. They both worked as laborers on the first four miles of the project.

When the company went bankrupt, further progress was temporarily halted just above the Halfway House. While Nathaniel returned to the farm, Jeremiah went to work in Gorham as a carpenter. He had married Susan Rogers of Jackson on January 10, 1858, and it was necessary for him to continue earning a living.

A few weeks after Jeremiah's wedding, Nathaniel had a painful misadventure. On January 31, he went on a solitary deer hunt that kept him out for four successive days. With the larder at home low on meat, he was determined to get a deer before returning.

Late into the fourth day he shot a 256-pound buck eight miles from the farm. Exhausted and cold, he gutted the animal and suspended it from a tree out of reach of other animals. He returned home to rest, and early the next morning he snowshoed back for it.

Dragging the animal through the deep snow, he arrived at the farm near noon. At 1:00 p.m., leaving his rifle behind, he set off again looking for another deer he had tracked near the spot where the first was shot.

Two hours later he picked up the track and followed it until dark. After stopping for a breather, he suddenly realized that he was lost. With the temperature at 34 degrees below zero, he still refused to turn back. Since it was a bright, clear night he decided to continue the tracking.

Hours later he heard a bleat from his exhausted quarry. When he speeded up the chase, the deep snow prevented the animal's escape. As it floundered helplessly, Nathaniel slipped out of his snowshoes, leaped on its back, and slit its throat with a hunting knife.

After quickly gutting it, he slipped the heart into a pocket as protection against possible starvation. With his feet growing numb he strapped on his snowshoes. With no sense of direction, he struck off blindly not knowing that one of the snowshoes was laced too tight.

At daylight he was still imprisoned by thick woods on every side. He did not see a familiar landmark until he came to the Wild River in Gilead, Maine, at midmorning. On the opposite side he stumbled on a farmhouse. In his twenty-one hours of circuitous wandering he had covered more than forty miles.

Alarmed over Nathaniel's prolonged absence in such deadly weather, late that day Hayes went to the neighboring farm of Thomas Culhane seeking assistance for a search. Culhane agreed to help, and brought along his hired man, John Goulding. Several hours later they came across the slain deer.

After enduring an experience similar to Nathaniel's, the next afternoon the three men showed up in Gilead. Led to Nathaniel's bedside, they found him delirious. With his legs badly affected by the ordeal, he did not walk for six months. And because he had laced the snowshoe too tight, he lost the toes on that foot.

As for Hayes and Culhane, they suffered from the effects of frostbitten ears for the rest of their lives. However, the greatest tragedy from the incident befelled the hired man. He had frozen both feet and they had to be amputated.

Following Nathaniel's recovery, Sylvia married Benjamin Potter on November 14, 1858. Surprisingly, she was only nineteen while he was fifty-five. According to his birth certificate, he was born in New Gloucester, Maine, on August 31, 1803. He was probably an old friend of Colonel Thompson of the Glen House where Sylvia could have met him while delivering her mother's handicrafts. Before taking over the Glen House, Colonel Thompson had operated a hotel in New Gloucester. Whatever the case, the marriage had Hayes' and Dolly's blessings.

The couple lived out their lives in Auburn, Maine.

In 1860 both Jeremiah and Nathaniel also left the area. Going first, Jeremiah moved his wife Susan and their year-old daughter, Marcella, to Littleton, New Hampshire, where he remained for the next forty-six years working as a carpenter.

Nathaniel left following his quiet marriage to Esther E. Willey, 24, on May 28. For years afterward he traveled the world as a circus employee. Hayes and Dolly seldom heard from him, or ever knew where he was.

With three of her children moved away, Dolly suffered deeply from their absence. For weeks at a time she was short tempered and sharp tongued with Hayes. When her mood darkened, long silent spells followed. Respecting her suffering, Hayes kept his distance. He was thankful they still had young Daniel.

Winters were hardest on Dolly through these years. Without "city folks" around to entertain, in the evenings she would just sit quietly at her spinning wheel, or gaze into the flames of the fireplace while she smoked a short-stemmed pipe. A sociable person who loved companionship, smoking helped her to pass long, lonely hours.

When she first took up smoking in her middle age, the importance of it was not lost on Hayes. When the season was favorable, he raised the tobacco she needed.

She suffered another type of grief when her friend, Colonel Thompson, met a tragic death on October 4, 1869. On that date high winds and heavy rains swept over the six New England states. Known as Saxby's Gale, the early autumn storm whipped through Pinkham Notch raising the Peabody River to flood stage. While attempting to protect some of his possessions in a mill near his house, the Colonel was swept away by high water. After hearing that he had drowned, Dolly was devastated.

When Daniel was twenty-four, her life turned another corner. In the summer of 1874 a refined, mature young woman named Lizzie Drew arrived at the Copp farm. From Oberlin, Ohio, she was sent there to regain her health. Having suffered from a long siege of typhoid, which was complicated by pneumonia, her doctors felt that New Hampshire's mountain air would not only restore her lungs but also her overall well-being.

During her recuperation, Daniel often took her for wagon rides, joined her on daily walks, and accompanied her to Sunday services and church socials. When the chilly nights of autumn arrived, they had long romantic fireside chats. On December 18, 1874, they were united in marriage by Reverend J.A. Hawks.

After the couple left for the bride's home in Ohio, Dolly grew more and more indifferent toward Hayes. Over the next eleven years their marriage continued to deteriorate. Perhaps the one thread that held them together during this time was Nathaniel's return home. Tired of his aimless wanderings, and with his childless union to Esther Willey ended, he finally came back to the place where he knew he was always welcome.

Shortly after his arrival, in the early summer of 1876 author Samuel Adams Drake arrived at the Glen House. Doing research on New Hampshire for his forthcoming book, *The Heart of the White Mountains, Their Legend and Scenery*, he had heard about Nathaniel's narrow escape with death while deer hunting. For that reason he wanted to interview him.

The next day, going to what he described as "the old Copp place," he later wrote: "The Copp farmhouse has a tale of its own, illustrating in a remarkable manner the amount of physical hardship that long training, and familiarity with rough out-of-door life, will occasionally enable men to endure."

Seeing Nathaniel and Hayes in the backyard, Drake walked over and introduced himself. He then sat down on a chopping block and entered into conversation with them. Describing what followed, he wrote: "By the time I had taken out my note-book I had all the members of the household and all the inmates of the barn-yard around me. I might add that all were talking at once. The matron stood in the door-way, which her ample figure quite filled, trifling with the gold necklace...."

In the interview that followed, Nathaniel told Drake the story as he remembered it. Apparently, though, he taxed Drake's patience in the process because Drake wrote, "I had literally to draw it out of him, a syllable at a time."

Finally, on November 3, 1881, the Copps celebrated their controversial Fiftieth Wedding Anniversary. Following a quiet observance, family and friends learned that Dolly and Hayes were considering separating. Since it appeared to be Dolly's decision, her judgment was questioned. When asked why, her famous reply was, "Hayes is well enough, but fifty years is long enough for a woman to live with any man."

Despite the decision, Hayes and Dolly stayed on at the farm. A few years later they had to admit that they were no longer capable of managing it. They then sold it to Nathaniel. The Coos County records show that the transaction took place in 1884. However, after the purchase, Nathaniel changed his plans and sold the entire property to E. Libby & Sons. Involved in lumbering, they only wanted it for the timber.

While the house was being boarded up, Nathaniel bought a farm eighteen miles above Gorham in the small farming community of Dummer. By then Hayes had moved to Stow, Maine, to live with Dolly's nephew, James C. Emery. On January 18, 1886, he gave Emery $400 toward the purchase price of the Elwood N. Bemis farm. In return, he had a home with the Emerys for the remainder of his life.

A Gorham newspaper item revealed that Dolly was still in the Gorham area in 1886. It noted that while spending a few weeks there among her many friends, she attended the Methodist Church service the previous Sunday. It added, "To a friend she made this comment upon the sermon: "When that minister read 'I go away to prepare a place for you but will come again and receive you unto myself,' it made me think of how Nathaniel had gone to Dummer to prepare a place for me, and is coming back after me."

For reasons unknown, this never happened. Before the year was over, she was living in Auburn with Sylvia. Sick of leading Hayes' type of life, this was more to her liking.

Now, from a historical perspective, what happened to this family in the years ahead?

In Hayes' case, he died shortly after his 83rd birthday on November 6, 1889. He is buried with the Emerys in the Austin Bemis Cemetery a short distance from where the Emery farm once stood.

As for Dolly, following her arrival in Auburn it is said that "she adjusted readily to life in the city, and she enjoyed the social life it offered." She died on October 4, 1891, at 84. She is buried in the Mt. Auburn Cemetery.

Following the death of his wife Susan, Jeremiah moved to Meredith, New Hampshire, where his daughter Marcella lived. Just before his 78th birthday, he died of unspecified internal injuries on September 5, 1910.

Unpredictable as ever, Nathaniel made front-page news for the last time when he dramatically appeared in the Lewiston-Auburn area of Maine on Friday morning, October 21, 1910. Auburn police were first alerted to his arrival when they began receiving reports that "an oddly dressed, elderly man was attracting a great deal of attention in his wanderings."

After one woman nervously called the police station to report that "he'd nearly scared her to death," and another young lady complained that "she took to her heels because she thought he was about to follow her," Nathaniel was ordered brought to the police station.

Accompanied by Deputy Marshall Stetson, the 76-year-old man looked like a figure fifty years out of the past. His face was covered by a week's growth of beard, the upper portion of his short body

DOLLY COPP AND FAMILY 63

was garbed in the voluminous folds of an old, heavy ulster, and his middle was girded by a broad belt with a large silver buckle. A red flannel shirt collar peeked out at the neck.

Adding to his peculiar appearance was the fact that his heavily patched and darned trousers were inside out. Also, they only reached a few inches below his knees so that only his bare legs bridged the gap between his trousers and heavy wool socks. Added to this, a tall, fuzzy, old-fashioned hat sat on his head, and he was carrying a walking stick almost as tall as he was.

In the interrogation that followed, the police learned that he had been an inmate at the Brunswick Town Farm only the day before. This was an institution maintained for the poor.

MR. COPP VISITS AUBURN
(Photo courtesy of Lewiston Evening Journal)

This sketch of Nathaniel Copp appeared on the front page of the Lewiston Evening Journal on October 21, 1910. Looking for his sister, Sylvia, Nathaniel had the city in an uproar as he wandered the streets.

"Are you saying that you ran away from there?" one of the officers asked.

"I didn't run away," Nathaniel protested. "I just told them I wasn't going to stay and left."

"Just bid 'em goodbye and left," the marshall remarked.

"I didn't even bid them goodbye!" Nathaniel snapped.

When Sylvia was notified that her brother was at the police station, she was surprised to learn that he was in Auburn. Told that he had come to the city looking for her, she went to the police station and took him home.

Unfortunately Nathaniel was suffering from hardening of the arteries. As his condition worsened, he was returned to the Brunswick Town Farm. He died there on February 27, 1912, at 77. He is also buried in Auburn. Tragically, the world to which he belonged had disappeared years earlier.

This U.S. Forest Service sign, located along Route 16 just five miles south of Gorham, pays silent tribute to the plucky and indomitable little woman named Dolly Copp who lived and labored on the grounds where thousands of campers now pitch their tents.

Daniel, Dolly's youngest son, died at 72 in Richwood, Ohio, on March 13, 1922. To her credit his wife Lizzie, who was involved in educational and philanthropic work, founded the Lizzie A. Copp Industrial School for Girls in Burma, the School for Orphan Girls in Oneida, Kentucky, and the Alvan Drew School at Pine Ridge, Kentucky.

Living almost into her 91st year, Sylvia was the longest lived of the family. Before she died at the Auburn Home for Aged Women on October 29, 1929, she saw her mother's name perpetuated through the establishment of the Dolly Copp Campground by the United States Forest Service in Martin's Location. In 1915 the Copp farm was purchased by the Federal Government and made a part of the White Mountain National Forest. Since 1921 the Copp land has been enjoyed by thousands of campers.

If alive today, Dolly would have liked that. In a manner of speaking, she is still sharing her home with the "city folks" whom she loved so much.

Murder at the Cog Railway

This early photo of Elie Gendron shows him as he often looked, wearing work clothes and with a cigar in his mouth. Also evident is his artificial left arm with the attached hooks.

(Photo courtesy of Ralph Martin)

LIKE MANY OTHER YOUNG MEN before him, Elie Gendron came to New Hampshire from Sherbrooke, Quebec, seeking a better life. Though he found it, there was a stiff price attached. A price that included both physical suffering and a violent death. Whatever happiness Elie knew came principally from his marriage to Retta Hart Martin. Their wedding was held in Campton on July 28, 1935.

Beyond this moment, his physical suffering began when he lost the lower half of his left arm in a finishing room accident at the Franconia Paper Company in Lincoln. Despite this traumatic experience, following his recovery he continued to operate one of the rotary cutters on which the accident had happened. First though, he had to adjust to an artificial arm with two steel hooks attached. Hooks that replaced his missing hand.

The years passed. Always frugal with his money, Elie prospered. But, for reasons peculiar to himself, he developed an eccentric sense of humor. For example, he seemed to derive pleasure from flashing his overstuffed wallet in front of his co-workers. Frequently they warned him to either put the money it contained in the bank, or to invest it before someone attempted to steal it. His response to the warnings was invariably the same. Chuckling, he would say, "If anyone ever tries to take my money, they'll have to kill me first to get it." As subsequent events proved, he meant what he said. The wallet cost him his life at approximately 12:15 p.m. on Sunday, July 26, 1959. He and Retta were just two days short of celebrating their twenty-fourth wedding anniversary. The tragedy took place when a short, stocky, middle-aged male with a crew cut pointed a .22 calibre revolver at him and pulled the trigger repeatedly. Retta was seated beside him when it happened. It was a day that haunted her to her grave.

Hours before, in mid-morning, she and Elie put a picnic basket and their fishing gear in the trunk of their '58 Dodge. After Elie locked their small house on Lost River Road in North Woodstock, they rode out to Route 3 and headed north.

Though it wasn't on their itinerary, they stopped at the Flume gift shop in Franconia Notch and enjoyed a cold soda. After a brief visit with some of the local help, they continued on to Twin Mountain. Here Elie turned east onto Route 302 and drove to Zealand Campground.

Shortly after Retta had put out their picnic lunch, and Elie had opened a can of beer, a dark-colored '49 Chevrolet parked near their car. Retta noticed that the driver appeared to be studying their license plate and writing on a piece of paper. She thought he looked familiar, but she couldn't place where she had seen him.

A moment later he emerged, and as he approached them he read off their plate number from the paper he was carrying. He asked if the number was theirs. Elie nodded that it was.

Standing in front of them, the stranger smiled and inquired, "Do you have a sick mother in Canada, Elie?"

Later Retta remembered being surprised at hearing her husband addressed by name.

When Elie replied that he did, the stranger said, "She's taken a turn for the worse, I'm afraid. Chief Everett LaPointe of North Woodstock asked me to drive out and find you. I'm to get you to a telephone so you can phone him back."

Not particularly upset by the news, especially since his mother had been ill for a long time, Elie felt a few more minutes wouldn't make any difference. Thanking the stranger, he said, "Why don't you sit down and have lunch with us. I'll phone him later."

Retta Gendron is seen on the porch of her home on Lost River Road, North Woodstock. Following the murder she was frightened of anyone who came to the house. After dark her door was never unlocked. She is buried next to Elie in the Woodstock Cemetery.

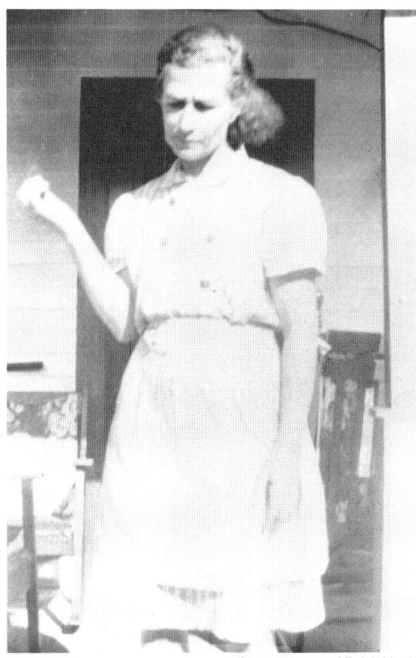

(Photo courtesy of Ralph Martin)

After they were seated, Elie asked, "How far do we have to go to get to a telephone?"

Speaking over a sandwich, the man told him, "I'll take you to a relay station in the woods. That will be the closest one."

Following the lunch, the trio piled into the Dodge. From the backseat the stranger directed Elie toward the Mt. Washington Base Station. As they approached the large Cog Railway sign, he had Elie turn left and cross the railroad tracks. From the Base Station road he had him turn right onto the narrow, secluded Clinton Road. At a point that was only 2 1/2 miles from the Base Station, he said, "Pull up here. We'll walk the rest of the way. It's only a couple of minutes through the woods."

As the two men left the car and started walking toward a path, Retta also got out. When she closed the door the stranger turned and told her, "Stay here and wait."

A few minutes later the men reappeared. Elie was walking slightly ahead. Immediately Retta sensed that something was very wrong. She later described Elie's face as being "white as a sheet."

"What's wrong, Elie?" she probed.

Instead of answering her, Elie's face remained grim and set.

Affected by a sense of urgency, Retta cried, "What's the matter, Elie?"

Suddenly Elie bolted for the car. "Get in quick!" he commanded. "We're getting out of here!"

Once they were both in the car, he frantically turned the ignition key. When the engine roared to life, his foot went down hard on the gas pedal. The rear tires spun furiously on soft ground before the car shot forward. When it did, Retta's right knee slammed against the dashboard.

Despite the confusion created by Elie's shouting and the stranger's shouting, Retta managed to glimpse the stranger's left hand disappear inside a trouser pocket. When it emerged, there was a gun in it. At that point Elie lost control of the car. The front bumper struck a sign post and a small tree, and the engine stalled.

Now in a complete panic, Elie desperately tried to get the flooded engine started. But he failed. At the age of 51, his life was about to end.

Walking toward them, the stranger pointed the gun at Elie and began shooting. The first two shots struck the car. Then, in one final defensive gesture, Elie held up his artificial arm. It absorbed the next shot. As Retta screamed, the man fired at Elie at point-blank range. Elie clutched his chest, twisted away from the steering wheel, and landed heavily in Retta's lap.

In shock, Retta screamed, "You've killed my husband!"

The man tore open the driver's door. He pointed the gun at her. His hands were trembling. "I'll kill you, too, if you don't get out of here!" he screamed back.

Nearly hysterical, Retta, who was only 4 feet 1, forced herself out from under Elie and headed for the woods.

Eventually her headlong flight brought her to the Ammonoosuc River. Following it for nearly two miles, she came to the road leading to the Mt. Washington Base Station.

Bruised, scratched, and near exhaustion, she arrived at the Bretton Woods Boys Choir Camp. Here she encountered Mrs. Ellen Teague, the camp nurse. Running up to her, Retta gasped, "My husband's just been murdered! Down there on the road. Oh, it's terrible. The man shot him in cold blood. Help me, please!"

After administering first aid to the distraught woman, Mrs. Teague telephoned the state police. Then leaving Retta at the camp, she drove to the site of the crime. Parking her car, she found Elie

Murder at The Cog Railway

still slumped over in the front seat. She checked for a pulse. There was none. Since there was nothing she could do for him, she returned to her car.

When the police arrived, she told them what she could and returned to the Base Station. She knew that her husband, Arthur Teague, manager of the Cog Railway, would be interested in learning that a murder had been committed almost at their doorstep.

The identity of the murderer was a shock that still awaited them.

Arriving in Twin Mountain, Assistant Attorney General Elmer Bourque of Manchester immediately took charge of the investigation. Moving quickly, he set up field headquarters at the Boulder Motor Court owned by Mr. and Mrs. Robert C. Jellison just off Route 302. Through questioning Retta, he obtained a precise description of the killer. It fit Robert G. Brown, 41, of Laconia. Brown was already wanted for a similar murder committed at Old Orchard Beach, Maine, on July 9. Another alarm went out for his apprehension.

Meanwhile, contact was established with Chief Everett LaPointe in North Woodstock. As a result, suspicions were confirmed that the killer's story, which lured the Gendrons into the woods, was pure fiction.

At the picnic site, police also learned that the killer's car was gone. Since it was at least five miles from there to the murder scene, they theorized that he had somehow obtained a ride which brought him back to the car.

Acting on that premise, local radio stations were contacted. They were asked to broadcast an appeal for anyone to come forward who had given a ride to a stranger that day. Before long the investigation struck paydirt. Miss Helen Long, a clerk at the Crawford House, called and said that a man answering the killer's description had been there that afternoon. She related that she arranged for Edward Torrence, 18, of Mt. Dora, Florida, a groundskeeper, to drive him to his car. A car, which he said, he had left at the Zealand Campground.

Two hours later another call came from the Crawford House. It was from a young lady who asked to remain anonymous. Given the necessary assurances, she then said she had seen the wanted man locally prior to the murder. Unable to pinpoint where, she said she would call back.

An hour later she did. "I've seen him before talking with a waitress in a Lancaster restaurant!" she exclaimed.

Following the leads she provided, police officers went to the restaurant. The waitress was off duty. Two hours later they located her at a nearby beach. After listening to the wanted man's description, she said, "You must be talking about 'Sonny' Gonyer."

When asked where he worked, she answered, "He's a trackman for the Mt. Washington Cog Railway."

The information was then relayed to the Teagues that Gilbert H. Gonyer, 44, of Bunker Hill Street, Lancaster, was strongly implicated in the killing. Fighting back dismay, Arthur Teague expressed doubts that Gonyer could be the man they were seeking. "He was sent to us by the State Employment Office three weeks ago," he said. "If he had any kind of a criminal record, they certainly told us nothing about it."

Certain that Gonyer was their man, the state police set up a stakeout at the Base Station boardinghouse where he quartered.

With the investigation moving forward, Elie's body was removed to the Stanard Funeral Home in Lancaster for an autopsy. That evening the Coos County Medical Referee announced his findings: "Death resulted from a .22 calibre bullet which entered the chest just below the breastbone, and passed beneath the sternum," he stated. "That same bullet was found on the left side of the victim's back near the surface."

Prior to this announcement, police gave Retta permission to return home. Not having a ride, she telephoned her daughter-in-law, Mrs. Patricia Martin of North Woodstock. Grief-stricken, in shock, and exhausted, she had difficulty in speaking coherently. By listening carefully, Mrs. Martin understood that Elie had been shot and that Retta wanted her son William to pick her up at the small Twin Mountain telephone office.

Ironically, at this point Retta was muddled about whether Elie

Murder at The Cog Railway

This photo of Gilbert Gonyer originally appeared in Front Page Detective magazine with an article entitled, "Murder Hits the Hotdog Trail." Shown while pondering his fate at the Boulder Motor Court in Twin Mountain, he was admitted to the New Hampshire State Prison at 4:15 on November 30, 1959, to begin a double life sentence.

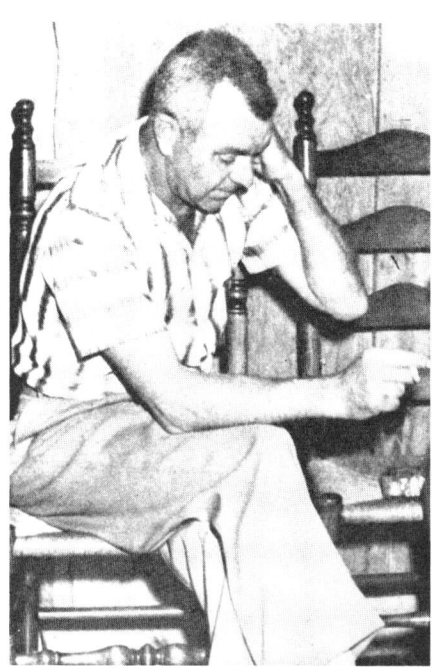

(Photo source: *Front Page Detective*, November 1959)

was actually dead. No one connected with the case realized in all the confusion that she hadn't been told that his death was officially confirmed.

Early the next morning she was taken to the local police station and was asked to examine selected photographs of criminals with similar physical characteristics. Leafing through them, she eliminated Brown as a suspect. When she came to Gonyer's picture she turned away from it, saying, "That's him."

With Gonyer's role in the killing now definitely established, at 10:00 a.m. a 13-state alarm went out for his arrest. Shortly afterwards, his criminal past emerged. As far back as 1938 he had been sentenced to the New Hampshire State Prison for forgery. Later he served 50 months in Connecticut for car theft. Now it was also learned that he had just been released from the Maine State Prison on June 1 after serving another 12 months for the same offense. And, as part of his record, it was noted that he was divorced and the father of a daughter.

Just before 1:00 p.m. that day, less than 25 hours after the murder had been committed, Gonyer's whereabouts surfaced. He was spotted still driving the '49 Chevrolet. But, even more unbelievable, at that very moment he was headed for Twin Mountain!

When he stopped at Garneau's Garage for gas, he immediately found himself surrounded by law enforcement officers. They included Bourque, State Police Corporal Lloyd Sherman, and Troopers

Walter Morse and Gary Waterhouse. And their service revolvers were all pointed at him. Having little choice, he surrendered without resistance.

Taken to the Boulder Motor Court, he was interrogated for several hours. Initially he denied the killing. When he finally confessed, he said, "I didn't want to kill him, but I got scared. The Gendrons didn't know it, but I was more frightened than they were. The boys in the pen told me it was easy to knock off picnickers, but they were wrong."

Asked how he knew Elie by name, and more particularly, how he knew about his sick mother, Gonyer told them he had lived in Lincoln at one time and knew all about Elie.

Toward the end of the questioning, he said his original plan was simply to rob Elie and then get away quickly. "The trouble started," he said, "when Elie refused to turn over his wallet." He added, "From then on everything went wrong."

After the stenographer, Mrs. Frederick Helm of Groveton, finished typing the confession Gonyer signed it. Afterwards he toured the crime area with Bourque and several officers. As they went along, he added details to what he had already told them. For instance, they learned that he paid $10 to young Torrence for driving him back to the campground. He also disclosed that the '49 Chevrolet belonged to his brother "Peanut," who worked as a dishwasher in Twin Mountain.

Discussing the gun, he said that he had purchased it the day before the killing and later threw it into the woods.

As to the amount of money he took from Elie's body, he shrugged and said he didn't know because he "lost" the wallet.

Police Chief Howard Sanborn of Bethlehem, who assisted in the investigation, estimated that the killing netted Gonyer about $200. He also noted that neither the gun nor the wallet has ever been recovered.

At 7:00 that Monday evening, Gonyer was transferred to the Whitefield jail to await a Tuesday morning arraignment. Police Chief Thomas Gage later said his prisoner "slept like a log" that night.

The next morning, at 9:53, Gonyer appeared before Judge

Harold L. Keir in the Whitefield Municipal Court. The fifteen minute proceeding was interrupted by the tearful entrance of Gonyer's mother, Mrs. Hugh Dingman. She was accompanied by her husband and a second son.

Confronting the confessed killer, the broken-hearted mother sobbed, "What did you do that for?"

Shaking his head, Gonyer replied, "I don't know."

After order was restored, and all the evidence had been presented, Judge Keir read the formal complaint charging Gonyer with premeditated murder by a pistol held in the left hand.

Gonyer asked the judge, "Does that mean I planned to kill him?"

Standing up, Assistant Attorney General Bourque repeated an earlier suggestion that the court appoint counsel for the defendant.

Gonyer said, "I see no sense in it. I plead guilty."

Ignoring the remark, Judge Keir ordered a plea of innocent to be entered on Gonyer's behalf.

Speaking in a low voice, Gonyer told the judge, "I only planned to rob him. I didn't plan to murder him."

Following the hearing, he was transferred to the Coos County Jail in West Stewartstown to await the fall term of the Superior Court in Berlin.

A few days after Elie's funeral, Gonyer had another confrontation with Retta. It occurred because she was asked to make a visual, physical identification of him. Riding to West Stewartstown with two state troopers, she entered the jail with her son Ralph and Chief Everett LaPointe. Taking a quick look at Gonyer, she said, "That's him," and left. His effect on her was evident.

Finally, on November 30, following the completion of all legal proceedings against him, Gonyer was sentenced to two terms of life imprisonment. The double sentence was to insure that he would serve out the remaining years of his life in prison.

But, when all was said and done, he beat the system!

Almost twenty years later, on March 3, 1979, he was released on parole from the New Hampshire State Prison. The following July he

(Photo source: *Front Page Detective*, November 1959)

This cruiser photographed at the murder scene belonged to Police Chief Howard Sanborn of Bethlehem. During the investigation, Gendron's '58 Dodge was impounded and stored in Chief Sanborn's garage.

absconded from parole supervision, and his present whereabouts to this day are unknown.

As for Retta Gendron, she lived a little more than 3-1/2 years after Elie was murdered. Always terrified that Gonyer would somehow find a way to come back and kill her, she died on March 3, 1963, at the age of 66.

In the final analysis, more than the gun and wallet are missing in this strange case. Now, so is Gilbert Gonyer!

A Hero Remembers

(Photo courtesy of New Hampshire State Police)
State Police Officer Leo Jellison

SEVERAL YEARS AGO veteran State Police Officers Leo "Chuck" Jellison and Wayne Fortier attended a ceremony held in their honor at the State House in Concord. At this time they not only received awards and commendations from Governor John Sununu, the FBI, and the state police, but they were also the recipients of the Medal of Valor, the highest award granted by the state police.

This recognition came to them for the heroic manner in which they ended the six-week cross-country nightmare of sexual sadism and murder that was being carried out by Christopher B. Wilder. It was a killing spree that may have claimed the lives of at least thirteen young women.

In apprehending Wilder, Officer Jellison almost lost his own life. While grappling with him in a stolen Pontiac Trans-Am at Vic's Getty Oil Station in Colebrook on Friday the 13th, 1984, the killer's .357 Magnum pistol went off twice. The first shot penetrated Wilder's heart, went out his back, and seriously wounded Jellison. The second shot slammed into Wilder's heart, literally causing it to explode.

Officer Jellison spent two weeks in the Upper Connecticut Valley Hospital recovering.

Ironically, Jellison, the 6 foot 4, 250-pound trooper that ended Wilder's lawless flight only twelve miles from the Canadian border, was the same nine-year-old boy who was living with his parents at the Boulder Motor Court in Twin Mountain when Assistant Attorney General Bourque set up his headquarters there during the Gendron murder investigation.

When asked if he remembered that moment from his childhood, the young officer laughed and said, "I sure do. Everywhere I looked, all I saw was police uniforms. I'm not ashamed to admit that I was scared to death. Believe me, I've never forgotten it."

A Chronicle of the Willey Family Tragedy

(Photo courtesy of Dick Hamilton Private Collection)

In 1884 Horace Fabyan repaired the Willey House and built a two-and-a-half story hotel on to it. The original Willey House and attached shed can be seen directly behind the table. The Bible and candle that are shown were in the house at the time of the landslide.

At THE DARK HOUR of 3:00 a.m. on Monday, August 28, 1826, ominous black clouds began to settle over the sparsely inhabited region known today as Crawford Notch. A deadly summer storm was gathering. Before the storm had shed its fury, it would claim nine lives in a nightmarish disaster. It is a tale that still tugs at the heart and chills the spine.

The wild and desolate fifteen-mile-long defile was then known as "The Notch" or "The Pass of the White Mountains." A steady stream of horse-drawn carts and wagons passed through here on a turnpike which was incorporated in 1803 at a cost of $40,000. The route was an important link between northeastern Vermont, northern New Hampshire, and Portland, Maine. Three habitations dotted the road and functioned as inns. They were especially important during the winter months.

At the northwestern end of the Notch, Ethan Allen Crawford's establishment was situated in a large intervale near the Ammonoosuc River four miles above the steep, narrow elevation called "The Gateway of the Pass." His highly respected father, Abel Crawford, operated "The Mount Crawford House" nine miles south of the Gateway.

In between them, Samuel Willey, Jr., of Bartlett had recently become the new owner of the small one-and-one-half story farmhouse called "The Notch House."

(Photo courtesy of Dick Hamilton Private Collection)

This scene, originally photographed and published by John P. Soule of 130 Tremont Street, Boston, sometime after 1884, shows the scar left by the northernmost slide. The longest of the three slides, it came down directly behind the Willey House and carried away most of the barn. Had the family stayed in the house, all would have survived.

Built in 1792, this house had been abandoned for several months and was badly in need of repairs. Its last tenant had been Ethan Crawford who had rented the property in the fall of 1823. Ethan had agreed to furnish it with hay and other necessities for travelers and their horses. But, during the winter of 1824 due to excessive demand, Crawford ran out of hay and had to buy more in Jefferson. After carting it over sixteen miles to the Notch House, he lost interest in the venture and gave it up altogether.

Willey moved his family into the abandoned house during the autumn of 1825, and set to work with his two hired men to make the house secure against the oncoming winter. And, when the winter did arrive, the howling winds, intense cold, and blinding snowstorms were unlike anything the young family had ever experienced at their previous residence in Bartlett. Yet, it was for this very reason that the traveling public welcomed the accommodations Willey provided.

Looking back, Samuel Willey, Jr. was a son of Samuel and Betsy

A Chronicle of the Willey Family Tragedy

This is a rare photograph of the original fireplace in the old Willey House. It was taken by Mrs. George Sawyer just four days before the house was destroyed by fire on September 24, 1899.

Glazier Willey who were originally from Lee, New Hampshire, and had been among the earliest settlers in Bartlett. But shortly after arriving in Bartlett, they moved to upper Conway to "The Bigelow Farm" where they lived out their long lives. The Bigelow Farm was on the east side of the Saco River, across from the Lovejoy Farm, home of Polly Lovejoy who became young Samuel Willey's wife.

When the couple married on September 12, 1812, Samuel was twenty-four and Polly was twenty-one. Their personalities complemented one another from the outset. He was a kind and gentle man, respected for his cautious, sound judgment, while she was a bright, attractive woman possessed of an amiable disposition and a lively personality. By nature, both were deeply religious.

To get established, the young couple rented a one-story farmhouse on the west side of the Saco River in lower Bartlett. Known as "The Humphrey Ledge Farm," it was the oldest farmhouse in the area. Through the thirteen years that they resided here they had five children. From oldest to youngest, they were Eliza Ann, Jeremiah, Martha Glazier, Elbridge Gerry, and Sally. They also raised David Nickerson, who later became one of their hired hands.

Though the farm afforded the family a comfortable subsistence, in 1825 well-intentioned friends convinced Samuel Willey that it would be a sound business investment to purchase the Notch House. Tragically, this was the move that sealed the family's horrible fate.

Encouraged by the profit he made there that first winter, Willey continued to enlarge the conveniences of the inn for entertaining guests. Helping him were Nickerson, who was now 21, and David Allen, 37, a powerfully built man who had a wife and four children living in Bartlett.

By early summer not only were the renovations progressing satisfactorily, but the area itself had taken on an attractive appearance. In front of the house there was a beautiful meadow which stretched to the base of 3,875-foot-high Mt. Webster. Fringed by tall rock maples, the meadow added a touch of beauty to the tranquil atmosphere surrounding the inn.

Directly behind the house Mt. Willey, which was not really named this until nineteen years after the tragedy, rose to a height of 4,260 feet. Between the house and the foot of this mountain Willey planted a patch of wheat of less than an acre. Unfortunately, due to the restrictive nature of the Notch, there was barely enough room for necessary buildings. And, since the meadow was so small, it was needed solely for forage for the cows, sheep, two oxen, and two horses.

The only other animal on the premises was the family dog.

As travelers "put up" at the Willey House, as it was now called, they spoke with gratitude of the kindness and attentions afforded them by their hosts. It was while speaking in this vein that one guest added, "Despite the presence of the children, order, peace, and cheerfulness also pervades the house."

It was also often noted that the children were "intelligent, well behaved, contented and happy."

The first hint of trouble came early that summer while Abel Crawford and a road crew were repairing the turnpike. A sudden heavy rain forced them to seek shelter at the Willey House. While they were in the house, a small slide with prodigious power came down Mt. Willey. Missing the barn by about fifty feet, the debris covered several hundred feet of road. It was immediately followed by a second slide of lesser magnitude.

The Willeys became greatly alarmed. Because the larger slide came so near to the house, Mrs. Willey panicked and attempted to leave the house carrying two of her children. Abel Crawford calmed her. He told her, "Don't be alarmed. You are much safer here than you would be on the road. Besides, there may be other difficulties in the way caused by other slides. And, if swollen waters have carried

Upon the spot where the remains of the Willey Family were temporarily buried in Crawford Notch, it was the custom for years afterward for visitors to place a stone on the gravesite. Over time, a large monument literally grew out of the ruins of the slide.

away some of the bridges, then they cannot be crossed."

Shortly after the road crew left, Samuel Willey searched about for a safer location than the house should a similar emergency arise again. Toward that end, a few hundred feet south of the house he constructed a "camp" from a large, overturned cart body. As a further safeguard, he placed a twenty-five-foot log behind the house to protect it from rolling rocks.

In the few months remaining to him, whenever discussing the two slides with guests, and the possibility of future ones, Willey stated, "Such an event, we know, has not really happened here for a very long time past, and another of the kind is not likely to occur for an equally long time to come. Taking things past in this view, then I am not afraid."

This was to prove to be a fatal attitude.

That summer, as improvements on the property continued, the weather remained excessively hot and dry. Coming into August, the earth turned to a powdery dust which was soon ankle deep. As the drought began to feed off itself, vegetation became parched and lifeless. Toward the middle of the month, a wind blowing in from the south brought a promise of rain. Occasionally light showers sprinkled the area, but they provided little relief.

Then on August 28 the storm struck! With night coming on, high winds and torrential rains savagely lashed the valley. Amid the flashes of lightning, peals of thunder, reverberations and echoes of innumerable landslides, the Saco River went on a rampage. Just before midnight the storm suddenly ceased. When the clouds cleared away, the remainder of the night passed in perfect calm.

Early the next morning Ethan Crawford was awakened by a young voice: "Father, the earth is nearly covered with water, and the hogs are swimming for life!"

Leaping out of bed, Crawford quickly discovered that his crops were lost, fourteen of his sheep had drowned, a ninety-foot shed had been washed away, and some of his best land was buried beneath sand and gravel. At its peak, the flood had come within eighteen inches of his doorway.

No matter in what direction Crawford looked, he saw devastation beyond belief. It was later estimated that more than a hundred slides had come down during the storm. Most of them centering around the Mt. Washington range.

Down in the valley Abel Crawford had also suffered heavy losses. Since he was away when the storm struck, his wife was home alone with the children. When the Saco River began to flow through their house, she hustled the youngsters off to an upper floor. She then spent the night at a window with a clothespole pushing away floating trees and logs that were threatening to knock their house off its foundation. When the lightning flashed, she could see their crops being destroyed, their sheep drowning, and their freshly cut lumber being washed downstream. She also witnessed the destruction of their new sawmill. And like Ethan, they also lost some of their best land.

In the truest sense, the greatest tragedy had occurred at the

A Chronicle of the Willey Family Tragedy 83

Willey House. However, due to the family's isolation, no one had any way of knowing that. The full horror of what happened there would slowly unravel.

In the meantime, on Tuesday morning warnings were being spread throughout Bartlett and Conway to remove all surviving cattle, sheep, and horses from the intervales to higher ground. Unbelievably, the Saco River had risen twenty-four feet.

At midday, a lone traveler named John Barker appeared at Ethan Crawford's. Having urgent business south of the Notch, he told Crawford he had to get through the Notch that day. Crawford urged patience. Particularly since the bridge that crossed the Ammonoosuc River was out.

This is Edward Melcher, the member of the rescue party who discovered David Allen's body. On the day of the storm his own three children had a narrow escape when the Stanton Bridge was destroyed by the Saco River minutes after they ran over it. That same night a landslide caused the Melcher Farm to flood.

At 4:00 p.m., after the river had receded somewhat, Crawford used a draft horse to swim Barker across. Once on the other side, Barker headed for the Gateway. With most of the road before him destroyed, he soon learned that it would be slow going.

While scrambling down the steep pitch of the tortured Gateway, he encountered washouts twenty feet deep. And in the valley it was no better. All he could see ahead of him were massive piles of debris, exposed boulders, and the remains of trees that had fallen from the high Notch walls.

Just before dark he finally arrived at the Willey House. Not only was it hauntingly quiet inside, but he was shocked to find the house surrounded by rubble caused by a great landslide that had come down directly behind it. When he climbed over the ruin to reach the back of the house, his investigation revealed that a large boulder had divided the destructive mass into two streams. Though the northern stream had destroyed the barn, the house and the attached woodshed had escaped intact. Then, after passing around the house, the slide had flowed back together.

After satisfying his curiosity, Barker worked his way past a flock of mud-caked sheep that were placidly nibbling grass on a narrow strip that had survived in front of the house. Unexpectedly he was stopped from entering the house by the family dog who appeared to be strangely agitated.

Patiently calming him down, Barker entered the house. Inside he found all the doors open, the beds unmade, and clothes scattered about. In the northwest bedroom, where the parents obviously slept, he found an open Bible with Samuel Willey's spectacles resting on the Eighteenth Psalm. Going to the dining area, he came across money still on the bar along with some business papers. He concluded that the family must have fled to Abel Crawford's place.

While he could still see, he helped himself to a cold supper. Afterwards he lay down on one of the unmade beds. As tired as he was, sleep proved impossible. Throughout the night he heard low moanings that raised the hair on the back of his neck. At dawn he was still awake.

Once it was fully light, summoning his courage he followed the sound to where the barn had stood. Poking around, he uncovered two dead horses in their stalls. Nearby he found a pair of oxen that were still alive. While one appeared to be unharmed, the other was painfully pinned beneath a fallen timber. Breathing a sigh of relief, he knew he had found the source of the moanings. Locating an axe, he chopped the animal free. Before leaving the premises, Barker looked for the dog. There was no sign of him. Later that day the broken-hearted animal showed up at the Conway farm of Polly Willey's parents, the Lovejoys. Whining pitifully, he approached different members of the family. He tried in vain to get them to follow him back to the Willey House.

Failing that, for some time afterwards he was seen running back and forth on the Notch road. Eventually he disappeared altogether.

(Photo by Floyd W. Ramsey)

On July 16, 1926, this special commemorative plaque was unveiled at the site of the Willey House by the Anna Stickney Chapter, Daughters of the American Revolution.

It was noon before Barker reached Abel Crawford's. His arrival had been partly delayed because so many of the bridges on the turnpike had been washed away. He sadly learned that the Willeys were not there. The worst was now suspected.

Later that day, as Barker continued to work his way south spreading word that the family was missing, an anxious Ethan Crawford turned up at the Willey House. Accompanied by a Connecticut guest, earlier he had been forced to abandon his wagon and they had walked the last five miles to check on the family. As they approached the house, the first sign of life that they encountered were some of Willey's unmilked cows.

After finding the house deserted, for reasons peculiar to the moment, the guest insisted on being guided back through the Notch. Overriding his concerns for both the Willeys and Abel's family, Crawford did the guest's bidding. After arriving back home around 4:00 p.m., his gnawing sense of tragedy concerning the Willeys compelled him to return there. A few hours later, as he again approached the desolate house he found several men milling around. One of his brothers was among them. This brother assured him that Abel's family had come safely through the storm. Following a limited search, the group was forced to agree that there was little hope the Willey family would be found alive. Having difficulty accepting this realization, Ethan became too upset to remain near the house any longer. Against his brother's wishes, he once more headed back through the soul-searing snarl. Engulfed by the black of night, he wearily groped and stumbled his way home.

Meanwhile, as word circulated that the Willey family had disappeared, more able-bodied men headed for the Notch. Among them was Benjamin D. Eastman of Conway. Describing the moment, he later wrote: "We immediately commenced moving in the direction of the Notch. Not only relatives, but all who could safely leave and endure the severity of such a trip. The strong and the athletic pushed on over every incumbrance, climbing over rocks, trees and brush, and wading through swift waters. Some who had not the power of endurance dropped into private homes until the next morning.

"Two of us from Conway pressed on to the old Crawford House, and there learned that a small party had left nearly an hour before. As it was now past midnight, we first thought we would stop until daylight. But after taking some refreshments we replenished our tin lanterns and resumed our journey. We were soon in with the others, they having been retarded in felling trees on which to cross some of the streams."

At this point Eastman was now traveling with a rescue party that included Abel Crawford, Edward Melcher, Richard Barnes, Samuel Tuttle and several other men. Earlier this group had struggled to reach Crawford's inn from Bartlett. Abel, who was with them even then, experienced difficulty trying to cross the Sawyer River. Appreciably older than the other men, he was unable to ford the swift current. Eager to get home to check on his family, he was determined to get across. Melcher finally solved the problem by carrying him over on his back.

After enjoying a brief family reunion, Abel was told about the losses he suffered from the storm. But, like his son Ethan, he was more upset over what must have happened to the Willeys. When the group left his inn for the Willey House that night he was with them.

About this time final confirmation of the disappearance finally reached both the Lovejoys and the elder Willeys. Because the messenger first carried the sad tidings to the Lovejoys, he found himself blocked on that side by the swollen Saco River. The Reverend Benjamin Willey, Samuel Jr.'s brother, later described what the messenger did next: "To get ears to hear his important tidings, he stood on the river's brink, the nearest point to my father's, and sounded a trumpet. It was the sound of the shrill blast after shrill blast through the darkness which startled the elder Willey and the entire neighborhood from their repose."

Awakened in this abrupt manner, the startled sleepers gathered on the river's bank and heard the dreadful news shouted across the roaring river, "News of the Willey family! All are gone!"

On Thursday morning, August 31, while James Willey, Samuel Jr.'s elder brother, directed the search around the rubble directly in front of the house, Samuel Willey, Sr., along with his sons Benjamin and Stephan, and other relatives, friends and neighbors, made their way up the Notch road.

Going on noon, as they neared the site, they could see that three slides had come off Mt. Willey. The southernmost slide had deposited its tangled debris thirty feet high in the intervale. The northernmost slide, which was the longest, had notched the skyline and had come down directly behind the house. The third slide had completely overwhelmed the cart body which Samuel, Jr. had planned to use as a "safe refuge."

With about fifty men now gathered to hunt for the bodies, the search turned southward toward the debris that had been washed along by the flood. Despite exhaustion, Ethan Crawford had arrived again in response to a message he had received at home requesting his assistance.

Shortly after noon Edward Melcher, following the southern division of the slide, brushed against a twig. When he did, he disturbed flies gathered around an entrance in the debris. Working his way into this opening, he discovered a man's hand jammed between two logs. Hearing his shouts, Stephan Willey and Thomas Hart came to his assistance with shovels. Their digging soon exposed the body of the hired man, David Allen. This find meant that there was now a widow with four children living in Bartlett who was left penniless and at the mercy of charity.

A short time later Mrs. Willey's body was found lying directly behind Allen. When both bodies were uncovered, they were found to be nude and terribly mangled. Particularly about the head. Allen's right hand was extended toward Mrs. Willey, and it was only separated from her left hand by two feet. It appeared as though he had been guiding her up to the moment of death.

While Melcher, Willey, and Hart continued digging out those bodies, Richard Barnes found Mr. Willey's body about seventy feet farther down the brook. One of Willey's knees was sticking out of the water. He was not only pinned under a timber from the barn, but he was also entangled in the top of an uprooted tree. After being removed, he was found to be fully clothed except for a torn-off coat sleeve. Since his injuries were much less severe than either Allen's or his wife's, he was much more recognizable.

As night came on, the search was halted. The three bodies were wrapped in sheets, and then placed in crude coffins that were hastily constructed. They were next set in a temporary common grave close to the house where they would remain until they could be moved that winter. Following the burial, Elder Samuel Hazeltine of Bartlett offered up a brief prayer of committal and read from Isaiah 40:12: "Who hath measured the waters in the hollow of his hand and meted out heaven with the span, and comprehended the dust of the earth in a measure and weighed the mountains in scales, and the hills in a balance?"

The next morning most of the searchers left. A few remained behind to look for the other six bodies. Before he departed, Ethan Crawford made a simple monument for his deceased friends. With a piece of red chalk he printed on a planed board: "THE FAMILY FOUND HERE." He then nailed the board to a dead tree, and returned home where he was badly needed.

The search for the other remains continued for the rest of the week without success. By Sunday, September 3, the only searchers still there were Benjamin Eastman and a small boy named George

Nickerson. Nickerson's older brother, the other hired man, was still missing.

About noon of that day, Eastman and the boy worked below the area where the other bodies had been found. From a large jam they saw what appeared to be a straw bed. In order to reach it, they had to build a raft. While removing some of the broken timbers from the jam, they disturbed more flies. Knowing what their presence could mean, Eastman and the boy began digging. Three feet down they uncovered a child's toes. Their efforts were interrupted by the arrival of friends who had come to help.

Put to work, the newcomers completed removing the body of Sally Willey, 3. In the meantime, Eastman and Nickerson had finished building the raft and had floated down to the bed. From that location they spotted what looked like another body.

It turned out to be the oldest child, Eliza Ann, 13. When she was removed from the water she was wearing only a large handkerchief. Presumably it was tied to her waist so that someone could lead her. Since there was not a single bruise anywhere on her body, it was evident that she had drowned.

In less than two hours that day the youngest and the eldest of the children had been found.

As the search through the rubble continued, young Nickerson sadly told Eastman, "I know my brother is dead, but I must see his body or I shall die."

On Tuesday, a week after the disaster, his wish was granted. David Nickerson's body was located four feet below the area where the first bodies were recovered. He was the last to be found.

That December the four Willey bodies were buried near "The Bigelow Place" in upper Conway, which today is known as Intervale. The father, mother, and two children were all laid to rest in one wide grave. However, their large gray slate headstone is inscribed with the names of the missing children as well.

David Allen's body was taken to the Bartlett cemetery. His headstone, which is no more than a rough boulder of red granite, is located in the far northwestern corner. In front of it there is an American flag designating that he was once a soldier.

The whereabouts of Nickerson's grave is unknown.

Today, though there is no way of knowing exactly why the family and the two men fled the house during the storm, the best answer seems to come from an unusual source: a dream of James Willey's. In the dream he spoke with his dead brother, asking him why they left the house as they did. Samuel, Jr., replied, "We did not leave the house until the waters rose so high in front, and came up so near that we found they would carry away the house. So to avoid being drowned, we took some coverings for shelter against the storm, and went out to the foot of the mountain back of the house. From there, soon after, we were carried away by the great slide that came down in that direction."

When all is said and done, perhaps the strangest aspect of this whole tragedy is the fact that Samuel Willey's last communication with his family appears to have come from beyond the grave.

(Photo by Floyd W. Ramsey)

This large slate headstone stands next to the entrance of the small Willey Cemetery which is located almost directly behind the Scottish Lion Restaurant in Intervale. The ages of the children are not necessarily accurate. For example, Eliza was thirteen at the time of her death.

The Haunting of Hannah Nute...
The Final Word

(Courtesy of Dartmouth College)
This is Daniel Webster at 22, three years after he graduated from Dartmouth College with William Farrar in 1801. Born in Franklin, New Hampshire, on January 18, 1782, his brilliant oratory not only got him elected to both houses of Congress, but he was also Secretary of State twice and mentioned for the Presidency several times.

IN 1818, while President James Monroe was still adjusting to his quarters in the White House, approximately 650 miles to the north, in the picturesque little frontier village of Lancaster, New Hampshire, a mysterious and frightening "presence" was establishing its residence in the home of Deacon William Farrar.

When the haunting began, Farrar was deacon of the local Congregational church, an active member in its choir, and an accomplished musician who played a large bass viol. He was also a very successful lawyer with a rather substantial practice. His justice docket was reputed to be one of the largest in Coos County. The fact that he graduated from Dartmouth College with Daniel Webster in 1801 added further weight to his reputation.

Yet, despite his standing in the community, this dark complexioned, spare little man is known to have suffered from chronic indigestion. This is not surprising, considering that he experienced two major misadventures after he permanently settled in Lancaster in 1811.

The first befell him when he went on a premature honeymoon. Supposedly he had been united in marriage to tall, dignified, and devout Margaret Kibbee of Bloomfield, Vermont, on December 9, 1811, by Judge DeForest. Unfortunately, as it was subsequently learned, marriage ceremonies were not one of the judge's legal functions.

Later, to make amends, the well-intentioned judge personally corrected the situation in early 1812.

The haunting was the second misadventure. And it began after Deacon Farrar hired young, delicate-looking Hannah Nute to assist his wife with the housework in their two-story house located on Lancaster's dusty main road.

When Hannah assumed her duties, a young man named George Kibbee, who was related to Mrs. Farrar, was also living in the house. This may have caused Hannah to develop the type of emotional stress believed necessary to unleash the invisible presence that selected her as its victim.

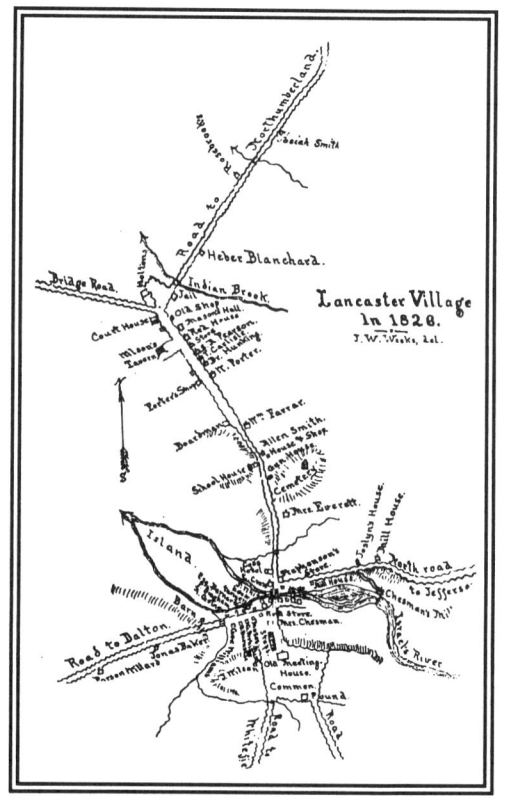

Despite a discouraging period of poor farming seasons, Lancaster continued to increase in population within the village itself. By 1826 there were more than 34 houses located there. Deacon Farrar's house is on the right, midway along the main road heading north.

Whatever the explanation, make no mistake about it. At this moment it was not the house that was about to be haunted. It was Hannah! The house would come later.

Her nightmare began one evening after she retired to her bedroom on the ground floor just off the large kitchen. Exhausted from her labors of the long day, she was soon asleep. Meanwhile, the other members of the household were already asleep upstairs.

Without warning, the still of the night was shattered by a loud rapping under Hannah's bed. Awakened by the sound, at first she

This is the All Saints Rectory, which is located at 163 Main Street in Lancaster. It now occupies the site where the Deacon Farrar House once stood. The property was purchased sometime after 1856 by the Reverend Isadore H. Noisseaux. Before the century ended, the Farrar house was taken down and replaced with more suitable quarters.

thought it was caused by the rats inhabiting the cellar. While attempting to get back to sleep, she was again disturbed. This time by three distinct raps from the same location. Now badly frightened, she jumped out of bed and ran through the kitchen to the hall.

Pounding up the stairs, she yelled, "Oh, Mrs. Farrar! Mrs. Farrar!"

Once she gained the second floor, she almost fainted in front of the Farrar's bedroom door.

Awakened by the commotion, Mrs. Farrar yanked open the door. After looking up and down the hall, she sighed, "I thought surely the house was on fire. What do you mean, Hannah, by giving me such a fright?"

Still gasping for breath, Hannah stammered, "There is someone under my bed."

"What nonsense," Mrs. Farrar snapped. "You have been dreaming!"

"Oh, no, I wasn't asleep!" Hannah cried. "They rapped three times very loud on the floor."

Finally noticing how frightened the girl really was, Mrs. Farrar softened her voice and said, "Oh, Hannah. I am truly surprised that you should be so foolish. If it will make you feel better, I will go down with you and look under the bed."

"Oh, hadn't you better get the deacon to go and look," Hannah pleaded. "I am certain someone is there."

Ignoring the plea, Mrs. Farrar headed for the stairs. Filled with fear, Hannah followed her.

In the kitchen Mrs. Farrar lighted a tallow candle from the coals still burning in the fireplace. Then, taking a deep breath, she went into Hannah's room and looked under the bed.

Afraid to enter the room, Hannah stood trembling out in the kitchen.

Once Mrs. Farrar was satisfied the room was empty, she said, "Hannah, come in here and look for yourself. You have my word there is no one here."

Hesitantly Hannah did as she was told.

Pointing under the bed, Mrs. Farrar asked, "Now, are you convinced you were dreaming?"

At that moment three loud raps sounded beneath Hannah's feet. Instantly she emitted a long, ear-piercing scream, and fled back to the kitchen.

Needless to say, Mrs. Farrar was right behind her.

Sobbing uncontrollably, Hannah begged her, "Please call the deacon. Please! Someone is in the cellar!"

In response to Hannah's scream, George Kibbee came rushing into the kitchen. "Good lord, what's the matter?" he shouted.

Just then Deacon Farrar also appeared. Nervously pushing his thin black hair forward to cover his baldness, he shrieked, "Wife, what is this all about?"

Doing her best to appear calm, Mrs. Farrar explained what had happened. No sooner had she finished when another succession of raps came out of the floor.

Hannah screamed again.

"To say the least," Mrs. Farrar exclaimed, "this is very alarming!"

Unable to conceal a mounting anger, the Deacon growled, "I'll soon find out what's making this disturbance." And with the long iron fireplace shovel in one hand, and his wife's candlestick in the other, he headed for the cellar.

Before the candle light could disappear altogether, he was followed by George, Mrs. Farrar, and Hannah. In that order.

Despite a thorough, tiring search of the musty cellar, nothing was found. Nothing, that is, except the growing realization that there was an unseen presence in the house with them.

Returning to the protective feeling thrown off by the fireplace, they decided the next best thing to do was to talk the matter over. Pointing a trembling finger at her husband, Mrs. Farrar said,

"Deacon, I think it is a warning. I have heard of such things."

George had an even stronger opinion. He stated, "Personally, I think your house is haunted."

Wearily shaking his head, the deacon replied, "Well, whatever it is, it's certainly a singular and startling phenomenon. In view of that fact, George, I think you had better go for Parson Willard in the morning."

Mrs. Farrar agreed, saying, "Perhaps it is best."

Throughout the night the blood-chilling rappings continued to be heard at short intervals. As a consequence, the Farrars were forced to summon nearby neighbors in a desperate attempt to calm Hannah. By the time Parson Joseph Willard arrived, the girl was completely distraught.

After listening to what the family had been subjected to, Parson Willard frankly admitted that he could offer no explanation for the strange disturbance. He did suggest, however, that it might be proper to hold a religious service. Without hesitation, George brought him the great family Bible from the parlor. The parson then read aloud a portion of the Scriptures. Prayers followed. When the service ended, the raps were louder than ever.

In the days that followed, the entire house was thoroughly investigated. Even the outside shutters were closely examined. But, as before, there was no discernible explanation.

And the rappings continued!

Word of the haunting spread to adjoining towns, and the Farrars found their house being thronged by both townspeople and strangers alike. Finally someone made two shattering observations. The raps only manifested themselves in the room where Hannah was. And they only followed her.

The situation now took an even uglier turn for the wretched girl. The decision was made to have her closely watched. For this purpose, four of the town's leading men were appointed to be an investigating committee.

Once they agreed on how they would handle the strange responsibility, the four men wasted no time in going to the Farrar house. On their arrival, Hannah was turned over to them. Despite her anguished protests, they tied her hands and feet. She was then placed on her bed, and they took up the chairs provided. Solemnly they sat, two on each side of her.

For an entire day and a night they never took their eyes off her. And the raps taunted them! They came from the walls, the floor, and the bed itself. But from nowhere else in the house. Only in Hannah's room!

When the four men felt it would serve no further purpose to remain, they solemnly informed the Farrars that they could neither explain the raps nor find their source. Their duty done, they left.

Despite these findings, many townspeople continued to believe that Hannah was somehow behind whatever was going on.

Acutely aware of their suspicions, and now in failing health, Hannah begged the Farrars to send her away. Reluctantly they agreed that it might be for the best.

On the day that she was preparing to leave, the raps were heard more frequently than they had ever been heard before. Then, while she was passing through the hall for the last time, they relentlessly followed her. With each step that she took, the floor was struck with tremendous force. When she left the house, it was believed that the invisible presence left with her.

Time proved otherwise. More than sixty-four years later, on September 29, 1882, the Lancaster Gazette published a letter written by Doctor Clark C. Norris of Colebrook. The letter said, in part: "I saw in the Gazette of the 22d instant, the story about the Deacon Farrar House some sixty or more years ago. In reading the story it brought to mind the time and noises which were heard by my father's family while living there during the early 1850's.

"When my father purchased the Farrar property off D.A. Burnside, locally it was known as the "Haunted House." Despite this fact, we moved into it shortly after the purchase, and all went "merry as a marriage bell." For awhile, at least.

"Then, of an evening the doors flew open, and banged shut on their hinges as if forced by a violent wind when all without was calm and serene. At other times shrieks were also heard in various parts of the house that would cause the hair on the head of a nervous person to rise on end.

"Other sounds included those of the most unaccountable log rolling which seemed to be going on up in the attic; and then a thud, as though someone, or something, had fallen from a height to

The Haunting of Hannah Nute

the floor below.

"These sounds were not heard by me alone, but by all of the family.

"One memorable scene will ever be remembered by my sister Sabeina. One evening she, with a candle in hand, went into the cellar for some potatoes. Before she reached the bin, she screamed and flew upstairs and fell upon the floor in a fainting condition. When restored to consciousness she would only say, "Oh, horrors. I never, never will go again into that cellar."

"We lived there a year or more after this, but she could not be induced to go back into the cellar.

"Grandfather, who was aged and did not sleep sound, often spoke of hearing strange sounds and queer noises in the dead of night. And mother often said she heard all these noises, yet she was not afraid to go by night or day with, or without, a light over the

Deacon William Farrar died on March 3, 1850, of "lung fever" at the age of 69. Buried in Wilder Cemetery just south of where he lived, his grave is located between those of his two wives, Margaret and Tryphena.

Four years after Hannah Nute left the house, Margaret Farrar died childless at the age of 35. Less than a year later Deacon Farrar married Tryphena Bergin on August 19, 1823. She bore him three children, and died the same year that he did.

house. She said she never harmed anyone, and therefore she feared no harm.

"Whatever may be the power or source of spirit manifestation, I don't pretend to say. But I do say, I know there was a force, or something unaccountable, hanging around and about the Farrar House."

Which all points to one final and inescapable conclusion concerning Hannah Nute: the poor girl got more than one "bum rap" while she was living with the Farrars.

A Melancholy Occurrence on Mount Washington

This is one of the portraits done of Lizzie Bourne following her tragic death on Mount Washington on September 13, 1855. Today it hangs in the Brick Store Museum at 117 Main Street, Kennebunk, Maine.
(Floyd Ramsey Photo, courtesy of the Brick Store Museum)

On TUESDAY, September 18, 1855, the funeral planned for beautiful twenty-three-old Elizabeth Greene Bourne of Kennebunk, Maine, had to be canceled for one day due to heavy rain. Five days earlier she had died on the summit of Mount Washington under circumstances that also played a role in the death of her well-known uncle, George Bourne, fifteen months later.

Prior to the tragedy, George Bourne had been highly successful in the Bourne family shipbuilding firm. Financially secure, he had retired in 1852 while only in his early fifties. From that time, until the death of his niece, he had shared his zest for life with his family, friends, community and church. He was also an active and influential member of the local Sons of Temperance, a group that favored complete abstinence from intoxicating beverages.

Following the tragedy he was a broken man.

Today Elizabeth Bourne is remembered as the first person to perish on the summit of New England's highest peak. But, just what were the circumstances surrounding her death there on the night of Thursday, September 13, 1855, that so deeply affected her genial Uncle George?

Built in 1812, this magnificent Bourne Mansion, which was the home of Lizzie Bourne, was entered in the National Register of Historic Places on January 24, 1980.

On the date in question, George Bourne, accompanied by his wife Jane, his twenty-five-year-old daughter Lucy, and his niece Elizabeth, checked in at the Glen House at the base of the mountain. It was early afternoon, and they had just completed their 120-mile journey from Kennebunk.

Elizabeth, or "Lizzie" as she was affectionately called, possessed a playful, coaxing manner. Despite her father Edward's concern for her fragile health, which was caused by a heart defect, she was able to obtain his permission to share in the holiday trip. He knew that, like her uncle, she possessed a love for the outdoors. Adding to her enthusiasm for going was also the prospect that a climb up Mount Washington in those days provided unparalleled adventure.

Though Lizzie knew that food and lodging could be obtained on the summit at both the Tip Top House and the Summit House, her primary purpose for making the climb was to witness the spectacle of sunrise from the top of New England's highest peak. This was a spectacle that she had heard a great deal about from friends, so she did not want to miss out on the opportunity to see it for herself.

With the Carriage Road still under construction, hikers had to use either existing footpaths or the bridle path. For a fragile girl like Lizzie Bourne, these choices posed a daunting challenge. However,

A Melancholy Occurrence on Mount Washington

This postcard from North Conway dated June 25, 1906, graphically shows how close the Bourne party was to safety when the fateful decision was made to halt the climb. One hundred yards above the Lizzie Bourne marker, the Summit House can be seen.

she evidently felt equal to it because she talked her Uncle George and Cousin Lucy into making the climb that very afternoon instead of waiting until the following morning.

When the trio began the eight-mile ascent at about 2:00 p.m., tragically none of them recognized the need for a guide. Their plan was to spend a warm, comfortable night at the Summit House, and to be up at daybreak so that Lizzie could see the sunrise from the top of the 6288-foot peak. As fate would have it, they were rushing to keep a rendezvous with death.

Within two hours of their departure, they reached the end of the Carriage Road construction. Soon after leaving it, they came to the "Camp House at the Ledge," which is now known as the Halfway House. At this point they were 3840 feet above sea level. Because Lizzie was showing signs of tiredness, they stopped for a brief rest.

While visiting with workmen who were staying at the camp, they were told word had just been received from the summit that there were signs of a storm brewing. With the mountain's reputation for sudden, arctic-like storms, they were advised to turn back.

Unfortunately, because the weather was mild at that particular level, the girls insisted on continuing. With the best of intentions,

George yielded to their arguments. This set the final stage for the tragedy that was soon to follow.

As they continued to use the remaining daylight to work their way up the bridle path, the late hour soon brought them to the "point of no return." Then when they were two miles below the summit, a strong wind suddenly whipped up that made further climbing extremely difficult.

With the mountain now wrapped in twilight, the wind reached gale proportions and the temperature dropped dangerously low. To make matters worse, Lizzie was also showing signs of exhaustion. George and Lucy were struggling to keep her moving. While assisting her up what they thought was the last steep slope, a thick cloud settled over the summit and created the illusion of an even higher climb. Momentarily discouraged, they halted.

As the Cog Railroad ascends the rock-strewn summit of Mount Washington, the passengers cannot help but notice the track-side cairn which secures Lizzie Bourne's modest wooden marker. The date refers to when the tragedy became known, and not to the date on which she died there.

Nine days later George would write of this experience: "To our sorrow another mountain stood before us, whose summit was far above the clouds."

And so it was, without the guide that they so badly needed they had no idea of where they were. The next day, when they found out, it was a shock from which George never recovered.

Before long they started upward again, but what little progress they were making ceased altogether as they became enveloped by

A Melancholy Occurrence on Mount Washington

the dark of the night and the wind's paralyzing cold.

Fighting back panic, George had the shivering girls stop and lie down on the path while he feverishly built a rock wall from the life-threatening cold. Occasionally he laid down to rest, and to share his body warmth.

Sometime later, when the wall was finally completed, it gave him the encouraging feeling that now they would all survive. Clinging to this hope, periodically he left the shelter to restore his body warmth by thrashing his arms and by stamping his feet.

However, whenever he was outside the wall, the roaring wind and bitter cold quickly engulfed him. Minutes later, gasping for breath, he would be forced to crawl back to the girls. At no time throughout the entire ordeal did he leave them alone for more than ten minutes.

This is the special stone monument that Judge Edward E. Bourne originally planned to place on Mount Washington at the site of his daughter's death. Ever since its completion, it has served as Lizzie's headstone in Kennebunk's Hope Cemetery.

(Floyd W. Ramsey Photo)

As the hours passed slowly, he began to suffer miserably. Then around ten o'clock, as he lay down next to Lizzie, he reached for one of her hands. It was icy cold! Trembling, he touched her forehead. That was cold, too! He shouted to her. She did not respond.

When he wrote about this moment, he simply said, "She was dead. She had uttered no complaint, expressed no regret or fear, but had passed silently away."

Driven by grief, over the next eight hours George spared no

effort to keep his daughter alive.

At dawn the two survivors left the shelter to seek help. And this was when they made the soul-shattering discovery that they had spent the night only one hundred yards from the Tip Top House. What an agonizing moment this must have been for George Bourne.

Immediately after the owners and guests had been awakened and alerted to the tragedy, two men and two women rushed down to the rock sanctuary to retrieve Lizzie's body. On returning to the house, for four hours they tried every method imaginable to restore life to her. In George's words, "For four hours they labored with hot rocks, hot baths, and used every exertion to call back her spirit, but all in vain."

Just before noon Lizzie's body was placed in an open, shallow pine box which was slung from a long pole. She was then carried off the mountain by two men, with two others acting as relief. Brokenhearted, George and Lucy traveled with them.

At the Glen House, while the grief-stricken Bournes were completing final arrangements for the journey home, early newspaper accounts of the tragedy were heralding the fact that Lizzie's persistent eagerness to view the "splendid sunrise" produced a "Melancholy Occurrence" which left her in a pine box and destroyed her uncle's health.

Before the story ran its course, it was a tragedy that stunned all of New England.

On Saturday evening, September 15, George, Jane, and Lucy Bourne somberly arrived back in Kennebunk, and Lizzie's body was delivered to her father's house.

The day after the delayed funeral, Edward Bourne wrote a letter to the Summit House proprietors expressing his wish "that no material change be made in the wall thrown up by my brother as I hope to place there some more enduring monument to the memory of my daughter."

To this day, this "more enduring monument" has never reached Mount Washington's summit. The Mount Washington's Road Company suffered financial failure after constructing the first four miles of the Carriage Road, and this bankruptcy removed the only route by which the marker could have been hauled to the site of the tragedy. Having no other alternative, Edward Bourne had the stone placed at Lizzie's grave in Kennebunk's Hope Cemetery. It is still there.

As evidence of the family's unwillingness to accept Lizzie's death, they had four portraits done of her by 1858 from daguerreotypes that she had sat for in the early 1850s. Three of them graced the walls of the Bourne Mansion for more than 109 years. As for George Bourne, following the funeral his health continued to deteriorate. Within fifteen months he became the second victim of that terrible night on the mountain. Referring to that fact, his brother Edward wrote: "The suffering of that night, both mental and bodily, without doubt, very seriously impaired George's physical constitution so that it became more accessible to attacks and ravages of disease."

Which it did. Thirteen months after the tragedy George was stricken by typhoid fever. Following two months of almost continuous bed confinement, he died on December 7, 1856. His grotesque nightmare that started on New England's highest peak was finally over.

The Light in the Window...
An Unusual Passaconaway Love Story

AT THE AGE OF EIGHTY-ONE, Mrs. Ruth Priscilla Colbath, the legendary "Hermit Lady of Passaconaway Valley," died quietly and alone at the Memorial Hospital in North Conway.

With her passing, an extraordinary vigil had ended. Every night, for thirty-nine years, she had placed a lighted lantern in the front window of her small farmhouse to guide the return of her husband, Thomas. Through that entire period she was sustained by the faith that he would return.

Back in the fall of 1891, while she was preparing his supper, Thomas said to her, "I'm going out for a walk. I'll be back in a little while." She had no reason to doubt him.

That night, for the first time, she placed the light in the window.

Sadly enough, she never saw him again. But she also never lost her faith in him. And, in the end, he didn't really fail her. At least, not completely.

Nearing the end of her life, Ruth Priscilla Colbath is seen sitting in front of her beloved farmhouse. Her neighbor, Ben Swinston, who looked after her in her later years, collected $500 from her estate for his services.

(Courtesy of Ann Croto, Albany Historical Society)

This is her touching story:

She was born in 1850 in Albany, New Hampshire, on the northern end of the Kancamagus Highway, in the clapboarded farmhouse built by her grandfather, Thomas Russell, between 1830 and 1832. Historically speaking, she was the great granddaughter of Austin George, one of the first settlers in the Valley.

At the time of her birth, her father, Amzi Russell, was a man of some affluence. He owned most of the Passaconaway Valley, and was one of the leading lumbermen in that area. He also ran a small store where Ruth, the fourth of five daughters, occasionally bartered with the Penacook Indians who came to trade with him. Though she was industrious, when she was about five years old she suffered a crippling hip injury that would always limit her work capabilities.

Since she was an exceptionally intelligent child, when she reached the proper age her father sent her to Wolfeboro, New Hampshire, where she attended the old Tuftonborough Academy. However, despite this educational opportunity, after she returned home she chose to continue to live and work on the family farm. She was the only daughter to do so. As her four sisters married, they moved out of the area.

Through these early years of her life she sadly watched the Valley become literally emptied of her friends and neighbors. Farm after farm was deserted as whole families were lured to the cities by the Industrial Revolution. Then, sometime after 1879 her father died. As if this wasn't enough, following on the heels of his death his sawmill operation was totally destroyed by fire.

Economically, the entire Valley was now brought to its knees.

Still, Ruth stayed on. She continued to live with her mother, Eliza George Russell. Even after she married Thomas Alden Colbath, a carpenter who was believed to be from Wolfeboro. And perhaps this was why their marriage was ill-fated from the beginning.

Whatever happened, the three of them lived together until that tragic day in 1891 when Thomas unexpectedly walked out on her.

Through the first fifteen years of his disappearance, Ruth maintained her financial independence by serving as the Passaconaway postmistress until her retirement in May of 1906. And, when her mother died on February 21, 1905, she inherited both the homestead and the rights to her father's timberlands. Whenever her back taxes mounted, or she needed money to live on, she simply sold off parcels of land.

It was shortly after the turn of the Century that the Conway area began developing as a popular summer retreat. As summer visitors began hearing of Ruth's strange vigil, many of them sought her out. During their visit she openly shared her life's story with them. Inspired by her faithfulness, some referred to her as "The Grand Old Lady of the Mountains," while others simply called her "The Winter Hermit."

In reference to this latter title, a reporter once wrote, "No other woman leads such a lonely life during the bleak winter months as this dear old lady of solitude."

The years passed. Still no word of Thomas. The lantern continued to burn in the window. By the time she was eighty Ruth had become so infirm that she could barely cross from one room to another. Even with the aid of a crutch and a cane. Whenever she tried to do so, her falls became more frequent.

Time was running out for her.

In one of her last interviews, which was with a *Boston Herald* reporter, she admitted that she had not been over her doorstoop in many months. While leading him into her front room, which was stacked high with books and magazines, she said, "I was born in this very house. I am still here. It is my home. I love it. I hope never to be obliged to leave it."

When asked what her life was presently like, she replied, "In the summertime visitors come frequently to see me. Perhaps out of curiosity, but I welcome them all. In the winter it may seem lonesome to some, but I am not lonesome. The mountains are grander than ever, and sometimes I aid a wanderer."

Asked how she lived through the winter, when the Valley was all shut in, she said, "Ben Swinston looks after me. He lives a mile down the valley. He comes on bright days to see I want for nothing. He chops my wood and looks after my fires. Also, the town of

Albany, in which this Valley is located, keeps the single road from Conway open. Should I become ill, a doctor could be summoned. For, yes, I have a telephone." When asked about her husband, she bowed her head and said softly, "I have tried for years to find him. He may still be alive. If he is, perhaps some day he will come back to me."

To the end her faith in Thomas remained intact.

In early November of 1930 she became seriously ill. Ben had her rushed to the hospital. A short time later she died. Again, quietly and alone.

Then, in late September of 1933, Thomas Alden Colbath returned. He had finally completed a walk which had lasted for forty-two years. Both he and Ben stood in front of the empty, darkened farmhouse. Ben told him of how Ruth always expected his return; of how she refused to leave the house; of how people said she was crazy, and were always telling her that her husband had to be dead.

Sadly shaking his head, Ben concluded, "But, she always put the lamp in the window no matter what they said."

An explanation followed, but Thomas was vague about why he had left her. Or, for that matter where he had gone. In a hushed voice he mentioned California, Cuba, and Panama. As he wound down, he also said that he would live in the farmhouse again if its present owners would permit him to.

It was not to be. He had returned too late. The estate had already been divided among Ruth's relatives.

Though it is not really known, Thomas' final years are believed to have been spent living with his sister in Wolfeboro.

Priscilla, along with other members of her family, is buried in the Russell Cemetery just a short distance from her house. Recently it was learned that her paternal grandparents are also buried there in unmarked graves.

As for the house, in these later years it has taken on a special dignity. Carefully restored by the Saco District of the United States Forest Service, it has been elevated to the status of being a living history rather than just a tourist information center. And since

THE LIGHT IN THE WINDOW 111

April of 1987 it has been officially entered in the National Register of Historic Places.

Though belated, perhaps this is Ruth Priscilla Colbath's final reward: the preservation of the house in which thirty-nine years of faithful love and patient devotion were lived out by a gentle and caring soul.

This was Ruth Colbath's home in Passaconaway where the light burned in the window each night for 39 years as she waited for her husband to return from his walk. Located on the north side of the Kancamagus Highway, it has been included in the National Register of Historic Places since April of 1987.

The Bugbee-Towne Mystery

BETWEEN the summer of 1880 and the winter of 1881 unusually tragic circumstances occurred in Lancaster, New Hampshire, that almost totally destroyed two prominent and highly respected families there. The Frank Bugbee family, which was the first to be struck down, was wiped out completely. The other family, the Townes, was brought to the brink of extinction. It was not until early August of 1881 that evidence finally surfaced which suggested foul play. The ensuing sensation that gripped the town is still talked about today as "the Bugbee-Towne murders".

Hattie Bugbee, 14, died in Lancaster, N.H., on Thursday, July 15, 1880. Her death was the beginning of a chain of tragic circumstances later referred to "as one of the most remarkable criminal cases that has ever occurred in our State."

(Floyd W. Ramsey Photo)

Seventeen years before the tragedy began unfolding, the two ill-fated families merged when Dr. Frank Bugbee married Maria Patience Towne on March 4, 1863. The young couple had met a few years earlier when Bugbee visited Lancaster with Maria's brother, Francis. At the time the two men were students at Dartmouth Medical College in Hanover, N.H.

Maria and Francis Towne were the only children of Barton and Harriet Towne who owned a farm on the Stockwell Road for many years. After retiring from farming, the Townes bought an attractive, three-gabled house on High Street in downtown Lancaster. Being public spirited, Mr. Towne remained active by holding several important positions in the community.

The Bugbees were particularly distinguished in the field of medicine. Dr. Ralph Bugbee, Sr., was a physician in Waterford, Vermont, for more than half a century. In addition to his son Frank, he had three other sons who also pursued medical careers. The oldest, Ralph Bugbee, Jr., had a practice in Littleton, N.H., and the other two had practices in and around Derby Line, Vt.

After Frank Bugbee and Francis Towne received their medical degrees, while Bugbee settled in Lancaster, Town— who later dropped the "e" from his name— was commissioned a first lieutenant in the United States Army and became an assistant surgeon. Years later, when the tragedy was running its course, he was stationed in the Territory of Washington. This fact, perhaps more than any other, may have helped him to escape the cruel death that befelled his brother-in-law and his mother and father.

(Floyd W. Ramsey photo)

Deeply devoted to her only child, Maria Patience Bugbee remained constantly at Hattie's bedside throughout her suffering. Worn down by care, watching and grief, within hours of Hattie's burial she also contracted the fatal disease and became the second member of the Bugbee household to die.

Soon after settling in Lancaster, Dr. Bugbee had an extensive and highly successful practice established. As a result, it wasn't long before he and Maria were living in a stately two-and-a-half story house next door to the elderly Townes. When their only child, Hattie, was born in December of 1864 their lives were complete.

As the years passed, they continued to prosper. Frequently they entertained their many friends in their beautiful home, and, as time allowed Dr. Bugbee served on civic improvement committees. Eventually he purchased a large farm where he went to relax.

Somewhere along the way, an attractive young lady entered the lives of the two families. Though they accepted her as Nellie Webb, they knew her real name was Nellie French. She was the daughter of a poor family that lived in the Guildhall, Vt., area. Her mother was

The Bugbee-Towne Mystery

of questionable character, and was suspected of having burned down a neighbor's barn. Despite this fact, Abigail Webb, wife of farmer Edward H. Webb, took young Nellie in so she could attend the Guildhall school.

Though Nellie was never formally adopted by the Webbs, she assumed their last name.

When Nellie's education could go no further in Guildhall, Mrs. Webb arranged for her to live with the Townes so she could enroll in Lancaster Academy. Since Mrs. Towne and Mrs. Webb were spiritual sisters in the Methodist Church, Mrs. Towne readily agreed to assist Nellie in every way possible.

(Floyd W. Ramsey photo)

Dr. Frank Bugbee, who died at 43, was an outstanding physician who was noted for his kindness, gentleness, and quiet humor. Sought after in the most difficult medical cases, he accurately diagnosed his own fatal illness as arsenical poisoning.

After Nellie graduated from the Academy, the generosity of the two women enabled her to attend Plymouth Normal School, a teacher-training institution in Plymouth, N.H. When she completed the two-year course there, she taught school locally for a brief period and then went into taxidermy. She supplemented her income by making hats for a very select clientele. Throughout this phase of her life, she still continued to live with the Townes. Because she had been an important part of their lives they looked upon her as a semi-adopted daughter.

Then, without warning, the warm and comfortable world of the Bugbees and Townes became a dark and dreadful nightmare from which there was no awakening. On the last happy afternoon of her life, Hattie Bugbee, 14, entertained a number of her companions at a child's picnic. That night she complained of a sore throat.

Despite her father's medical expertise and her mother's tender care, the next day her illness had grown worse. By Monday morning patches of grayish membrane were evident on her tonsils and throat. With their appearance, her father was able to diagnose the malignant character of her sickness. She had contracted diptheria, an acute and infectious disease.

That evening Richard P. Kent, a prominent Lancaster businessman, accompanied by his wife, Emily, called at the Bugbee residence. Their two granddaughters, "Bertie" and Annie Kent, were concerned about their sick friend. Struggling to maintain a show of professional composure as he admitted the couple, Doctor Bugbee sadly informed them that Hattie had diptheria of the most virulent type.

After returning home, the Kents conveyed this information to their family. They made sure that their granddaughters understood that there was little hope for Hattie's recovery so they prepared for the worst.

On Tuesday, while Mrs. Bugbee remained by her daughter's bedside, Dr. Bugbee sent his stable boy to the South Groveton home of Cornelius Regan to fetch Regan's daughter, Hannah, 18. The Bugbees often called on her whenever they had need of a hired girl.

As the young "coachman" drove into the Regan's yard, Hannah spied him from a kitchen window. Watching him step from the carriage, she suddenly felt a strange chill. Then, after he entered the house and explained the nature of his errand, Hannah had a premonition that if she went with him she would never see her home again. At this point she broke down and began crying. When her mother, Lizzie, asked her what was wrong, Hannah skirted the issue and began making excuses for staying home.

Not knowing the reason behind her daughter's odd behavior, Mrs. Regan grumbled, "Stop acting so foolish, girl. Go with the man. You know we need the money."

Later, arriving at the High Street residence, Hannah was greeted in the kitchen by an emotionally drained Dr. Bugbee. Wanting to be honest with her, he said, "As you know, Hannah, diphtheria is very contagious. If being in this house bothers you in any way, you may feel free to leave whenever you wish."

THE BUGBEE-TOWNE MYSTERY

Hattie Frances Towne, 70, and her husband, Barton G. Towne, 71, both died from the arsenic poisoning that struck down their son-in-law. Married on February 9, 1834, they were originally from Littleton, N.H.

Despite her premonition, Hannah agreed to stay. After getting settled, she was assigned to work under Nellie Webb's supervision. From the beginning of Hattie's illness, Nellie had moved into the house to help.

By Wednesday it was obvious that Hattie had only a short time to live. The diphtheria had produced a poison that was steadily weakening her heart and nervous system. During a brief rally, she requested to see her two companions, Bertie and Annie Kent.

Shortly after Dr. Bugbee sent for them, the two girls appeared in the yard beneath Hattie's bedroom window. Hattie was gently lifted up so that she could wave to them. When she became exhausted by the effort, she was placed back in bed.

That evening, attempting to capture the courage displayed by his granddaughters, Richard Kent wrote in his diary, "This is a striking instance of coolness in the midst of suffering."

Hattie's life ended the following night at 11:00. Due to the nature of her illness, a short, private funeral was held in the house the next afternoon. Afterwards her casket was placed in her father's waiting carriage. As the Bugbees sorrowfully rode the short distance to the new cemetery just off Summer Street, a procession of twenty carriages followed. Just inside the iron gates, on the hillside to the right, the Reverend D.J. Smith of the Methodist Church performed the interment service.

That night Mrs. Bugbee contracted the sore throat!

Over the next several days, as the diphtheria ran its course, Dr. Bugbee waged another desperate struggle against death. Regardless of his efforts, on the following Tuesday Maria became "unexpectedly and alarmingly worse." The next morning, which was now July 21, she died at the age of 42. Among her final words, she said, "I place my trust in my Savior and submit to his will."

At 4:30 that afternoon she was laid to rest next to Hattie.

Two days later the community was shocked to learn that death had struck again in the Bugbee house. This time it was Hannah Regan, the hired girl. Just a few weeks short of her nineteenth birthday, her premonition about never returning home had come true. Later that day she was buried in the Catholic cemetery off Spring Street.

Following the three deaths, many people now considered the Bugbee house an unhealthy place in which to live. Nellie Webb, however, continued to stay there to look after grief-stricken Dr. Bugbee. When advised by well-intentioned friends to move out, she told them she felt no fear about remaining because she knew the Lord would look after her.

A short time later she offended members of the Methodist Church when she began attending Sunday services wearing a coat which had belonged to Mrs. Bugbee, as well as Mrs. Bugbee's watch and chain. Put on the defensive concerning the latter, she made it known that Mrs. Bugbee had given her the watch, and that Dr. Bugbee gave her the chain because it went with the watch.

Unfortunately the misunderstandings that she was creating didn't stop there. By staying in the Bugbee house she also strengthened the gossip that she believed Dr. Bugbee, who was twice her age, would eventually marry her.

Dr. Bugbee himself fell victim to the same wagging tongues.

The Bugbee-Towne Mystery

When he was frequently seen traveling down the South Lancaster road to the home of his friend, the Honorable James W. Weeks, an ex-Judge of Probate, it was rumored that he was calling on Weeks' daughter, Clara. The fact that Clara, 28, had been an invalid for some time, and that her condition was growing worse, seemed to carry little weight. (She died several months later, on May 5.)

It isn't too surprising, either, that the gossip mongers weren't stopped by the fact that Nellie was engaged to young H. Burton Mayo, a brakeman on the Boston, Concord & Montreal Railroad. The gossip aside, the situation took an extremely cruel and brutal turn after Dr. Bugbee retuned from Derby Line, Vt., with a demijohn of whiskey.

Reproduction photo by Bart Sheridan, Lancaster Historical Society

Nellie Webb Mayo, 22, was the only suspect in the poisoning deaths of Dr. Frank Bugbee and Mr. and Mrs. Barton Towne. Surprisingly, public opinion was strongly in her favor throughout the three days of Grand Jury hearings. Despite this fact, she severed all of her New England ties and moved to the Midwest.

On Friday night, September 3, he informed Nellie that he was retiring early because he wasn't feeling well. After he was comfortable, Nellie brought him a liquid preparation which included some of the whiskey. A few hours later he developed acute gastrointestinal irritation and was seized with a terrible vomiting. From that time on he was unable to retain anything in his stomach. By Sunday morning he had become comatose.

A number of physicians were summoned to examine him. Among them was his brother, Dr. Ralph Bugbee of Littleton. All of them were puzzled by his condition. The next morning, around

8:00, knowing that he was not going to recover, Dr. Bugbee rallied just long enough to dictate his will and to give final instructions concerning his funeral. Just before he passed away, he suddenly sat up in bed and said, "I wish I knew what is killing me." Startled, one of the physicians asked, "What would you say if you had a patient in your own condition?" The dying man gasped, "I should say that it was arsenical poisoning."

Just twelve days short of his forty-fourth birthday, Dr. Bugbee joined his wife and daughter. His death was attributed to a mixture of blood poisoning and diptheria. The immediate cause was listed as "the infusion of blood around the heart." Since Dr. Bugbee was high in the Masonic Order, his funeral was a colorful affair conducted by the North Star Commandery, Knights Templar. Following a brief prayer service at his home the next afternoon, the Knights and a brass band led the funeral procession of about 50 carriages to the gravesite. A week later James W. Weeks gave public notice that he had been appointed executor of the estates of both Dr. Bugbee and his wife Maria. Shortly after that, on October 2, 1880, Nellie Webb and H. Burton Mayo were quietly united in marriage by the Reverend D. J. Smith.

Just when things were finally settling down in Lancaster, Barton and Harriet Towne took a long carriage ride to the small town of Bethlehem on Thanksgiving Day. Following their late return home, Mrs. Towne complained of feeling chilled. Nellie Webb Mayo, who might have been staying with them while her husband was on a Boston run, administered a liquid preparation to Mrs. Towne that included some of the whiskey Dr. Bugbee had brought back from Derby Line, Vt. Due to breakage, however, it was now in a different bottle.

As was the case with her deceased son-in-law Dr. Bugbee, Mrs. Towne was soon raked by continuous vomiting. Her attending physician treated her for a disordered functioning of the liver. As her condition worsened, her heart, kidneys, and other organs showed signs of being seriously affected.

The seventy-year-old woman succumbed to her malady at 3:30 a.m. on Friday, December 10. Though her obituary notice stated that she died of "chronic difficulty and bilious fever," a private funeral service was held for her that afternoon because of the suspicion that diptheria might be involved.

Then, on Monday morning, February 21, 1881, her husband Barton, 71, also died. When his illness first began on February 12, his doctor treated him for a bilious attack. When he failed to respond to the treatment, the diagnosis was changed to "blood poisoning."

Again, diptheria was suspected. For that reason, another private funeral was held in the house.

The only surviving member of the two families now was Major Francis Town, who was stationed in Walla Walla, Washington. Early that spring he sent an order to Lancaster authorizing Doctor Ezra Mitchell, Jr., to exhume his father's body in order to have the stomach analyzed by a chemist.

On May 25, after the request had received the proper legal sanctions, Mr. Towne's body was disinterred and the stomach removed by Dr. Mitchell and Dr. Emmons F. Stockwell. Dr. Stockwell accompanied the organ to Harvard Medical School in Cambridge, Massachusetts, where it was turned over to Professor Edward Stickney Wood. Professor Wood not only taught chemistry at Harvard, but he was also a pioneer in the field of toxicology.

It was not until August 5 that the Lancaster authorities finally received word that a considerable quantity of arsenic had been found in Mr. Towne's stomach. That day, for whatever reason, Dr. Stockwell took it on himself to inform Nellie Webb Mayo that she was under suspicion of having committed murder and that she probably would be arrested.

Angrily declaring her innocence, Nellie told Dr. Stockwell that she was ready to meet the charge at any time. Immediately after this exchange, she consulted with friends concerning her predicament. Then, acting on their advice, she engaged Attorneys William Heywood and his son Henry in the event legal proceedings were instituted against her.

Soon all of New England began talking about her as Boston newspapers headlined what had happened in Lancaster. For example, in the *Boston Journal* dated August 9, its four-decked headline read, "A YOUNG WOMAN SUSPECTED OF WHOLESALE POISONING"; the final deck even provided the motive: "To Secure a Paltry Sum of Money."

In the lengthy article that followed these incriminating headlines, it was reported that "From the Bugbee estate Mrs. Mayo received $500 and some presents, and from the Towne property only some furniture."

Local editors objected to these out-of-state articles and wrote, "The sensational reports published in Boston and other papers, we understand were sent from Concord and ought to have been suppressed. Additional facts are every day coming to light regarding the Bugbee-Towne case, which we sincerely hope will soon place all suspicion at rest."

Among the facts alluded to was the bottle of whiskey which had made its way from the Bugbee house to the Towne house. Following Mr. Towne's death, the bottle was removed from the nightstand next to his bed and the contents were tested by the local druggist, Parker J. Noyes, who was also a chemist. It was identified as the source of the arsenic.

Now convinced that Nellie was guilty of murder, James W. Weeks went to Concord, N.H., for a conference with Attorney General Mason Tappan. After their discussion, the Attorney General directed Weeks to have the bodies of Dr. Bugbee and Mrs. Towne exhumed.

The following Sunday, which was August 14, the Lancaster authorities received confirmation from Tappan that the exhumations were not only to begin immediately, but they were to include Mrs. Bugbee as well.

The next day Drs. Mitchell and Stockwell were at the cemetery overseeing the removal of the bodies. When Mrs. Bugbee was disinterred the excellent state of her preservation surprised them. They felt this indicated the presence of arsenic in her body.

In early September the first autopsy report was received in Lancaster. In it Professor Wood stated that he could not find any traces of arsenic in Mrs. Bugbee's organs. It was now established that she definitely died from diphtheria. A week later the autopsy reports of Dr. Bugbee and Mrs. Towne were also received. Tragically, like Barton Towne, they had died from arsenic poisoning.

An anonymously written letter published in the *Boston Globe* demonstrated the mounting belief that Nellie Webb Mayo was a murderess. Penned in Littleton, N.H., it said, "The Lancaster poisoning case is still attracting a great deal of attention here, and nearly every one has a theory in regard to it. Before the report of the analysis of the stomachs of Dr. Bugbee and Mrs. Towne there were many people who questioned whether a series of murders had really taken place.

"All the evidence went to show that whiskey which was used during the sickness of Dr. Bugbee and Mr. and Mrs. Barton C. Towne was taken from a bottle which was probably replenished from the demijohn in which Dr. Bugbee brought the whiskey to Lancaster. Rather than believe in the fiendishness of someone who must have been often in and about the house during the sickness of these three persons, these people were willing to believe that by some terrible mistake or blunder a bottle which had contained Fowle's Solution of Arsenic had been used for the whiskey.

"This theory, however, is overthrown, and the fact is undeniable that a series of awful murders took place, and that the deaths of Dr. Bugbee and Mr. and Mrs. Towne occurred as the direct result of poison."

Fortunately for Nellie, the Coos Grand Jury did not agree with the letter writer. On Thursday night, October 18, after listening to nearly three days of testimony, the jury ruled that the evidence necessary to indict her was "insufficient and circumstantial."

Following this finding, no charges were ever again brought against her. And this didn't set too well with some people in Lancaster. This becomes all too evident from a diary entry made by Richard P. Kent on December 15, 1881. He wrote: "Mr. J.W. Weeks made a lengthy call at our house and talked over the incidents connected with the poisoning of the Towne and Bugbee families. He has no doubt of the guilt of the suspected party, although the Grand Jury failed to indict her."

At this point in Nellie's life, Weeks' attitude was inconsequential. Knowing that the damage done to her name and reputation locally was irreparable, she severed all of her New England ties and permanently moved to the Midwest with her husband.

To this day no one really knows where the arsenic came from that caused the deaths of Dr. Frank Bugbee and the elderly Townes. The final answer is a part of the mystery that still lingers over this fascinating case.

The Rest of The Story...

IF COLONEL FRANCIS TOWN thought his nightmare had finally ended with the departure of Nellie Webb Mayo from Lancaster, he was sadly mistaken. In a bizarre twist to the unfortunate chain of circumstances that affected Town's life so grievously, in the late 1880's author Mary R.P. Hatch of Stratford, N.H., wrote a book entitled *The Upland Mystery*. It was a murder mystery that blended fact and fiction, and, unfortunately, it was based on the Bugbee-Towne arsenic deaths.

The Old Well in Which the Poison was Found.

In the book, the entire Brown family dies. A relative, Dr. Carber, who is practicing medicine in Hong Kong, develops a suspicion that their deaths were due to foul play. A dull-witted detective then appears on the scene. A white powder is found, and also a bottle of poison in a well. Miss Marah Connel, who becomes Dr. Carber's romantic interest, manages to make herself the center of suspicion. Though she is arrested, she is later proved innocent.

Sad to say, in the book Dr. Carber and Marah Connel closely resembled Colonel Town and Nellie Webb, who were the real life prototypes for the fictional characters. Persons reading the book were confusing the romance between Carber and Connel as one that might have actually existed between Town and Webb.

As a consequence, Colonel Town advertised in the newspapers for copies of *The Upland Mystery*. Angrily he bought up and destroyed all that he could lay his hands on. However, some copies eluded him, and though the book is now extremely rare, a copy can be found in Lancaster's Weeks Memorial Library. It does not circulate, but can be read there.

FWR

New Hampshire's Famous UFO Kidnapping

BARNEY HILL nervously braked his 1957 Bel Air hardtop to a stop near the middle of the highway. He purposely left the headlights on and the engine running. His wife Betty quickly handed him the binoculars.

Opening the car door, he stepped out on Route 3 in Lincoln, New Hampshire. As he did, the huge circular disc that had been following them drifted silently past him to the left and hovered over the open field.

Struggling to overcome his fear, Barney entered the field determined to identify the strange, wingless object. As he passed the shuttered vegetable stand, the object tilted downward by a gnarled apple tree and descended toward him. Focusing the binoculars, he could see several humanoid-like figures dressed in black watching him from the windows.

Mrs. Hill, still in the car and concerned for his safety, heard him say repeatedly, "I don't believe it! I don't believe it! This is

(Floyd W. Ramsey Photo)

Located just north of the Indian Head Resort, Parker's Motel could easily have been the end of the Hill's UFO experience if they had stopped here. However, low on money, they were forced to continue their journey homeward.

ridiculous!"

From where she sat, she could not see the craft descending.

This was the night of September 19, 1961. The Hills were about to become the central figures in one of the most famous and fascinating UFO abduction cases on record.

Precisely what happened to them that night, and what became of them in the years to follow remains an incredible story to this day.

Following a vacation trip to Niagara Falls on the Canadian side, the Hills and their little dachshund Delsey were headed home to Portsmouth by way of Route 3. Stopping in Colebrook, they had their car serviced. After a late snack at a nearby restaurant, they returned to the car at about 10:05 p.m.

Based on this fact, Barney estimated they would arrive home no later than 3:00 a.m.

Just south of Lancaster Betty spotted a bright starlike object above Jupiter. As she watched, it grew brighter and began moving across the face of the moon. At this point Barney felt that she was seeing a satellite.

(Floyd W. Ramsey Photo)

Located just off Route 3 in Lincoln, New Hampshire, this is Clark's field today. It is somewhat altered by neglect and the encroachment of I-93. The apple tree, center, is where the UFO hovered not more than fifty feet from where Barney Hill stood, and a historic moment unfolded.

A short time later Delsey grew restless so they stopped to let her out. During this stop Barney and Betty took turns watching the object through the binoculars. As they walked Delsey back to the car, they saw the object change directions and fly eastward toward them. Barney now decided that it was a military plane flying over to check them out.

Shortly after they had passed through Whitefield, Betty noticed that the object's movements had become erratic. Once she shouted, "Barney, look at it! It's jumping in the sky!"

Barney became more puzzled than ever.

When they came to the Cannon Mountain area in Franconia

Notch, the object again turned and headed directly toward them. Braking, Barney turned sharply to the right and drove into a picnic turnout.

Standing in the chilly night air, he again sighted it through the binoculars. He made out a shape like the fuselage of a plane, but one without wings. He also saw what seemed to be a series of blinking lights running in an alternating pattern along a rim.

Just as he handed the glasses to Betty, the object passed in front of the moon. As she followed it, she could see thin shafts of light which were flashing red, amber, green and blue. However, because Delsey was whining and shivering and Barney was showing signs of irritation, she handed him the binoculars and got back in the car. When he followed her a few minutes later, he said he thought the craft was now playing games with them.

(Floyd W. Ramsey Photo)

Though the Hill's 1966 bestseller was entitled, "The Interrupted Journey," their startling UFO experience is often referred to as "The Indian Head Incident." This is in reference to the famous resort that they passed just minutes before their dramatic confrontation in Clark's field. While trying to find their capture spot, Barney and Betty Hill visited here on more than one occasion.

Though he did his best to conceal his growing fear, Betty sensed how he felt.

As they passed "The Old Man of the Mountains," a famous rock profile located at the southern tip of Cannon Mountain, the object continued to move with them. Seven miles down the road, near the turnoff for the Flume, they stopped again. They almost got another good look at it, but tree interference forced them to move on.

A half mile beyond the Flume they passed Parker's Motel on their left. As they went by, they saw a man standing in the lighted doorway of an end unit. At that moment Betty thought, "Something is going to happen. I don't know what it is, but whatever it is I'm prepared for it."

Looking up, she was surprised to see that the huge object was only a few hundred feet above them. During this time she also noticed that the blinking light pattern had changed to a steady white glow. The binoculars helped her to clearly see a double row of windows. Excited, without thinking she rolled down her car window and waved to it.

Just south of the Indian Head, which is a well-known resort complex, they both noticed two wigwams just off the highway to their right. They were part of an attraction named Natureland. It was just a short distance from here that Barney stopped the car, asked for the binoculars, and then walked into the area called Clark's field.

His confrontation with the UFO was about to begin!

Watching the object through the binoculars, he estimated that it was no more than 80 to 100 feet off the ground. He could see two fin-like projections sliding out from the sides, each with a red light on the end. He could also see that the windows curved around the object, which was now revealed as a thick, pancake-shaped disc. The windows glowed with a cold, bluish-white fluorescence. It was now within 50 feet of him.

Back in the car Betty had been nervously watching for the headlights of approaching cars. She was suddenly aware that Barney had disappeared in the blackness of the field. She screamed, "Barney, Barney, you damn fool! Come back here!"

He didn't hear her. He was too absorbed in watching at least a half dozen small humanoids who were standing behind the windows staring down at him. When all but one stepped back, Barney could see a large panel in the craft where they began pulling levers. The craft came down lower, the two lights came out farther, and an extension appeared from the underside.

Sharpening the binocular focus on the one face still staring at him, Barney realized that he was looking into eyes unlike any he had ever seen before. When he tried to pull the glasses away from his eyes, he couldn't. He now realized that he was about to be captured.

From strength born of hysteria, he tore the binoculars from his neck and ran back to the car screaming, "We've got to get out of here! They're going to capture us!"

Flinging himself into the car, he jammed it in gear and they went speeding down the highway. Repeatedly he ordered Betty to look out the window to see where the craft was. She did as he asked, but she could see nothing. When she told him, he yelled at her that it was directly overhead. She looked again. All she could see was blackness. Even the stars seemed to have disappeared.

Suddenly a strange sounding beeping noise came from overhead. The car vibrated. An odd tingling sensation, which was followed by drowsiness, overtook them. They stopped talking.

Later Betty would remember that Barney left Route 3 just below North Woodstock, and that he turned left and took Route 175. She also remembered Barney braking the car, and making another left turn onto a dirt road. She saw what she thought was the moon setting. Then everything blanked out.

Sometime later they heard a second series of beeps, and for the final time the craft flew over them. Barney yelled, "Oh, my God! Not again!"

As their drowsiness slowly lifted, they found themselves trying to return to Route 3. Finally Betty saw a road sign that indicated they were in Ashland. She then said to Barney, "Do you believe in flying saucers now?"

He abruptly replied, "Don't be ridiculous!"

They did not fully regain consciousness until they saw the U.S. 93 sign that read: CONCORD–17 MILES.

On the outskirts of Portsmouth they both discovered that their watches had stopped. It was not until they saw their kitchen clock that they learned it was after 5:00 a.m. They looked at each other. They wondered why they had arrived so late. Though they didn't know it then, the night's events had been erased from their memory.

Before the day was over they would be puzzled by other disquieting questions. For example, after unloading the car why did Barney feel compelled to go to the bathroom to examine his lower abdomen? Why were the tops of his best shoes severely scuffed? What were the shiny spots that Betty discovered on the trunk of the car that caused a compass needle to spin erratically? Why were they both left with the feeling that something very puzzling had happened to them?

As a result of this strange experience, over the next two years

Barney's health deteriorated to the point where it was difficult for him to continue his work as an assistant dispatcher at the South Boston Postal Annex. Sometimes while commuting to work, if he saw any suspicious looking lights in the sky he'd panic, turn around, and drive back home.

He was also haunted by the memory of the humanoid staring down at him in Clark's field. He knew the humanoid said something to him, but what? Frustrated, he'd walk around the house, bang his fists and cry, "Why can't I remember what he said?"

A series of warts also began to develop in an almost perfect circular ring on his groin. They added to his concern.

Betty's health also suffered.

About ten days after the sighting, she began having nightmares that lasted for five nights. Later they became a reality for her and Barney under time-regression hypnosis. At no time prior to the hypnosis did she directly discuss the nightmares with him. She also suffered several bouts of pneumonia, but she thinks that the stress of her job as a child welfare worker helped her to overcome the stresses produced by the experience.

(Floyd W. Ramsey Photo)

Betty Hill is a graduate of the University of New Hampshire. Beyond UFOs, she is also greatly interested in archeology and trends in the political arena. She is seen standing in her back yard with her dachshund Brandy. Delsey died on December 24, 1968, just a few months before Barney's death.

While being treated for high blood pressure and ulcers, Barney's work attendance became more and more erratic. Finally he stopped responding to his medication, and was totally out of work for a year. In the summer of 1962 his doctor finally referred him to the distinguished Exeter psychiatrist, Doctor Duncan Stephans.

In his sessions with Doctor Stephans, Barney tended to ignore the UFO incident. It was not until September of 1963, in their

Unitarian Church discussion group, that he and Betty spoke publicly for the first time about their UFO experience. Also attending the meeting was another guest speaker, Captain Ben Swett, from nearby Pease Air Force Base. After listening to their story, he thought it was interesting that both their memories cut off moments after they fled the Indian Head area. He suggested hypnotic recall, but only if it was administered under the direction of a psychiatrist.

Doctor Stephans agreed. He referred them to the prominent Boston psychiatrist, Doctor Benjamin Simon.

Beginning on December 14, 1963, Barney and Betty each had separate sessions with Doctor Simon every Saturday for seven months. Each was hypnotically regressed back to the beginning of the experience, and then carefully brought through it. Since each session was recorded, near the end of the treatment program they listened to the tapes and learned the following:

(Floyd W. Ramsey Photo)

Betty Hill still continues to occupy the first floor of the residence she and Barney were living in on State Street in Portsmouth when they were kidnapped by humanoids on September 19, 1961. Over the years, a stream of famous figures have stopped here while pursuing their own interests in UFOs.

In Clark's field, as Barney stood looking up at the humanoid, he was told, "Don't be afraid. You are going to be all right. Just stand there and look at me."

Later, after they left Route 3 for Route 175, they were several miles south of the Russell Pond area when they again turned left on to a dirt road. It was here that the object was waiting for them. And it was here that eleven humanoids, all about five feet tall and dressed in black, flagged them down. When Barney stopped the car, the engine died and he was unable to restart it.

As the humanoids approached, Barney and Betty fell under their control and entered a sleep state. Barney, whose eyes remained closed through the entire ordeal, was helped from the car and held up by two of the aliens.

While walking along a path through the woods, Betty forced

her eyes open and broke the trance. Looking behind her, she saw Barney being somewhat dragged along. The tops of his shoes were scraping over the rocks.

Several times she commanded him to wake up, but each attempt failed. Finally the alien leader assured her that no harm would come to them. She was also told that they were going to be tested and then be put back in their car.

Despite this reassurance, as they approached the UFO ramp she balked. The alien leader got angry. When a feeling of helplessness came over her, she quietly headed for the doorway. Inside they turned left and went down a corridor to a wedge-shaped room where Betty was to be examined. Barney was led past her to the next room for the same purpose. Only the UFO leader and the examiner remained in the room with her.

In the testing that followed, her eyes, ears, nose and throat were checked. Next, hair, fingernail, and skin samples were taken. After inspecting her hands and feet, the examiner had her slip out of her dress and lay on a table. Following a study of her spine, he ran a multiple needle device over her that he said recorded her central nervous system. Later, when she reacted to the pain caused by the insertion of a long needle in her navel, the testing was discontinued and the examiner left to study Barney's bone structure.

Alone with the leader, Betty coaxed him into giving her a strange looking book as a proof of her experience. Also, when she asked him where he was from, he produced an oblong "sky" map that seemed to materialize out of the wall. He explained that the heavy lines she could see were trade routes, the solid lines were places they went occasionally, and the broken lines represented expeditions.

When Betty failed to pinpoint where the earth was on the map, he put it back in the wall. Shortly after that, the examiner and several other aliens excitedly entered the room. Immediately the examiner began to inspect her mouth. They were confused over why Barney's teeth came out and hers didn't.

Among other things, Betty explained dentures to them, old age, a human life span and how we measured time. When asked about food, she had difficulty explaining what vegetables were.

At this time Barney returned. The testing was over. Under hypnosis he would later recall a cup-like object being placed on his groin as part of his examination.

As they were ready to go down the ramp, some of the humanoids became highly agitated. Consequently, the leader took the book away from Betty. Angrily she reminded him that it was her proof.

He said, "That is the whole point. They don't want you to know what has happened. They want you to forget all about it."

Betty forcefully replied, "I won't forget about it. I'll remember it if it is the last thing I do."

He told her, "It won't do you any good if you do. Barney won't remember a single thing. And if you should remember anything at all, he is going to remember it differently from you."

In his final statement, the leader said to her, "I'm going to leave you here. Why don't you stand by the car and watch us leave."

Minutes later Betty found Barney sitting in the car. Though his eyes were open, he appeared to be in a fog. Surprisingly, he responded when she invited him to join her outside the car. Reaching into the car, she picked up a shivering Delsey.

As she leaned against the car fender, Barney stood beside her. While they watched, the object began to glow. Soon it was surrounded by a swirling, orange-red fiery mass.

Betty cried out, "Look at Delsey! She may be the only dog in the world who has ever seen anything like this, and she's hiding her head under my arm!"

Once the craft had left, and they had found their way back to Route 3, Betty said, "Well, Barney, now try to tell me that you don't believe in flying saucers."

He abruptly replied, "Oh, don't be ridiculous."

The confusion had just begun.

In the years that followed, the Hills never released their experience to the news media. As advised, they reported it only to the authorities at Pease Air Force Base. If discussed at all, it was only with members of their immediate family. Eventually, however, two Pease Air Force officers talked about it with an investigative reporter at a Boston cocktail party. When the reporter approached the Hills, they shied away from him.

Despite this fact, the *Boston Herald Traveler* broke the story on

October 26, 1965. It instantly made headlines around the world. Unfortunately the reporter had only half the facts, and the Hills came close to being held up to ridicule. They were now forced to go public.

With their telephone ringing constantly twenty-four hours a day, they soon had to invest in an answering service. They didn't stay home any longer than was necessary.

In time they established contact with the author, John Fuller, who was researching UFOs in the Exeter area. He told them, "The best way to get the public off your back is to write a book."

With Doctor Simon's blessings, they collaborated with Fuller. In 1966 their bestseller, *The Interrupted Journey*, came out. With its appearance, they went on a nationwide TV tour. Years afterwards, Betty was still doing TV programs.

Tragically, Barney was felled by a stroke on February 25, 1969. According to Betty, they were playing pool downstairs in their State Street home when Barney put his hand to the back of his head and said, "A hornet just stung me."

Betty told him, "Barney, there are no hornets in February."

Going upstairs to rest, a short time later he slid off the living room couch and fell to the floor. Rushed to the Portsmouth Hospital by ambulance, he slipped into a coma and died at 7:15 that evening. He was forty-six years old.

Ironically, proof of the Hills' experience surfaced that year with the publication of the 1969 *Gliese Catalogue* which contained the latest findings in astronomy. Following the publication, Marjorie Fish, a former teacher and a nuclear researcher at Oak Ridge, Tennessee, identified two of the stars which were a part of the "sky" map that Betty had re-created while under hypnosis in Doctor Simon's office.

This pattern of stars is known today as the Fish-Hill Pattern.

In 1970 Marjorie Fish announced that the humanoids were coming here from a star known as Zeta Reticuli I.

When Betty's "sky" map was set up by scientists on computers, it was found that the map reflected earth looking outward from Zeta Reticuli I. They concluded that no one on this planet had the capability of creating such a map.

It was also in 1970 that Betty was promoted to Supervisor of Intake and Referrals at her Portsmouth Public Welfare office. Five

During the summer of 1964, while Barney and Betty Hill were traveling through the Thornton-Campton area looking for a campsite for her parents, she and Barney immediately recognized the exact location where they were taken aboard the UFO. Subsequent measurements taken there revealed the craft was sixty-to-sixty-five feet across. Betty is seen sitting in her living room with a bust of the UFO leader made from her description of him.

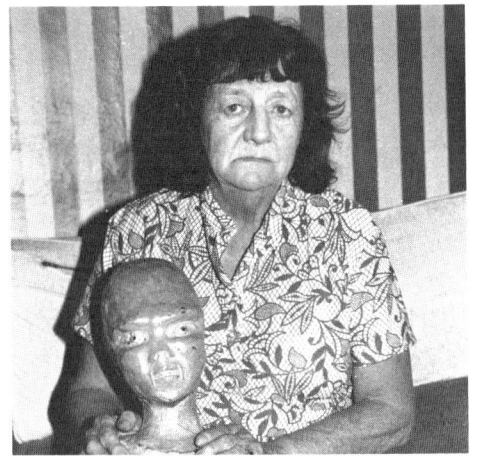

(Floyd W. Ramsey Photo)

years later she retired for health reasons.

On October 20, 1975, a made-for-NBC TV movie entitled *The UFO Incident* dramatized the Hills' experience. It starred James Earl Jones as Barney, and Betty was played by Estelle Parsons.

For many years after the UFO encounter, Betty remained in contact with scientists throughout the world who shared UFO reports with her. And, until recently, she also traveled around the country doing radio and press interviews as well as giving lectures on the college and public school circuit. Over time, she has also appeared on every major TV talk show in the United States. She has even been on Japanese and Chinese television. Though she still gets requests from the media for personal appearances, she now prefers a quiet life to the limelight and has learned to say no to these requests.

Active by nature, she is still carrying on limited UFO investigations. Occasionally she travels to an isolated spot southwest of Portsmouth that she has identified as a UFO corridor. She has taken many UFO slides, and she states that the UFOs coming in now have a different purpose than those that arrived earlier.

During the early period of their appearances, which she calls "The Time of Exploration," she says they were just looking over the landscape. The later, or second period group, are now in what she refers to as "The Period of Infiltration." She says this group is doing an in-depth study of mankind.

She warns that there is a danger associated with UFOs. She attributes this to too many people shooting at them over the years. When a UFO assumes a defensive posture, she says, it will either make darting motions at a person or it will shoot colored balls of light called "fire bullets." When this happens, she warns, the person becomes disoriented and confused.

Quietly she concludes, "If you see a UFO stay your distance but be friendly. Remember they are astronauts from a different solar system, and they are a long ways from home. Be friendly to them, and they may respond in a friendly way."

She also states that there are still UFOs flying over New Hampshire in large numbers, and she adds that during her travels people often ask her why there are so many here. She replies, with a smile, "Haven't you been to New Hampshire to find out? We're simply a beautiful state."

Today, despite the encroachment of I-93 through the area, the old, gnarled apple tree still stands in Clark's field. It remains as the silent witness to the strange confrontation that took place there between Barney Hill and the humanoids so many years ago. And, like Betty Hill, it perseveres.

The Taft Visit...
A Tender Moment for an Unhappy President

(Photo courtesy of Littleton Historical Society)

This was a proud moment for thousands of Littleton, New Hampshire, townspeople as President William H. Taft addressed them in front of the Carnegie Library on the afternoon of October 9, 1912. As can be seen, the decorating committee outdid itself when it dressed the Library for the occasion.

ON WEDNESDAY afternoon, October 9, 1912, the townspeople of Littleton, New Hampshire, extended a warm and enthusiastic greeting to President William Howard Taft and his lovely wife as they rode down Main Street in an open Pierce Arrow sedan. It had been at least thirty-five years since a President had last visited the area, and regardless of party affiliation, Littleton residents were going to make the most of Taft's visit. This held true whether they were Progressive Republicans supporting independent candidate Theodore Roosevelt, conservative Republications loyal to Taft, or Democrats for New Jersey Governor Woodrow Wilson.

Oddly enough, it was the bitter factional quarreling taking place within his own party that had brought Taft to the North Country. The week prior to his visit, when he stated that he was making a trip to Massachusetts and Vermont for non-political reasons, he meant just that. He had decided to visit ancestral homes in both states simply to get away from his political headaches.

As strange as it sounds, this was a man who never wanted to be President in the first place. The first twenty years of his working life were spent as a lawyer and a judge. A quiet, pleasant man, he had a strong distaste for the political arena. His mother, Louise Torrey Taft, confirmed this once when she remarked, "I do not want my son to be President. His is a judicial mind, and he loves the law."

Ironically, it was his father's importance in the Republican Party that kept pushing Taft in the very direction that he did not want to take. And it was his wife Helen's ambitions that kept him on that road. Despite his feelings to the contrary, she persuaded him to leave the bar and the bench to pursue a life in public office.

Briefly tracing Taft's rise to political power, he first gained national prominence when President William McKinley appointed him to head the commission charged with ending military rule in the Philippine Islands. Once that was accomplished, McKinley next appointed him to be the first governor there.

In 1901, following McKinley's assassination, Vice President Theodore Roosevelt ascended to the White House. Though he and Taft were complete opposites, they became close personal friends. Eventually Roosevelt talked him into becoming his Secretary of War.

It was while in this position that Taft became Roosevelt's top "trouble shooter." Not the least of his duties included taking charge of the Panama Canal construction. While juggling that responsibility, he also helped negotiate a solution to the revolution threatening Cuba.

Later that year he wrote to Helen, "Politics, when I am in it, makes me sick."

Over time, Roosevelt leaned more and more towards Taft becoming his political successor. To that end he praised him mightily. For example, during one interview he said, "Everything is all right in Washington because Taft is sitting on the lid."

Thus it was, when Roosevelt announced he would not seek re-

The Taft Visit

(Library of Congress Photo)

This 1911 family photo shows President Taft sitting with his wife Helen and their three children. From left to right, they are Charles, Helen and Robert. Taft is the only man in the history of the United States who served first as President, and then as Chief Justice. He died on March 8, 1930, one month after he retired from the Supreme Court.

election in 1908 that Taft accepted the Republican nomination against his better judgment. The rest is history. By more than a million votes he handed the Democrat's heavyweight, William Jennings Bryan, his third and final knockout as a presidential contender.

Despite this margin of victory, Taft harbored strong doubts that he had all the necessary qualifications to be President. These misgivings were reflected in a remark he made when a blizzard swept through Washington on March 4, 1909, the day of his inauguration. He moaned, "Even the elements do protest."

Sad to say, it was the beginning of four of the most unhappy years of his life.

Looking at the bright side, he was our first Chief Executive to receive a yearly salary of $75,000 plus an additional $25,000 for travel expenses. Not wanting this latter amount to go to waste, during his four years as President he traveled more than 150,000 miles.

On the human side, though he may not have been our most successful President, he certainly was our largest. When he was sworn in he weighed 332 pounds. Shortly after he moved into the White House, word leaked out that he got stuck in the presidential bathtub.

Needless to say, a larger tub was quickly installed.

His immense girth could be partly attributed to his prodigious appetite. Which, in itself, was sometimes a source of embarrassment for his wife. During the course of consuming a huge meal, it was not unusual for Taft to fall asleep while engaged in conversation with White House guests. After several minutes he would wake up, resume the conversation, only to fall asleep again.

(Photo courtesy of Paul Dovholuk)

President William H. Taft addresses townspeople and schoolchildren in Lisbon Square on the morning of October 10, 1912. With him are his military aide, Major Thomas L. Rhoads, his wife Mrs. Taft, and Miss Mabel Boardman, who was President of the Red Cross in Washington, D.C. The photo was taken by Lisbon photographer Irving E. James.

Perhaps this is why his wife preferred entertaining guests at small teas.

To his credit, during his term as President he did his best to provide the Nation with a good Administration. Though he succeeded in this respect, by the same token he failed to excite the public imagination along the way. It was partly due to this particular ineptitude that he found himself alienated by the progressive element of his party. His wife, who had a better head for politics, might have been able to help him control this faction if she had not suffered a stroke in the winter of 1909.

Taft's problems worsened after the Democrats captured control of the House in 1910. The "Progressive Republicans," as they eventually became known, turned completely against him. And, when they did, they once more rallied around their old champion,

The Taft Visit

Theodore Roosevelt.

Encouraged by their backing, Roosevelt entered the Republican primaries the following year. Ironically, though he carried most of the states, Taft was still nominated on the first ballot at the nominating convention. This pill was a little too much for Roosevelt to swallow quietly. Accusing Taft of stealing the nomination from him by "steamroller" tactics, he entered the presidential race as an Independent.

Deeply hurt by his old friend's political rancor and opposition, Taft campaigned until the month before elections. Knowing that his divided party faced inevitable defeat by the Democrats, he publicly announced that he was going to visit ancestral homes in Massachusetts and Vermont.

Shortly after he arrived at his summer White House in Beverly, Massachusetts, he received a special delivery letter from George H. Tilton of Littleton, New Hampshire. It was an invitation to visit there during his New England trip. Flattered by the request, he immediately sent the following reply through his executive secretary, Rudolph Foster:

"The President greatly appreciates the cordial invitation which you extend to him in your letter of October 3, in behalf of the Littleton Board of Trade, and asks me to thank you warmly. In view of the necessity for returning to Beverly October 11, the President's trip through Vermont will necessarily be a hurried one, but he will be glad to stop at Littleton briefly Wednesday in case he finds it possible to do so."

Upon receipt of this letter, Tilton, who was a prominent Littleton realtor and president of the Board of Trade, immediately appointed about fifty townspeople to a planning committee. As he contacted each of them, he stressed the importance of the moment. He urged them to be at the police station courthouse on Monday evening at 8:00.

Almost without exception they were there. The purpose behind their attendance fired their enthusiasm and evaporated their political differences. Consequently the meeting ran smoothly. Individual committee assignments were accepted without argument, and the decision was made to receive the President at the Carnegie Library grounds on his arrival.

Early the next day Dr. George W. McGregor and Dr. Millard Young, a local dentist, worked with grocer Fred H. English in ironing out plans for the construction of a speaker's platform on the library sidewalk. At the same time Deputy Sheriff Albert E. Strain's group organized a squadron of 12 police officers that would be trained to maintain crowd control, and also lead the community band down Main Street.

On an unusual note, the decorating committee found itself composed of four Democrats and one Republican. Taking advantage of the situation, the four Democrats—James McLeod, Walter Parker, Edward Cummings, and Revel Eastman—ganged up on Charles Gosselin, the lone Republican. They assigned him the responsibility of hiring the man who had just decorated St. Johnsbury, Vermont, which was also on the President's itinerary.

To their dismay, Gosselin reported back that the man would not do the job for less than $150. At that price they knew they would have to do the work themselves. And they did.

The school committee, which was comprised of Myron Richardson, George Boule, and D.F. Carpenter, who was the first superintendent of the Littleton Union School District, carefully mapped out a way to have all the students present at the library for the occasion. Knowing how much the President loved children, they wanted the students to stand as close to him as possible.

As other committees also worked on their assignments, the town bristled with excitement. Many residents compared the moment to President Rutherford B. Hayes' visit in 1877. Older residents recalled Ulysses S. Grant's 1869 visit. None of them, however, could top the memory of James R. Jackson, 74. He was just a student in Judge Harry Bingham's law office in 1864 when there was an unexpected knock at the door. When he answered it, there stood former New Hampshire President Franklin Pierce and his friend Nathaniel Hawthorne. Since Bingham was out of town, Jackson had the singular honor of entertaining the two men personally.

By the time the afternoon of the Taft visit arrived, the town was ready for him. As luck would have it, the first house he would pass was that of Mr. and Mrs. William B. Hurd, staunch Democrats. Though they couldn't be persuaded to take down their picture of Woodrow Wilson, they honored Taft by also hanging out his pic-

THE TAFT VISIT   145

This is Lisbon High School's class of 1903. George C. Morgan, standing directly behind Professor Wallace, not only shook hands with President Taft during his visit, but he also owned the photo showing Taft in Lisbon Square. Morgan's inscription on the back later helped to identify the location.

ture along with a display of the flag.

Just down the street, a loyal Taft supporter named Harry Green literally had his house covered with flags. It was at this location that the work of the decorating committee had actually begun. In front of Green's house there was a great canvas sign stretched across the road which read, "WELCOME TO OUR PRESIDENT." And from the Masonic Temple to the end of the Opera Block not only did the committee have the entire business district ablaze with red, white, and blue buntings and American flags, but the library and speaker's platform as well. As a result, the air was charged with a contagious spirit of patriotism.

At 3:00 p.m., with both sides of Main Street alive with thousands of people, George Tilton and his reception committee rode out of town and traveled eight miles to the east side of the Waterford Bridge to await the arrival of the President. Once there, they found themselves visiting with one another for an hour.

Finally, at about 4:10, the presidential entourage reached the toll house on the Vermont side of the Connecticut River. Much to the reception committee's amazement, the attendant on duty charged the presidential party the fare necessary to cross over into New Hampshire. Whoever the attendant was, he certainly didn't bow to authority.

Once the transaction was completed, it was only a matter of seconds before Tilton was welcoming the President. After he had finished, Taft introduced him to his wife, to Miss Mabel Boardman, who was a prominent Red Cross worker, and to his military aide, Major Thomas L. Rhoads. As for the other two cars, he pointed out that they carried three secret service agents, his Japanese maid, his personal valet, and a fair amount of luggage.

Once the formalities at the bridge were concluded, the presidential party headed for Littleton. Riding in the lead car, Tilton was pleased that the President had consented to give a brief speech.

In the meantime, the community band had completed its march down Main Street and was giving a concert from the library grounds. The music stopped, however, when the President's car was seen approaching Henry Green's house. When it reached the Congregational Church, Elbridge Young gave the signal that set off the roar of a 44-gun salute. Besides serving as a welcome, the explosion was also the cue for the band to begin playing again.

With the crowd eager to get a closer look at President Taft, Deputy Sheriff Strain and his men moved quickly to keep the shoving and pushing to a minimum. Particularly in the area where Taft alighted from the Pierce Arrow.

Flanked by Tilton and another committee member, Dr. William Beattie, Taft gave a long dignified wave to the throng cheering him along the sidewalk. Directly behind the speaker's platform there were no less than 800 school children happily waving small flags in glad greeting.

Just before the President ascended the platform steps, little Catherine Beattie, 7, broke out of the school group and ran over to her father. Looking up at him with a surprised look on her face, she exclaimed, "Why, father, you here! I didn't spect to see you round Taft!"

The President was still laughing when Tilton announced, "Ladies and gentlemen, I have the great honor to present to you the President of the United States!" After the applause died down, the President immediately turned to the children. Speaking to them in a loud authoritative voice, he said, "First I am going to talk to you, but after I am finished you must agree to keep quiet while I am talking to everyone else."

The children nodded in innocent agreement.

He then asked them three simple questions: "Do you know what office I hold? Did you get a half holiday to come down and greet me? Is your interest in me the same as in the American flag?"

With each question answered in the affirmative, Taft then told them it would be a memorable event in their lives to be able to say they had seen a President. Having said that, he then turned and addressed the crowd.

"Ladies and gentlemen of Littleton, I am here on a trip for pleasure," he told them. "Neither for business nor politics. And I only wish to give you my thanks for this cordial greeting."

Unexpectedly, the children cheered.

Smiling at them, Taft continued, "There was a time in the early history of the Country when we didn't have our present means of transportation. When we had to travel in coaches, it was difficult to get around. Now that we have automobiles I believe it will become more and more the custom for presidents to travel about through the various sections of the Country. My trip has been full of pleasure, and not the least of it are the expressions of loyalty to the Office which indicate the desire of all to be loyal to the man who for the time represents the Country."

The children cheered again.

Laughing, the President told the crowd, "You have factories in your town, and I have no doubt they are sharing the prosperity which the rest of the Country is enjoying. We may have reforms, but nothing is so important as good business so that people may have good wages and a reasonable share of the comforts of life."

Another cheer came from the children.

Respectfully nodding to them, Taft concluded, "After that let us have the reforms. But first let us get business and have it constant and well grounded. With the hope and belief that you are sharing in this prosperity, I will say goodbye."

A thunderous applause erupted from the crowd. Waiting it out, Taft then turned and lightheartedly accused the children of breaking their contract with him.

His affection for them was obvious.

Upon leaving the platform, Taft noticed little Catherine Beattie being held in her father's arms. Stepping over to her, he talked quietly with her, and then he kissed her hand. After he said goodbye to Dr. Beattie, he worked his way back to the Pierce Arrow while the band gave a rousing rendition of "America." Among the few people he shook hands with along the sidewalk was Thomas Colby, an old veteran.

Minutes later, much to the embarrassment of the Bethlehem Welcoming Committee, they found their car traveling behind Taft's as he left Littleton for Bethlehem. Caught off guard by the brevity of his remarks, they had failed to return to their vehicle in time to depart ahead of him. When his motorcade turned right to cross the bridge just off Main Street, they made a record run through town and headed for the Apthorp Hill road. They arrived at farmer Edward E. Bishop's place on the upper corner just ahead of Taft.

Following introductions, with a collective sigh of relief the committee led the way to the Sinclair House, one of Bethlehem's leading hotels.

Having spent less than 15 minutes in Littleton, Taft spent even less time here. Without leaving his car, he arose and addressed about 100 people. A larger group had been planned, but it didn't show up until after he was gone.

Though Taft was a man who could never be hurried, this day seemed to be an exception.

That night he relaxed in the lobby of the majestic Mount Washington Hotel at Bretton Woods, New Hampshire. The next morning, due to a downpour, his plans for a few rounds of golf were cancelled. After he and Helen said goodbye to hotel manager W. S. Kenney, the motorcade left at 9:40 a.m. for the final leg of its journey through New Hampshire.

After passing through Bethlehem and Littleton once more, the President was greeted at the Lisbon town line by Dr. Edgar O. Crossman and his committee. It was going on 11:00 when they reached Lisbon Square. Here Taft saw that the school children were out in force, along with about a thousand townspeople.

With more stops just ahead, he again spoke from the car. Local photographer Irving E. James captured the moment on film. Then, after Taft shook hands with the townspeople closest to him, the motorcade moved on to Haverhill for the same purpose. This was followed by a stop in Hanover, where he met with Dartmouth College students.

By day's end Taft arrived in Dublin, New Hampshire. He spent the night here at the summer residence of his Treasury Secretary, Franklin McVeagh. The next day he returned to Beverly, Massachusetts.

The Taft Visit

Less than a year after welcoming President Taft to Littleton, Dr. William J. Beattie was killed on September 26, 1913, while walking across the highway in front of the Crawford House. Struck by an automobile, he died instantly. He had gone there to make arrangements for moving one of his patients. A trusted physician and skilled surgeon at Littleton Hospital, he had also gained national prominence as a tuberculosis specialist.

(Floyd W. Ramsey Photo)

A few weeks later the election results proved to be catastrophic for the Republican Party. For Taft in particular. He had only carried Utah and Vermont. And Roosevelt didn't fare much better. He received only 88 electoral votes to Wilson's 435.

In 1913, as Taft left the White House for the last time, he said to President Wilson, "I'm glad to be going. This is the lonesomest place in the world."

Eight years later, when he finally achieved his goal of being appointed Chief Justice of the United States, he declared, "This is the highest honor I have ever received."

Or was it? Perhaps the reception he received during his 1912 visit to Littleton, New Hampshire, carried within it the seeds of a higher honor that went unrecognized. Particularly when the school children cheered him from their hearts.

Even if it did mean breaking their contract with him.

The Unsolved Murder of Orville Gibson

WHILE SHROUDED in early morning darkness, one of the most senseless murders ever committed in New England took place in Newbury, Vermont, on December 31, 1957. Despite a thorough, painstakingly drawn-out investigation, Lieutenant Chester A. Nash, Commander of the St. Johnsbury barracks of the State Police, eventually told a local reporter he felt the case had been "solved but not broken." He also stated, "We were aware of what happened that very first day. The evidence was conclusive. But, we can't get a conviction."

The beautiful Vermont village of Newbury was chartered in 1763, and in 1902 local historian Frederick Wells proudly stated, "Our town can boast of no criminals in its history." That statement was irrevocably destroyed by Orville Gibson's murder on December 31, 1957.

After all these years the case is still not broken. With that in mind, this is basically what happened on the day of the murder and in the long days that followed.

On the last morning of his life, dairy farmer Orville Gibson shut off his alarm clock at 3:30. After dressing warmly and stoking the furnace, he had a cup of coffee with his slight, attractive blonde wife, Evalyn. He then picked up the lard pail he used to carry fresh milk back to the house, and left the warmth of the kitchen.

Bracing himself against the cold morning air, it was shortly after 4:00 when he walked briskly across Route 5 to his large barn which was located on the south edge of Newbury village. Inside there were a hundred purebred holsteins, sixty of them waiting to be milked. First, though, their stalls had to be scraped, and grain put in their mangers. After the milking, Gibson would feed them their ensilage and then return to the house for breakfast.

At 5:00, 19-year-old Ralph Shephard would be coming in to help. Recently Gibson had fired his regular hired hand of five years, Eri Martin, because "bad blood" had developed between them.

Entering the barn, Gibson hit the main light switch and walked around the old pickup truck that was parked facing the door. It was half full of ensilage. As he passed the tailgate, an unseen assailant blackjacked him viciously across the back of the head. He crumpled to the floor, crushing the lard pail.

By the time young Shephard entered the barn by a side door, Gibson had been lugged away. Despite his absence, Shephard began his chores.

When 7:00 went by, and her husband hadn't returned for breakfast, a worried Evalyn Gibson hurried to the barn looking for him. Just beyond the light switch, in the narrow passageway formed between the wall and the truck, she found the crushed lard pail. Badly frightened, she ran back to the house and telephoned the state police and her brother-in-law, Freeman Placey, who was also a Newbury farmer.

When State Troopers William Graham and Lawrence Washburn arrived just before 8:00, she led them to the barn. In the ensuing search all they found were odd bare spots every few feet on the barn floor. They concluded they were contact points where Gibson's heavy body sagged as he was carried out of the barn.

Just outside the barn door they also found where he had apparently been dragged for several feet. Where the drag ended, there was a small pile of ensilage. It was evident that he had been picked up again, and probably carried to a waiting vehicle.

If so, where had he been taken? And for what purpose?

While the state troopers were busy at the barn, Freeman Placey had gone sleuthing on his own and had made an interesting discovery on the town's old iron bridge. This rusting span, which crossed the Connecticut River, was the connecting link between Newbury and Haverhill, New Hampshire. Halfway across it, Placey found more ensilage which he was certain had come from Gibson's barn.

Based on this find, the State Police immediately realized that Gibson must have been dumped into the river. The bridge ensilage, along with ensilage from Gibson's silo, was quickly relayed to Dr. Thomas A. Sprotson, Professor of Botany at the University of

Though a new bridge now occupies the site of the old iron bridge, this is where Orville Gibson met his tragic death in the Connecticut River. Eighty-five days after being thrown over the railing, he was found floating face-down seven miles below here.

Vermont, to determine if the samples were a match. In the meantime, until Gibson's body was found the case could only be treated as a kidnapping.

While waiting for the laboratory analysis, Lieutenant Nash directed a two-day search of the river. It then froze over, and the drag had to be suspended.

When Dr. Sprotson's report arrived, it stated that the two samples of ensilage were identical and from the same source. This finding fueled Mrs. Gibson's nagging belief that her husband was dead. Later, while reflecting on this moment, she said, "This was the worst time for me. The gradual realization, but not actually knowing, that he was down there under the ice."

The state police were now wrestling with a very ugly question: If it turned out that Gibson was in the river, why had he been so brutally murdered?

The answer at first appeared connected to an unpleasant incident that had occurred between Gibson and Eri Martin on

Christmas Day. At that time, Martin had received a $25 bonus for his five years of service to the Gibsons. Instead of sharing the gifts with his wife and four children, who awaited his return at the farm's tenant house where they quartered, he went into town and got drunk.

(Life Magazine photo, Nov. 2, 1959)

Martin, 56, was a small, skinny man who only weighed 120 pounds. This fact by itself limited the amount of alcohol his system could tolerate.

Eri Martin, 56, who was Orville Gibson's hired hand until "bad blood" developed between them, is shown with two of his daughters, Beverly, 9, and Deborah, 5. Following Gibson's murder, he became the first suspect in the killing because of their fight on Christmas Day. It was soon learned that he was the excuse, not the motive for the crime.

Unfortunately, his thirst exceeded that tolerance. Later that day, when he showed up at the barn, he staggered through the evening chores. Then, while wheeling two 40-quart cans of milk down the ramp leading to the milkhouse, he got into trouble. Not only was the milk dumped, but as the wheelbarrow overturned one of its handles whacked him across the ribs. The blow drove him into the milk-soaked dirt.

Befuddled, he was crawling around in the mud searching for his glasses when Gibson came across the accident. He lifted Martin to his feet, located his glasses for him, and then advised him to go home to bed. Thinking the matter was closed, he righted the wheelbarrow, picked up the empty milk cans, and headed for the barn.

Martin followed him. With his judgment still fogged by the alcohol, he insisted on knowing what Gibson intended on doing about the spilled milk. With a hint of anger in his eyes, Gibson told him he would probably take the loss out of his pay.

Martin instantly fell into a rage. He stomped on his hat and spit out profanities at Gibson. With his patience exhausted, and shocked by Martin's behavior, Gibson slapped the little man and forced him out of the barn.

The Unsolved Murder of Orville Gibson 155

(Floyd W. Ramsey Photo)

By 1957, through eight years of hard work, the Gibsons had made their farm a showplace. Today the barn shows severe signs of deterioration. It was just inside these open doors that Orville Gibson was brutally struck down, and the crumpled lard pail was found.

That night the local doctor was summoned to the tenant house. He treated Martin for three cracked ribs.

Over the next few days, as word of the fracas circulated throughout Newbury, some of the villagers dropped by to visit Martin. During their stay, Martin told them, "Gibson not only beat me up, but he also ruptured my kidneys."

Martin failed to mention that he had also been struck by the wheelbarrow. As a consequence, Gibson, who was a solidly built man who weighed 190 pounds, had suddenly become a "hot-tempered bully."

When unsigned, threatening postcards began arriving in his mail, Gibson felt that he had no choice but to fire Martin for the trouble he was causing. Despite this decision, with the best of intentions he continued to allow the Martins to occupy the tenant house.

So, without interruption, Martin's visitors continued to call. Among them was "Ozzie" Welch, the popular school janitor.

Welch would later testify in court that he stopped by to offer Martin the use of his telephone if he ever decided to sue Gibson for damages.

And for his own personal reasons, Walter B. Renfrew, one of Newbury's most prominent citizens, also supported Martin. Serving the town at this time as a special deputy sheriff, Renfrew had also been a selectman, state senator, and a successful cattle dealer.

Despite his position in law enforcement, while in neighboring Bradford Renfew told Deputy Sheriff Roy Hood, "Gibson should be tarred and feathered and rode out of town on a rail for what he did to Eri Martin."

On one occasion he also angrily complained to State's Attorney Harvey B. Otterman, Jr., telling him, "Gibson has no right running around loose! Why hasn't something been done about him?"

Knowing that the State had filed a complaint against Gibson for breach of the peace, Otterman quietly replied, "Walter, the law will take care of the matter. Just let it run its proper course."

Meanwhile, encouraged by all of the unexpected attention and sympathy he was receiving, Martin instituted a $15,000 civil suit against Gibson for his alleged injuries.

On December 30, Henry Miller of East Burke, Vermont, made a frightening telephone call to the Gibson farm from a nearby Newbury shop. Several men, who were hanging around in the shop, dared him to make the call. When Evalyn answered, Miller growled, "Tell your husband we heard about the Christmas party he gave Eri Martin. If he comes to the village, we might be able to arrange a New Year's party for him."

Over time the state police established that Miller was also the author of the threatening postcards.

Later that same day the Reverend Myron Wilder, the elderly parson of the Congregational Church, visited Gibson in his barn. His purpose was to warn Gibson about the storm of indignation that was building up against him.

That evening, about the time the Gibsons retired at 8:30, there were two parties warming up in Newbury. One was being held in the village at the home of Gaylord Hosmer, a well-to-do gravestone dealer. The other was taking place at Charles Kalberg's farm on Route 5, several miles south of the Gibson's. Many villagers referred to it as "the old pig farm."

Between the flowing whiskey, and the self-righteous anger that had been brewing, Gibson's fate was sealed that night. During the pre-dawn darkness he disappeared. And Eri Martin was the first suspect.

Much to Martin's relief, the investigation that followed soon cleared him of all wrongdoing. Once he was free to leave Newbury, he moved his family to Brookfield, Vermont. Later he settled his legal suit against the Gibson estate for $1500.

Now that the police knew that he was only the excuse for the kidnapping, they began searching for the motive. Turning to Evalyn Gibson, they asked her to review Orville's life. Knowing that they were searching for possible enemies, she told them, "The people who did this awful thing to us we considered our friends. Or, at least, not our enemies."

Life Magazine photo, Nov. 2, 1959

A gentle, cultured woman, Evalyn Gibson was 43 years old at the time of her husband's murder. Stricken by grief, she broke down and cried while looking at an old newspaper photo of herself and Orville.

She went on to relate that Orville was born in Newbury in 1910, and that he started life as a poor farm boy from "in back of town." She then explained, "By working hard he overcame the hardships of poverty, and went on to graduate from high school in 1930 as the valedictorian of his class."

Ironically, his valedictory address was titled, "Respect for the Law."

Continuing, Evalyn said, "After graduation he saved the money he earned as a traveling salesman so we could get married. Just behind him in school, I was his boyhood sweetheart. He was anxious to settle down, so we got married in 1936."

Asked how they came to own their 500-acre farm, which they named "Bonnie Acres," she replied, "In 1943 Orville returned to farming with the dream of one day owning his own place. In 1949 he learned a bank in Woodsville, New Hampshire, had foreclosed on this property, which was then known as the Greer Farm. Recognizing it as the opportunity he had been waiting for, he rushed to Woodsville and bought it out from under several other locals who wanted it as badly as he did."

Acting on this information, the police renewed their efforts. They now pursued the theory that jealousy over Gibson's ownership of the farm was the motive underlying his disappearance. However, they suffered a setback when the villagers became tight-lipped at the suggestion that he might have been murdered. Many of them believed that Gibson was nothing more than the victim of an unusually cruel prank, and that he would show up unharmed.

Despite this obstacle, the police got 84 townspeople to ride to Concord, New Hampshire, to take lie detector tests. They considered these tests vital to uncovering any clues that could lead to Gibson's whereabouts. They also continued searching for a vehicle used in the kidnapping.

Eventually State Police Sergeant Nelson Lay, who was noted for being a hard-nosed investigator, turned up Dr. John Perry Hooker, 36, a physician who owned a farmhouse in South Newbury. When found, he was living in Wells River, Vermont, with his grandfather.

According to Dr. Hooker, at 3:35 a.m. on December 31, while driving north on Route 5 he saw a car parked on the right side of the road about a hundred yards south of the Gibson farm. Among the several men that were either in, or standing around the car, he said he recognized Ozzie Welch sitting by the window in the rear seat. He noted that Welch was one of his regular patients.

He also said he "thought" the man behind the wheel was Frank Carpenter, and that the car was an old two-toned Kaiser. It was then quickly established that this was precisely the type of car that Carpenter owned.

While on the subject, Hooker told the police that he had once been threatened by Carpenter following the vandalizing of his

South Newbury farmhouse. The crime was traced to a young man who was visiting in Newbury. Shortly after his apprehension, Carpenter warned Hooker, "Lay off that kid or you'll get a bullet in the back."

Needless to say, the young man was never prosecuted.

Then Gibson surfaced! In March of 1958, eighty-five days after he had disappeared, his body was found in the Connecticut River. The ice had gone out, and Vermont State Trooper William Graham spotted him around 1:00 p.m. floating face down seven miles below the Newbury bridge. His body wasn't retrieved until late afternoon when all of the proper authorities were present. They included both the Vermont and New Hampshire States' Attorneys, state police from both states, photographers, and the Vermont State Pathologist, Doctor Richard Woodruff.

Performing an on-the-spot examination, Dr. Woodruff commented that the body appeared to be well preserved by the icy water. More obvious was the fact that Gibson had been trussed up with a quarter-inch rope. His wrists were bound under his thighs, and tied to his lower legs. His ankles were also tied together.

As for his clothing, he was still dressed the way his wife last saw him. Even his wallet was intact. It still contained three one-dollar bills. Only his woolen cap was missing.

Now that it was established that Gibson had been murdered, the question arose as to what state the crime had been committed in. If he had been thrown off the bridge while still alive, it was a New Hampshire case. On the other hand, if he had been murdered in Vermont and then thrown off the bridge, it was still Vermont's case.

Following the completion of the autopsy shortly after midnight, Doctor Woodruff ruled in favor of Vermont. In announcing his finding, he said, "Boys, I couldn't squeeze enough water out of that man's lungs to justify labeling it a drowning."

Later, when testifying in court, he attributed Gibson's death to asphyxiation but he was unable to identify what caused it.

Pressing on with the investigation, the Vermont State Police showed Ozzie Welch the rope that was used to bind Gibson. Looking at it, he exclaimed, "By God, boys, that's my rope!" As a result of this startling admission, Welch was also asked to take the lie detector test in Concord, New Hampshire, since Vermont did not own a polygraph machine at this time. He agreed to do so, but he specified the exact conditions under which the test would be administered. Since taking it was voluntary, the police accepted his terms.

On the morning of the test, before leaving Newbury with his wife Myrle, Welch hurriedly filled a last-minute prescription he got from Dr. Hooker. Following his arrival in Concord, he was so heavily sedated that the test technicians had difficulty keeping him awake.

Regardless, in early November he and Carpenter were both charged with kidnapping and manslaughter. Then on November 19 the Grand Jury, which was convened in Chelsea, Vermont, returned a first degree murder indictment against both men after listening to the testimony of twenty witnesses who were provided by the State. Judge Albert W. Varney, Jr., set bail at $40,000 each.

Appearing on the scene, Special Deputy Walter Renfrew put up the bail money for Welch, while Carpenter was bailed out by his brother Herman, a plumber living in Essex Junction, Vermont.

Following the completion of the necessary paperwork, while impatiently waiting for Welch's release Renfrew callously remarked, "Now Welch won't be left over here where you guys can get to him."

On October 12, 1959, Welch's trial finally began at the Chelsea Courthouse. It was presided over by Judge Nat L. Divoll, Jr., of Bellows Falls. Welch was defended by Henry Black, who was an able, high-priced lawyer and a well-known political figure. The State was represented by Attorney General Frederick M. Reed and Harvey B. Otterman, Jr., who was designated a Special Attorney so he could assist Reed.

During the trial, Reed and Otterman earnestly pieced together shreds of evidence through the twenty-eight witnesses they called to the stand. Nervously chewing gum, Welch listened carefully and scribbled notes.

During a break in the proceedings, Walter Renfrew boasted to reporter Joe Heany of the *Burlington Free Press,* "They haven't got the right boys yet. There were at least four of them, and they haven't got any of them."

At the end of the third day, after the State rested its case, Black announced that he was not going to ask Welch to testify. After informing the court that no witnesses would be called, he then

Following Ozzie Welch's acquittal, Defense Attorney Henry Black, right, raises his client's hand in triumph as Welch's wife Myrle smiles with relief. Shortly afterwards Welch went to his grave insisting he knew nothing about Gibson's murder.

moved for a directed verdict of not guilty. Since the evidence against Welch was thin and circumstantial, Judge Divoll ordered the directed verdict. In doing so, he noted that the testimony presented was "open to conjecture," and that the citizens of Newbury had confronted the police with a "solid wall of inconsistency."

So, in one bold stroke Welch had become a free man. By the same token, the first-degree murder charge against Carpenter was also dropped. This meant that he would only have to stand trial for the manslaughter charge.

While Welch was home celebrating his acquittal, the *Burlington Free Press* issued a $500 reward offer to anyone writing them an anonymous letter which would lead to a resolution of the murder. At the same time, the State posted a $1000 reward. Later, the *Press* reward went as high as $2000.

Surprisingly, by November 2 seventeen letters were turned over to the Attorney General's office. The police rekindled the investigation, and twenty-four more people were questioned. As a result, Gaylord Hosmer, the gravestone dealer, was arrested. He was charged with lying under oath concerning his whereabouts and activities at the time of Gibson's kidnapping.

After posting $7500 bail he was released. His trial was scheduled for the following June.

Special Deputy Renfrew also found himself under public fire for his controversial remarks. Since most of the remarks were a matter of record, he voluntarily resigned his position on November 1. He eventually died of an infected gall bladder.

Death was also stalking Ozzie Welch. Suffering from severe abdominal pains, he was admitted to Mary Hitchcock Hospital in Hanover, New Hampshire. Subsequent tests revealed that he had cancer of the large intestine. Only two months after his trial, he died at Cottage Hospital in Woodsville.

If he had any knowledge of the Gibson murder, it died with him.

The wheels of justice continued to turn. On April 18, 1960, Judge F. Ray Keyser banged the gavel at the Chelsea Courthouse, and Frank W. Carpenter's trial began.

The new Attorney General, Thomas Debevoise, was confident he would get a conviction. He had a strong case built around Carpenter's impounded 1953 Kaiser. There was still ensilage in the trunk that was identical to the samples previously tested by Doctor Sprotson. Also, Debevoise hoped to prove that the carbon monoxide found in Gibson's bloodstream was caused by the car's defective muffler.

In addition, the testimony of Dr. Harold C. Harrison, a noted Rhode Island criminologist, would establish that fibers taken from Gibson's clothing matched fibers found in the trunk. Also, that paint chips which came from the lard pail were found as well.

Despite Debevoise's expectations, his case began to unravel when experts testifying for the defense negated Dr. Harrison's testimony. More damage occurred when Dr. Joseph W. Spelman, a former Vermont State pathologist, along with Dr. Richard Ford, head of the Harvard School of Legal Medicine, testified that Gibson's death could have been a suicide.

After selling her farm, Evalyn Gibson moved to Orford, New Hampshire, where she married Charles McMackin. They lived quietly and happily together, pursuing a mutual hobby of rock collecting. Following her death in 1971, her wish to be buried beside Orville in Newbury's Oxbow Cemetery offered mute testimony to the fact that he was not "the meanest man in town," as he had been branded by some newspapers.

To prove that it was possible, Dr. Ford tied himself up exactly the way Gibson had been tied. Taken to the bridge, he then ran into problems. No matter how hard he tried, he was unable to show the jury how Gibson could hoist himself over the high railing and fling himself into the river.

Strangely enough, for reasons peculiar to himself, Dr. Ford later committed suicide.

On the witness stand, as the case continued, Dr. John Perry Hooker's testimony proved to be extremely ineffective. Of little value in the Welch trial, it did even less to bolster Debevoise's case. The fact that he "thought" the man driving the car was Carpenter legally meant nothing.

On May 5, like Welch, Carpenter was acquitted.

Once the trial was behind him, Carpenter moved to Essex Junction to work for his brother. Restless, he next moved to Colchester, Vermont, where he died of lung disease in 1972.

Several weeks later, on June 7, the Attorney General's office dropped the perjury charges against Gaylord Hosmer. The gravestone dealer then settled his affairs in Newbury and moved to

Franklin, New Hampshire, where he died many years later.

The investigation, however, was far from over. By November of 1968, more than 500 lie detector tests had been administered to people who were thought to know something about the crime. Yet, despite the full treatment the murder was given, its final solution still remained a legally impenetrable mystery.

In time, even Evalyn Gibson left Newbury. She sold Bonnie Acres to Charles Kalberg, the owner of "the pig farm." Moving to Orford, New Hampshire, she married Charles McMackin. When she died in 1971, she was buried beside Orville in the Oxbow Cemetery just north of Newbury village.

Today, though the quiet, dignified village appears to be calm and settled on the surface, it is still living under the heavy shadow of the unsolved Gibson murder. And, as the Reverend Myron Wilder once said, "Things will not be normal in Newbury until the truth is known."

Farr Memories:
Shattered Glory and Unfinished Dreams

SIMPLY STATED, this Civil War saga is a quiet tribute to the heroic and accomplished lives of Evarts and Ellen Farr of Littleton, New Hampshire. As their story unfolds it will dramatically illustrate the accepted adage that truth is often stranger than fiction.

The Civil War began at 4:30 a.m. on April 12, 1861, when Confederate Captain George S. James ordered a signal shell fired over federally-owned Fort Sumter which sat in the harbor at Charleston, South Carolina. Just minutes after Lieutenant Henry Farley yanked the lanyard which sent the signal shell arcing skyward, shore batteries commenced firing on the fort.

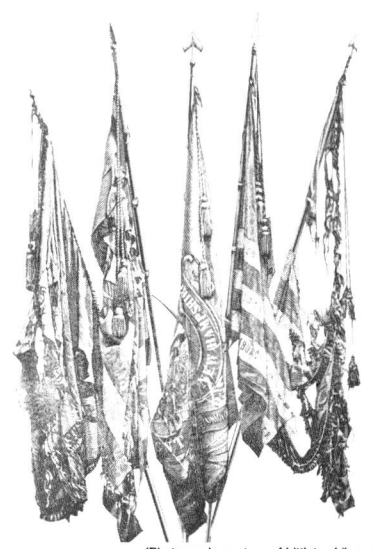

(Photograph courtesy of Littleton Library)

Tattered, ripped, and mutilated by the violence of war, these New Hampshire Civil War battle flags offer silent testimony to the sufferings of the men who followed them. They are on public display at the State House in Concord.

During the four years that followed these opening shots, our Nation suffered through the convulsions of a nightmare in which 618,000 young men sacrificed their lives, the once-proud South was reduced to rubble, and a legacy of hatred was spawned which still festers to this day.

Within twenty-four hours after the South made its ill-fated bid for independence from the Union, the urgent call for military volunteers could be heard echoing throughout both the North and South. In the North, when President Abraham Lincoln asked for 75,000 men to serve for three months, New Hampshire Governor Nathaniel S. Berry responded by instructing the State Adjutant General to muster a regiment of volunteers. In addition to this response, Berry also appointed one of his own staff members,

Colonel Henry W. Rowell, to be the recruiting officer for northern Grafton County.

Early on the morning of April 26, Rowell hastily set up a recruiting office in an unoccupied, unfinished building on Main Street in Littleton. At this time Littleton was a dynamic, thriving town which had just recently completed the transition from agricultural village to manufacturing community. As soon as Rowell opened his door, he found William Weller waiting to enlist. Weller entered the office, and was immediately followed by Evarts Farr. Though both young men were sworn in together, Weller was offered the honor of being listed as the first man who signed up from Littleton. When he declined the offer, the honor passed to Farr.

Captain Evarts W. Farr of Company G, the Second Regiment, New Hampshire Volunteers, lost his right arm at the Battle of Williamsburg on May 5, 1862. With unfaltering courage in the face of extreme danger, he went on to become one of our Nation's greatest heroes during the Civil War.

Beginning with this singular distinction, Farr went on to become the most notable of the seven children of John and Tryphena Farr. His fighting instincts may have been honed by the hardships of his early life. Born on October 10, 1840, he was tied to long hours on the family farm from early spring through late fall. Due to economic necessity, he was only allowed to attend school during the winter months. At fifteen he rebelled against this regimen, and left home without his father's consent.

Lured to the city by its offers of a better life, he arrived in Boston hungry and penniless. Perhaps because of his background, in time he was hired to drive a milk wagon from dawn to dark through the congested city streets. However, between the drudgery of this position and steadily growing homesickness, he soon realized that he had been better off at home. Without laboring the matter

Captain Leonard Drown of Fisherville, now named Penacook, was the first commissioned officer from New Hampshire who was killed in the Civil War. The circumstances leading to his death were described in the official report as "exasperating treachery."

any farther, he turned in his work apron and headed in that direction.

His father, who was now an established attorney, welcomed his return. In a show of gratitude, he gave Evarts greater latitude in attending school. Educationally starved, before long Evarts exhausted the local educational resources. Both surprised and pleased, his father next allowed him to attend the outstanding academy at Thetford, Vermont.

While attending Thetford Academy, Evarts not only finished growing into a tall, handsome man with a broad brow and expressive blue eyes, but he also fell in love with Ellen Burpee. This attractive young lady, who came from New Hampton, New Hampshire, was not only his intellectual equal, but she also possessed considerable artistic ability.

After both graduated with honors in July of 1859, Ellen returned home to teach art while Evarts entered Dartmouth College as a member of the Class of 1863. However, perhaps hoping he could hasten the day when he and Ellen could marry, he left Dartmouth at the end of his freshman year and took up the study of law in his father's Littleton law office. Unfortunately his studies there were interrupted by the shelling of Fort Sumter.

In the days that followed the bombardment, Littleton townspeople fell under the spell of an atmosphere that was now continuously charged with excitement. Throughout the entire week meetings were held at Rounsevel's Hall where the eloquence of the speakers kept their audiences aroused with enthusiasm for the war effort.

Sundays also reflected the change that had infected the town.

Instead of the quiet tread of devout people walking to their places of worship, the air was filled with the sounds of marching recruits and the shrill strains of war-like music such as "The Marseillaise Hymn," and "Washington's March."

On Tuesday, May 7, the time had finally come for the recruits to depart for their regimental camp at Portsmouth, New Hampshire. Upon arriving at the railroad station, they found that a large crowd had turned out to bid them goodbye. The subsequent arrival of the Coos Company from Lancaster added to the holiday-like atmosphere. With the Littleton Brass Band playing in the background, many of the recruits expressed the opinion that their show of force would soon bring the Rebel hotheads to their senses.

Following their arrival at Camp Constitution that afternoon, the recruits were disappointed to learn that the ranks of the First Regiment were already filled. Told to be patient, on May 19 they were rewarded with a directive from Governor Berry which gave them the first opportunity to enlist for three years under President Lincoln's call for 42,000 more volunteers. Immediately 496 of them signed up.

On that same day Evarts Farr and Ellen Burpee were united in marriage at the Franklin House in Portsmouth.

The following day the new enlistees were appointed to the Second Regiment, New Hampshire Volunteers. Of the one hundred men who were assigned to Company G, Ephraim Weston of Hancock was elected from their ranks to be Company Captain. Evarts Farr was then elected Company First Lieutenant, and Sylvester Rogers of Nashua became the Company's Second Lieutenant. Once the elections process was completed, the entire regiment was given a short furlough in order to make arrangements at home for a longer absence.

After getting Ellen settled in Littleton, on June 20 Evarts left for Washington, D.C. with the Second Regiment. During the protracted journey the New Hampshire recruits were given elaborate receptions in Boston and New York City. It was not until they reached Elizabethport, New Jersey, and were transferred to boxcars fitted with unplaned boards, that they learned not all of their travels would be on cushioned seats. And when barrels of overly-ripe cooked beef were opened, they finally got their first taste of army

FARR MEMORIES

The military career of Captain George E. Pingree of Littleton, New Hampshire, closely paralleled that of Major Farr's. The wound he suffered at the battle of Williamsburg later caused him to be transferred to the Veterans Reserve Corps. He remained on active duty until January 1, 1868.

(Photograph courtesy of Littleton Library)

chow.

On the morning of June 23 the Second Regiment, New Hampshire Volunteers, along with the Seventeenth New York Regiment and one from Pennsylvania, nervously marched through Baltimore with loaded rifles. Only their number kept a mob of southern sympathizers at bay. At noon they arrived in Washington without serious incident. That evening, after parading past President Lincoln at the White House, they were marched to their designated camping area on Seventh Street. With very few trees to shade them from the oppressive heat that had settled over the city, it proved to be an uncomfortable location.

Once quartered, the Second Regiment had finally begun its official duty of defending the Union.

Over the next few weeks drill and discipline necessary to battle became a daily part of camp life. But then, so did poor diets and unsanitary living conditions. In addition to these two health threats, New Hampshire's Second Regiment was brigaded with the First and Second Rhode Island Regiments and the Seventy-First New York Regiment. This also meant deadly exposure to "city sicknesses" such as smallpox, measles, hepatitis, and tuberculosis.

On the afternoon of July 16, when the regiments broke camp to march against the enemy, many of the New Hampshire men were unable to follow their regimental flags across the bridge leading into Virginia. Evarts W. Farr was among them. At that moment he was lying under a canopy of mosquito netting at nearby Douglas Hospital fighting for his life.

His fellow officer, Captain Ephraim Weston, was also suffering from a recently contracted disease but he stubbornly refused to be left behind. Like many, he believed that the Union Army was about to deliver the death-blow to the rebellion. For that reason he was with the 35,000 Federal soldiers marching toward the tragedy that soon became known as "the First Battle of Bull Run." In the ranks with him was Private George E. Pingree of Littleton who would later be commissioned a captain in the Eleventh New Hampshire Regiment.

Unfortunately General Irvin McDowell, who was commanding the inexperienced army, had no way of knowing that he was leading his men into a trap. Espionage agents in the city had informed the Confederates of his plans for capturing the railroad junction at Manassas 25 miles southwest of the Capital. On receipt of the information, Confederate Generals Joseph E. Johnston and Pierre Beauregard acted quickly to concentrate 30,000 troops just south of Manassas in anticipation of McDowells arrival.

On July 21 McDowell's army clashed with the Confederates near the small stream named Bull Run. In the heat of battle total confusion took over. Organization and tactics evaporated. It simply became one armed mob against another.

Later that afternoon, when the Federals appeared to be on the verge of victory, a determined stand by Virginians under General Thomas J. Jackson turned the tide. When last-minute reinforcements arrived from the Shenandoah Valley, the Rebels completely routed the Federal forces.

Though both Captain Weston and Private Pingree survived the battle, Weston's illness ended his life several months later.

Following his return to Washington, Pingree visited Lieutenant Farr at the hospital. While they were discussing the battle, Farr asked him for the casualty figures. Pingree sadly shook his head and told him that 13 men from the Second Regiment were killed, 35 were wounded, and 63 were missing. This tragic news strengthened Farr's resolve to recover.

In the months ahead, while Farr continued his convalescence, a complete lull settled over the Potomac. Faulty intelligence gathering

Professor Thaddeus Lowe of Jefferson Mills, New Hampshire, creator of the first air force in America, made more than 3000 ascents in his balloons to spy and report on Confederate activities. Pictured in 1862 during the Peninsula Campaign, he became the most shot at man in the entire war.

by Federal operatives failed to reveal that the Battle of Bull Run had left Confederate General Johnston short of fresh troops, food, and ammunition. Not knowing this, Major General George B. McClellan worked feverishly to whip badly needed discipline into the mushrooming Federal Army while constructing fortifications around Washington. During the construction he continually anticipated a southern attack which never came.

Then, on October 21, another Federal disaster occurred at Ball's Bluff near Leesburg, Virginia. This tragedy was set in motion when McClellan dispatched orders with the intent of finding out if any Federal movements in that direction would cause the Confederates to abandon Leesburg. This led to an unexpected battle in which Colonel Edward D. Baker and 49 other Federal soldiers were killed. The tragedy was compounded when another 100 Federal soldiers drowned while trying to swim the Potomac River after they panicked and fled the battle.

The death of Colonel Baker was particularly hard on President Lincoln. The two men were close friends. As for General McClellan, from a military standpoint, he was left firmly convinced that his "Army of the Potomac" was not ready for a major confrontation.

For this reason, despite President Lincoln's constant urgings to engage the enemy, on November 1 McClellan ordered the Army of the Potomac into winter quarters. Then, when McClellan next came down with typhoid fever, Lincoln lamented, "The bottom has dropped out of the barrel."

During this period of military inactivity Farr returned to his Company. On January 1, 1862, he was promoted to captain to fill the vacancy caused by Ephraim Weston's death. Outwardly, though Farr appeared to be fully recovered, tragic circumstances years later would prove otherwise.

In early March McClellan was well enough to resume his command. At this time Confederate General Johnston secretly began withdrawing his troops from northern Virginia. He knew that his position was now untenable in the face of McClellan's superior forces. At first startled by this unexpected retreat, McClellan finally seized the moment and sprang into action. On Monday, March 17, he launched his massive Peninsula Campaign. Its objective was the capture of the Confederate Capital, Richmond, Virginia.

(Photograph courtesy of Littleton Library)

Though he survived his wounds at the battle of Fredericksburg, Colonel Edward E. Cross of Lancaster, New Hampshire, lost his life at Gettysburg. On July 2, 1863, while leading his men near the base of Round Top, he was struck in the abdomen by a mini ball. He was the first colonel the Fifth Regiment lost in battle.

Over the next three weeks nearly 400 Federal vessels transported more than 112,000 men, 14,500 animals, 1,150 wagons, 44 batteries of artillery, 74 ambulances, and innumerable pontoon bridges, telegraph wires and other equipment to the tip of the Virginia Peninsula where McClellan secured a base at old Fortress Monroe.

On April 5 the advance on Richmond stalled when McClellan stopped his army on the marshy ground facing Yorktown. Once again misled by faulty information, he actually believed that he had the whole force of the enemy on his hands. During the stalemate, the Second New Hampshire Regiment arrived aboard a steamer. Late on the afternoon of April 11 it disembarked at Ship Point six

As a reward for valorous service in the field, Evarts Farr was promoted to the rank of major on September 9, 1862. The following December he fought with distinguished gallantry at the Battle of Fredericksburg despite having only one arm. Ironically, his brilliant military career was destroyed when he became entangled in state politics.

(Photograph courtesy of Littleton Library)

miles below Yorktown. Here the men joined their brigade on a flooded meadow. Five days later they marched to the besieging lines in front of Yorktown.

Their camp was located to the right of the Williamsburg Road, and just across from the headquarters of Brigadier General Samuel Heintzelman and General Joseph Hooker. Professor Thaddeus Lowe was also a nearby neighbor, along with his observation balloon and its accompanying apparatus. Lowe, who created America's first Air Force, was an inventive genius who grew up just 25 miles east of Littleton in the small farming town of Randolph, New Hampshire. Almost every day the men of the Second watched him make ascensions for the purpose of looking inside the Rebel redoubts and camps. While a ground crew held the balloon by a dragrope, angry Rebel gunners attempted to shoot it out of the sky. Its continual presence filled them with rage. At this time shell fragments often burst throughout the Second's camp, forcing them to seek shelter in a nearby ravine.

When they weren't watching Lowe, the men of the Second were kept busy digging trenches for an elaborate system of Federal redoubts. Soldiers from other companies were assigned the construction of a giant mortar battery which would be used to fire 13-inch shells at the Rebel works.

By May 2, with siege guns and mortars finally in place, McClellan completed his plans for wiping Yorktown from the face of the earth. However, the Confederate commander, Major General John B. Magruder, had no intention of waiting around to be shelled out. On the night of May 3 he evacuated Yorktown and retreated up the Peninsula. To cover his movements he ordered a rapid and continuous firing of guns until shortly after midnight. When the shelling ceased, a suspicion of what he was doing ran through the Union lines.

At daylight, men of the Second again assembled around Lowe's balloon to watch him and General Heintzelman ascend a few hundred feet. Immediately the General shouted down to the signal officer, "Telegraph to headquarters that there are no men to be seen in the enemy's works, and that a body of our men will advance after them as skirmishers."

The assignment fell to the men of the Second Regiment. Striking camp, they took up the march towards Williamsburg. During the pursuit it was learned that deadly cannon shells with detonators attached to them had been planted in the road, and that they were being activated by body weight. Several soldiers were blown up by the barbarous devices. General McClellan angrily assigned Confederate prisoners the task of locating them and digging them up.

That night a heavy rain added to the Regiment's miseries. As the road turned to a quagmire of mud, the men stumbled over stumps and exposed roots. By 11:00 the order was given to bivouac by the side of the road.

Though the torrential rain continued without letup, the men were aroused before dawn. While slogging through the mud, at 5:30 a.m. they were halted by a barricade of trees and a line of earthworks that the Confederates had constructed months earlier. Rifle pits also dotted the open plain beyond the obstructions.

Anxious to engage the enemy, General Hooker ordered Companies B and E to chase enemy skirmishers out of the fallen timber. While these companies were deployed to the left of the road, the remaining companies formed a line of battle in the woods to the right. At 7:15 these men were moved forward to within 250 yards of the outer margin of the fallen timber.

For more than six hours they remained there, constantly under fire from the enemy's batteries. Throughout the deadly shelling

Companies B and E managed to chase the Rebel skirmishers back, and to also empty the rifle pits. When their Company sharpshooters turned their attention to the Rebel cannoneers, their aim was so deadly that for brief periods the cannons were completely silenced.

As the downpour continued, at 3:00 p.m. the enemy fire suddenly increased. Hurriedly ordered out of the brush, the Second Regiment was broken up while making its way through impenetrable thickets. To distract the enemy, Captain Leonard Drown of Penacook, New Hampshire, led some of his men from Company E toward nearby Rebels. He was firing his revolver and cheering his men on when a Rebel leader waved a white flag and yelled, "Don't fire! Don't fire! We are friends!"

Believing the group wanted to surrender, Captain Drown ordered his men to hold their fire. Without warning the Rebels stood up and shot him. He was killed instantly, his body riddled with bullets. Several of his men also fell.

On the heels of this treachery, Company G emerged from the woods. Captain Farr moved quickly among his men speaking words of encouragement. His aide, Alec, was at his side. Suddenly a bullet smashed into Alec's chest and he fell dead. Farr turned in the direction from which he thought the fatal shot had been fired. While aiming his revolver at one of the enemy, a mini ball shattered the elbow joint of his right arm. His weapon flew out of his hand, and dropped into the mud. In shock, Farr reached down and retrieved it with his left hand.

Soon ordered off the field, he stumbled through the rain trying to find medical assistance. Eventually he came across a dilapidated shack without any windows. Weak from a loss of blood, he fell into the building and passed out for several hours.

That night Farr was awakened by excruciating pain and the discomfort caused by his wet clothing. Forcing himself to his feet, he moved on to a field hospital. His suffering was finally relieved that morning by a liberal dose of chloroform. When he regained consciousness, his arm had been amputated halfway between the elbow and the shoulder.

Following the surgery, he was placed in a horse-drawn ambulance for the jolting ride back to Fortress Monroe. Later that day he was joined by Private George Pingree who had been wounded by a shot fired by a member of the Fourteenth Louisiana Company. In his case, however, the bullet had passed through his right arm without doing the damage that necessitated amputation.

The brief but violent Battle of Williamsburg had cost the Federals 2,239 men, 456 of whom were killed. The Confederates lost an estimated 1,603 men. Though McClellan held the field, it was essentially a Rebel victory. The Confederate intent behind the engagement was simply to hold the Federals at bay while their army continued to escape up the Peninsula. And this had been successfully accomplished.

The next day, when McClellan once again prepared to crush the Rebels, to his frustration he found that they had made another full retreat during the night.

On Monday, May 19, Captain Farr quietly arrived in Littleton for a brief convalescence. Once his wound had healed he became restless and eager to rejoin his Regiment. Leaving home at the end of June, he caught up with it at Harrison's Landing in Virginia.

Despite his good intentions, on August 9 he was ordered to return home for badly needed recruiting service. This was the end of his career with the Second New Hampshire.

On August 22 he ran the following ad in Littleton's leading newspaper, The People's Journal: "To Arms! To Arms! The hardy sons of New Hampshire are now called upon to come to the rescue of their brave brothers who have won imperishable laurels. THE FOLLOWING INDUCEMENTS ARE OFFERED: bounty from the State, $60; bounty from the U.S. Government, $25; one month's pay in advance, $13; a premium of $4. In addition, each recruit will also receive the bounty of his respective town."

By August 29 the number of men who had answered Farr's summons was sufficient to ensure a full company. Farr's older brother, George, was among the 59 Littleton men who enlisted. So were the Kilburn brothers, Edward and Benjamin, who would later become world famous for their stereoscopic work. Tragically all of these men, including Evarts Farr and George Pingree, were to become participants in one of the worst Federal blunders of the war–the Battle of Fredericksburg!

Following the conclusion of his recruiting drive, Farr was notified that he was promoted to major and was being assigned to the

Congressman Evarts W. Farr as he looked shortly before his death at 40. In paying tribute to him, Senator Henry Blair of Plymouth, New Hampshire, stated, "There may have been better men, but I have not known them." (Photograph courtesy of Littleton Library)

Eleventh Regiment. Two days later George Pingree received word at his Littleton residence that he had been commissioned a captain in that same regiment. Both men would now be serving under Colonel Walter Harriman of Hancock, a well-known political figure in the State. It was a relationship that would end in bad blood.

In the meantime, the Eleventh Regiment, and the Thirteenth Regiment to which George Farr and the Kilburn brothers were assigned, were both joined to the Ninth Army Corps. The Commander of this Corps was General Ambrose E. Burnside who would soon succeed McClellan as the head of the Army of the Potomac.

Following this change of command, on November 9 Burnside explained to President Lincoln the bold new strategy he had devised for the capture of Richmond. In essence, he stated that he would move his army rapidly southeastward from Warrenton, Virginia, to Fredericksburg, which was on the Rappahannock River. He would take Fredericksburg before the Confederate's top commander, Robert E. Lee, could block him. Then he would quickly move south and seize Richmond.

Apparently seeing doubt in the President's eyes following the explanation, Burnside added, "I know everything depends on speed. Fredericksburg will be attacked as soon as the army arrives in front of the place."

President Lincoln reluctantly gave his approval to the plan with the observation, "The plan will succeed if you move rapidly; otherwise not."

Less than two weeks later Burnside's army of 111,834 men looked across the Rappahannock River at the trembling little city of Fredericksburg. In the entire area there were only four Confederate companies, one cavalry regiment, and a battery of light artillery. All Burnside had to do was get his forces over the river and the city was his. Due to high water, however, he made the fatal decision of holding his army back until the pontoon bridges arrived.

The ensuing delay gave General Lee all the time that he needed to maneuver his main force on to the heights commanding the southwest side of the city. By the same token, Confederate Lieutenant General James Longstreet was also able to anchor his men on the high ground known as Marye's Heights. For added insurance, two ranks of infantrymen were positioned behind a stonewall at the foot of this location. The Confederate batteries were also strategically placed.

By December 12 Burnside was still moving his troops across the river. Even worse, he did not have a clear-cut battle plan in place. Later that day he finally decided to pursue his original intention of concentrating his main force in Fredericksburg for a run past Lee's right flank. When he asked two junior officers what they thought of this idea, Colonel Rush C. Hawkins replied, "If you make the attack as contemplated, it will be the greatest slaughter of the war."

Colonel Joseph H. Taylor bluntly concurred, adding, "The carrying out of your plan will be murder, not warfare."

Totally ignoring this counsel, Burnside put his plan into operation. Early the next morning the Eleventh New Hampshire Regiment was moved to the lower part of the abandoned, Federally-looted city. At 11:30 Farr's commanding officer, Colonel Walter Harriman, received orders to move the Regiment forward for the attack. Being the first to advance, Harriman's men were exposed to a murderous fire.

In the first charge up Marye's Heights men fell dead or wounded by the hundreds. A Pennsylvania regiment lost its nerve, broke ranks, and ran towards the rear. As it did, the Eleventh continued to press on. Colonel Harriman was at the right wing, Companies D and F were in the center, and Major Farr was with the left wing.

A highly skilled artist, Ellen B. Farr died in Naples, Italy, on January 5, 1907, at the age of 66. Born to a life of suffering, she was widowed at 40, and predeceased by her daughter, Edith May, who died at 18, and her son, Herbert Augustus, who died at 37. In 1993 she was honored by the State of California as one of the outstanding women artists of the West. A few of her early paintings can be seen at the Littleton Library in Littleton, N.H.

(Private Collection of Floyd Ramsey)

As reinforcements arrived, the enemy increased its firing. When it did, Farr raised his sword and shouted above the din, "Boys, we've got to go up there. And the sooner we get there, the better it will be for us. Come on!" He then started up the hill on the double-quick, faithfully followed by his men.

In order to observe and report on the battle's progress, Professor Thaddeus Lowe was riding high in his balloon over Burnside's headquarters. Before long he was staring in horrified disbelief at the slaughter he was witnessing.

Throughout that day all attempts to storm the heights were repulsed. Seven divisions were hurled against the soldiers positioned on Marye's Heights, and not a single soldier reached the stonewalls. The Fifth New Hampshire, led by Colonel Edward E. Cross of Lancaster, earned the sad honor of having left their dead closest to that objective.

Earlier, during a charge up the slope, a shell exploded directly in front of Colonel Cross at eye level. Fragments struck him in the face, chest, and one hand, and the blast smashed him to the ground. After regaining consciousness, he struggled to his hands and knees while spitting out blood, sand, and two teeth. He collapsed again as shells burst around him. When a shell fragment struck his scabbard, the impact rolled him over.

Throughout the long hours that Cross lay on the battlefield awaiting death, he was repeatedly trampled by both charging and retreating troops. Finally someone discovered that he was still alive. It was dark when he was carried to the mayor's house, which was being used as a hospital. As he was being brought in, an officer asked, "What happened to Colonel Cross?" One of the litter bearers mistakenly replied, "He is dead." Cross raised his head and snapped, "Not by a damned sight!"

During the battle Farr's friend, Captain Pingree, was also knocked senseless by an exploding shell. Because he was not seriously injured, he managed to rally to his feet and fought on. In Lieutenant Edward Kilburn's case, his health was so severely shattered by the trauma of the battle that he retired from the service soon afterwards and returned to Littleton.

By day's end, Burnside had made a total of six large-scale assaults against Lee's entrenched army. In the process his losses soared to more than 12,535 men while the Confederates lost less than half that number. At the height of the massacre Lee observed, "It is well war is so frightful, otherwise we should become too fond of it."

The next day Burnside held a council of war. He concluded that there would be no further attacks under the existing circumstances. That night the Eleventh Regiment was put on picket duty near the enemy's lines. It remained there until the following night when Colonel Harriman unexpectedly ordered a withdrawal to the opposite side of the river.

After completing the crossing, Major Farr confided to Captain Pingree that it was his belief the Colonel had acted without proper authorization. This suspicion was confirmed when General Ferrero, Commander of the Second Brigade, angrily approached Harriman and asked, "In the name of God, where are you going? How came you here? Who ordered you to desert your post?"

Harriman replied, "Nobody ordered me back. I took my regiment off because I was afraid you had forgotten us. I thought the whole army had re-crossed."

Furious, Ferrero shouted at him, "I was going over to order you back! I just got the orders from General Burnside!"

After being confined to camp, Harriman submitted a report in which he attempted to justify his actions. He claimed that following a consultation with Lieutenant Colonel Collins and Major Farr, both advised him that an immediate withdrawal was definitely in order. It was quickly established that such a consultation had never taken place. In addition to his existing problems, Harriman now lost the confidence and respect of his men.

The following May, while the Regiment was quartered at Stanford, Kentucky, Farr filed charges against Harriman which accused him of "desertion of his post while on duty before the enemy, and conduct unbecoming an officer and a gentleman." Farr then asked that the charges be investigated by a military commission.

Once the commission found that the charges were justified, sixteen of Farr's fellow officers also signed them. In desperation, Harriman furiously argued that both Farr and Pingree were guilty of leading a conspiracy to drive him from the regiment.

On June 2, 1863, Farr read the full charges and specifications to Harriman while they stood before a military tribunal. Three days later Harriman resigned his commission and returned to New Hampshire. Despite his departure, Farr and Pingree had not seen the last of him.

In the meantime, both men briefly saw action again in the Vicksburg Campaign while under the command of General Ulysses S. Grant. Once this last major Confederate port on the Mississippi River surrendered on July 4, 1863, Farr and Pingree were granted badly needed furloughs.

On their return to Littleton, they were shocked to learn that political proceedings had been instituted to restore Harriman's commission. In an attempt to block the effort, on August 15 they attended a meeting at the State Capitol that was being held by Governor Joseph A. Gilmore for Harriman's benefit.

After Farr, Pingree, and Harriman had all addressed the question of restoration, Governor Gilmore beckoned to Harriman and they left the Council Chamber together. They soon returned and the Governor announced, "I have handed Colonel Harriman back his commission." Then looking directly at Farr and Pingree he strongly stated, "And if you gentlemen do not like it, you may court-martial the Colonel."

A turbulent scene of recriminations followed. When it was over, Farr and Pingree both knew their military careers were finished. Despite their unblemished military records and exemplary acts of heroism they had fallen victims to state politics.

On January 26, 1864, Major Farr was assigned to detached service under General Burnside. For the remainder of the war he primarily served on court-martial duty. As for Captain Pingree, he was eventually transferred to the Fifth Regiment, Veteran's Reserve Corps. He was on duty at the prison camp at Indianapolis when his regiment was disbanded in the fall of 1865.

The Civil War ended on April 9, 1865, when General Lee's Army of Northern Virginia found itself surrounded at the small village of Appomattox Courthouse. With his fighting force reduced to no more than 28,000 ragged, starving men, Lee knew that he had no choice but to surrender his command that day to General Grant.

Though it had been accomplished at tremendous cost, the Union had been restored and four years of national anguish were almost over. In less than a week, however, the Nation's feeling of jubilation over the war's end would be transformed into one of deep shock and mourning following the assassination of President Lincoln.

Farr was mustered out of the service on June 4. He then returned to Littleton to resume his life with Ellen and their two-year-old daughter, Ida Louise. Over the next several years they would have two more children, a son, Herbert Augustus, and another daughter, Edith May. Following a period of study, in October of 1866 he was admitted to the Bar at Lancaster. Finally he was able to enter into a law partnership with his father.

That same year he was also drawn into state politics when he learned that his old nemesis, Walter Harriman, was running for governor. In an effort to thwart Harriman's political ambitions, he lent support to a scheme to place Onslow Stearns of Concord in the campaign as an independent candidate. When the plan failed, he was left no choice but to back Harriman. Harriman then went on to win the election.

In 1869, when Onslow Stearns succeeded Harriman as governor, Evarts Worcester Farr suddenly became a respected political influence in the state. As a consequence, over the next few years he

The oldest daughter of Evarts and Ellen Farr, Ida Louise became a noted society and club woman. Following her graduation from Wellesley College, she married Edwin C. Miller, in Wakefield, Massachusetts, on January 30, 1884. Numbered among her many accomplishments, she became a founder of the society, "Daughters of New Hampshire." Through her efforts, fifty books written by New Hampshire women were sent to the Atlanta Exposition.

(Private Collection of Floyd Ramsey)

was not only elected to a seat on the Governor's Council, but he was also twice appointed State's Attorney for Grafton County.

In 1878 he resigned this position when he received the Republican nomination to run for the Third District's seat in the United States Congress. Though he came from a stronghold of Democrats, he won the election by a 1045-vote margin over his opponent, Henry O. Kent of Lancaster. On March 4, 1879, he proudly took his seat as a member of the Forty-sixth Congress. After doing so, he was immediately appointed to the committee on Invalid Pensions.

A short time later, while discussing committee matters with Congressman Updegraff of Ohio, Updegraff felt moved to ask him, "Evarts, have you ever regretted the loss of your arm?" Farr replied, "No, it is less than I had expected to give to my country."

As Farr continued to carry out his congressional duties with unfailing devotion, Congressman Joshua G. Hall of Dover, New Hampshire, began to notice that his colleague was showing signs of serious illness. His suspicions were confirmed when, in the closing weeks of the 1880 spring session, Farr was advised by his physician to take a leave of absence for reasons of health. Though it troubled Farr to set aside his work, he and Ellen went on a badly needed ocean voyage.

After tolerating the absence from his work as long as he could, Farr returned to his duties just two days before the close of the summer session. Though Congressman Hall was pleased to see him improved in both appearance and spirits, it would be the last time he would see Farr alive.

The curtain was already dropping on Farr's life when he ran for re-election in the latter half of 1880. His opponent this time was the highly respected Littleton Democrat, Judge George A. Bingham. The campaign was an exacting one, and it took its toll on Farr's fragile health. Though he managed to retain his congressional seat by a narrow margin, the effort left him too exhausted to immediately return to Washington as he had planned. In an attempt to regain his strength, he remained in the quiet comfort of his Pleasant Street home.

Towards the end of November he unexpectedly took a turn for the worse. Suddenly stricken by double pneumonia, at the age of 40 the end came quickly for him. Ellen was at his side when the family doctor pronounced him dead at 9:00 a.m. on Tuesday, November 30. The subsequent post-mortem revealed that his death was the result of a combination of pneumonia and an advanced liver disease. There was little doubt in the coroner's mind that Evarts had contracted the fatal ailment while serving with the Army of the Potomac.

Tributes to his memory began at his elaborate funeral which was held in Littleton on the afternoon of December 2. They did not end until the following March when Congress honored him by passing a joint resolution which authorized the printing of 12,000 hardcover books entitled, *Memorial Addresses on the Life and Character of Evarts W. Farr.*

Additionally, Ellen was relieved of immediate financial strain when the House of Representatives passed a resolution which enabled her to receive the balance of Evart's salary due him as a member of the Forty-sixth Congress, and six thousand dollars in lieu of the salary he would have received as a member of the Forty-seventh Congress.

In the years ahead, Ellen suffered through another tragedy when a sudden illness claimed the life of her youngest daughter, Edith

This monument, located near the entrance to Glenwood Cemetery in Littleton, N.H., was erected to the memory of Evarts W. Farr. Buried with him are his wife, Ellen, his daughter, Edith May, and his son Herbert Augustus. The last line of the elaborate inscription reads, "To live in hearts we love is not to die."

(Floyd W. Ramsey photo)

May, just after her graduation from St. Mary's School in Concord, New Hampshire. After accompanying the body back to Littleton for burial next to Evarts, Ellen opened an art studio for a brief time in the old Rounsevel Block.

It was not until she took up permanent residence in Pasadena, California, in 1895 that she finally began to receive artistic acclaim for her still-life paintings. As her fame as an artist continued to grow, beginning in June of 1906 her life was about to begin a bizarre downturn. At that time she mortgaged her home on South Fair Oaks Avenue to finance a journey to Europe. When her friends questioned her about it, she happily told them, "All my life I have looked forward to going abroad with all the longings of an artist and a lover of travel."

Planning to be gone for more than two years, she stopped in Wakefield, Massachusetts, for a short visit with her daughter Ida. While here she fell ill with a debilitating ailment that was diagnosed as "gastric fever." Bedridden for several weeks, she finally recovered enough to sail for Europe in November aboard the steamship Canopic.

Shortly after she checked into the Bellevue Hotel in Naples, Italy, the illness struck again. Failing to recover, she died at the hotel on January 5, 1907. Following her death, plans were immediately made to ship her body to New York City aboard the same ship on which she had arrived. However, when the sailors learned that there would be a corpse aboard, they became paralyzed by superstition and refused to sail.

A brief delay in shipment followed. The problem was finally resolved by encasing Ellen's coffin in zinc and then placing it in a large wooden crate labeled "STATUARY." When this strange cargo arrived in New York on January 30, it was received by Ida and her husband, Edwin Miller.

On Sunday, February 3, a quiet funeral service was held for Ellen at the All Saints' Episcopal Church in Littleton. The following spring she was laid to rest beside Evarts at Glenwood Cemetery, a hallowed ground which overlooks the meandering Ammonoosuc River.

With her burial the final chapter was written on two lives that deserve to be remembered.

The Kahlers of Bethlehem...
A Family Footnote to History

> *Let this man come right in.*
> *A. Lincoln*
> *Dec. 12, 1864*

(Courtesy of Barbara Kahler Newcombe)

This small business-type card, signed by Abraham Lincoln, the 16th President of the United States, opened the door to the White House for Peter Kahler, Sr. It was found among the personal effects of Frances "Pat" Kahler of Bethlehem, New Hampshire. Today it is in the possession of Barbara Kahler Newcombe, who also resides there.

FRANCES ELVA KAHLER of Bethlehem, New Hampshire, was a small, attractive woman who projected a quiet, commanding dignity. Known simply as "Pat," for over twenty years she worked in the cosmetic department at Parker's Drug Store in Littleton. Beyond this information, most locals knew little else about her.

Following a long, lingering illness, she died at the Littleton Hospital on July 26, 1980, at the age of 71. Following her burial beside her mother, Elva Kahler, at the Maple Street Cemetery in Bethlehem, a family member found a small business-type card among Pat's personal effects. It was dated December 12, 1864, and it read: "Let this man come right in." Surprisingly it was signed "A. Lincoln."

Could this be a card that was actually signed by Abraham Lincoln, the Sixteenth President of the United States? And, if it was, what was it doing in Bethlehem, New Hampshire?

In answer to those questions, this is the story behind that card as preserved by members of the Kahler family. In the fullest sense of the word, it is a true footnote to American history.

In 1850 an expert shoemaker named Peter Kahler immigrated to this country from Germany. Accompanied by his wife, Elizabeth, and his year-old son, Charles Otto, he spent his early years in New York City. While living there, his second son, Peter, was born in 1851. Peter was followed by two daughters, Elizabeth and Henrietta, who were born in 1855 and 1858, respectively.

Following Henrietta's birth, Kahler moved his family to Scranton, Pennsylvania. After settling there, he located his shop in the basement of the Hunt Building on Lackawanna Avenue. Being an ambitious young man, he soon took out a full-page ad in the city directory in which he advertised his business as "the largest boot and shoe establishment in Luzerne County." Despite eccentric mannerisms, before long he developed a local reputation for being a "true artist in his trade." To this end he meticulously measured his clients' feet, and he painstakingly handcrafted their footwear.

At the age of 36 he came to a turning point in his life. While reading an 1864 newspaper he learned that President Lincoln suffered from sore feet. It was with more than a passing interest that he read, "It is not unusual for the President to walk around in his slippers because his boots fit poorly."

Inspired by the realization that President Lincoln probably never had a comfortable pair of boots in his entire life, Kahler sat down and composed a letter to him. In it he stated that he recognized the importance of comfortable footwear to a man in such a prominent position. He also stated that all of the boots that he made were constructed scientifically from his personal, exacting measurements. He termed the process "autographing the feet." Before closing, he assured President Lincoln that affairs of state would only be set aside momentarily during the measurement procedure.

Receiving the letter, President Lincoln was pleased with what Kahler had to say. He quickly forwarded a letter back in which he expressed delight with Kahler's offer. Then, apparently expecting Kahler to arrive at the White House on December 12, he wrote on a card, "Let this man come right in." He then dated and signed it, and stuck it in his pocket.

Perhaps due to travel delays caused by the Civil War, Kahler did not arrive at the White House until early on the morning of December 13. After entering the Reception Room, he was momen-

A very weary Abraham Lincoln sat for this portrait following his arrival in Washington, D.C. on February 23, 1861. Part of the feet problems that he suffered from could be attributed to the fact that no right and left shoes were manufactured in America until the Civil War period. Peter Kahler finally made him the comfortable boots that he so badly needed.

tarily discouraged to find a crowd already gathered there. Soldiers assigned to keep order were brusque and abrupt. Every person present seemed to be clamoring to see the President at once.

Working his way through the confusion, Kahler managed to explain his reason for being there to one of Lincoln's people. He was told that the President was in a Cabinet meeting and could not be disturbed. Lincoln, however, somehow learned of his presence and immediately sent out the card he still had in his pocket. Accompanied by one of the President's secretaries, Kahler was bursting at the seams as he entered the Cabinet meeting.

As Kahler later told the story, he said that when the President spotted him he proceeded to slip out of his boots without a pause in the remarks that he was making to the men before him. Kahler then quickly spread out a sheet of brown paper, the President stepped onto it, and Kahler traced the outlines of his feet.

While Lincoln continued addressing his Cabinet, Kahler worked quietly and efficiently jotting down necessary dimensions in metric measurements. Not once throughout the entire procedure did the President pause in his remarks. By the same token he did not address a single word to Kahler. When Kahler was finished, Lincoln stepped off the paper, slipped on his boots, and was still speaking to the Cabinet when Kahler left the room.

Kahler later told his listeners that the intensity of the President's concentration amazed him.

Kahler also added that before leaving Washington he not only had the opportunity to visit Lincoln, but he had also measured his wife, Mary Todd Lincoln, for a pair of slippers. He said that in appreciation for these services Lincoln let him keep the card which admitted him into the Cabinet meeting, and that he also signed and dated the sketch done of his feet.

When he arrived back in Scranton, Kahler set to work crafting a pair of 14-B, knee-high boots for Lincoln that were made of the finest black, soft calfskin leather. When both the boots and slippers were completed they were shipped to the White House.

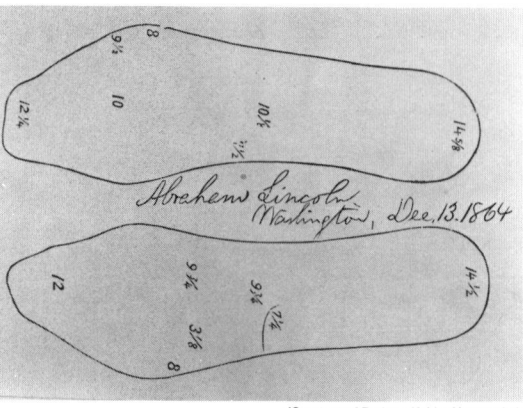

While Peter Kahler was preparing this "foot autograph" of President Lincoln during a Cabinet meeting, the President did not allow the measuring process to distract him in any way. As a consequence, Kahler later told friends that he felt like he had just experienced a strange pantomime while in his presence. Particularly since Lincoln never spoke a single word to him throughout the entire procedure.

Before doing business with Kahler, Lincoln was often known to remark, "When my feet hurt I can't think." Now, with the problem behind him, in a subsequent meeting he told several irascible Cabinet members, "The state of your minds indicates to me that you also need to be measured for new shoes."

Not long afterwards Kahler proudly told friends, "Almost immediately I had four new customers."

As it was destined to happen, on the night of April 14, 1865, while President Lincoln was attending a play at Ford's Theatre he was viciously assassinated by John Wilkes Booth. Later that night, when he was stripped of his clothes, his Kahler-made boots were removed for the last time.

According to Kahler, for unknown reasons he never received payment for the boots. Whenever he mentioned this, friends advised him, "Forget the payment. Just tell everybody that the President liked your boots."

Rising to the occasion, Kahler did better than that. Working from the original foot autograph he made a duplicate pair. He then

The Kahlers of Bethlehem

Dr. Peter Kahler, Sr., was highly esteemed as an artistic, old-time bootmaker. This page from his 1882 pamphlet, "Dress and Care of the Feet," reflects his creative strength. In appreciation for the comfortable boots he made, President Abraham Lincoln rewarded him with the card and the autographed foot sketch that are shown.

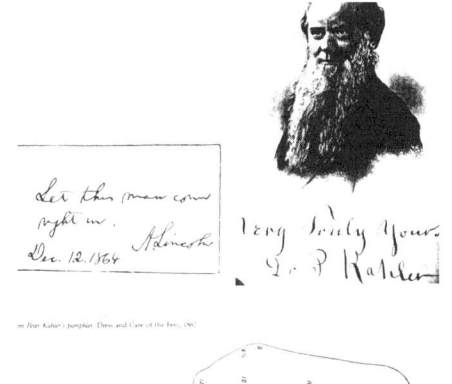

(Courtesy of Lisabeth M. Holloway, Curator, Pennsylvania College)

displayed them in his shop window along with a letter he had received from President Lincoln which praised his work. He also now began referring to himself as "Doctor Kahler, official bootmaker to the President." And he acted accordingly.

As his reputation spread, orders for boots came pouring in. Among them was one from President Andrew Johnson, Lincoln's successor. Now outgrowing his shop, Kahler was forced to move to larger quarters at 117 Wyoming Avenue. The following year, which was 1868, he realized that even greater opportunities awaited him back in New York City.

After settling his family in Manhattan, with the exception of his son, Charles Otto, who had married and remained behind in Scranton, he proceeded to found a large shoe business at 813-15 Broadway, naming it "Dr. P. Kahler & Sons." Once it was fully operational, he sent his business card to members of New York's high society. Particularly to all of its millionaires. Before long his boots and shoes commanded premium prices. As his renown grew, he affected a distinguished appearance by wearing a stove-pipe hat and kid gloves. He also rode to his office in a handsome horse-drawn carriage.

About this time the second generation of Kahlers had begun establishing themselves. Most notably, Charles Otto. In 1870, having arrived at the age of 22, he moved his wife, Laura, to Chicago where he set up a practice both as a bootmaker and a surgeon-chiropodist. Having learned from his father, he ran the following ad in the local newspapers: "Dr. C. Kahler, Chiropodist. Ladies' Boots and Shoes for Tender Feet; All Ailments of the Feet Successfully

Treated."

During the seventeen years that Charles Otto and Laura lived in Chicago they had four children. Born between December of 1877 and February of 1887, from oldest to youngest they were named Elizabeth, Peter, Henrietta, and Charles Lincoln. For whatever purpose, these were the same forenames that Peter Kahler, Sr. had given to his children. The end result was confusion in later years for historians who were interested in the family's accomplishments.

The same year that Charles Lincoln was born, Peter Kahler, Sr. began talking about retiring. Approaching sixty, he wanted time to enjoy the comfortable fortune he had amassed. In a manner of speaking, he felt that Charles Otto was the logical choice to fill his shoes.

Agreeing with his father's decision, Charles Otto moved to New York City. And, not long after his arrival, in order to strengthen the family's image as experts in the care of feet he founded the "Dr. P. Kahler's Sons' School of Surgical Chiropody."

Located at 928 and 930 Broadway, as the school gained in prominence it became the most visible of the pre-professional schools for training students in the treatment of foot ailments. It was not only advertised as "America's First Correspondence School of Surgical Chiropody," but it also boasted that it was "the only school in the United States where Chiropody is correctly and skillfully taught." And, for those who were interested, it offered a three-month course.

Also, beginning in the 1880's the Kahlers enhanced their reputations by publishing booklets which not only advertised their product and services, but themselves as well. The first booklet appeared in 1882 and was titled "Dress and Care of the Feet." On the title page Dr. P. Kahler was listed as the author. His full-bearded portrait adorned the opposite page. Eleven years would pass before Charles Otto began producing similar booklets under his own name. When he did, they were embellished with his portrait which revealed the fact that he favored mutton-chop whiskers.

In the meantime, Peter Kahler suffered through much of his retirement seeking relief for severe digestive difficulties. To this end, he was drawn to Harvey's Lake. It was not only the largest body of fresh water in Pennsylvania, but it was also a popular summer

(Photos courtesy of Barbara Kahler Newcombe)

Dr. Charles Otto Kahler, left, and his son, Dr. Peter Kahler, both demonstrated pride in their achievements as a family. Under their united direction the Kahler shoe dynasty was extremely successful. In 1918 Peter updated the family booklets on footcare, adding the x-ray as an invaluable diagnostic tool in establishing a proper diagnosis for difficult foot ailments.

resort.

While there in 1888, Kahler conceived the idea of establishing what he called the "Kahler Sanitarium and Mountain Village." Thinking that the scheme would add to his wealth, that fall he paid Mrs. Betsey Worden $9,000 for her sixty-acre farm. Upon assuming ownership, he immediately had a survey made with the idea of laying out winding streets and building lots.

When the survey was completed it revealed that his land was not properly shaped for the plans he had in mind. The solution to the problem necessitated his buying adjoining land which was known as the "Lake Hotel" property. He offered $20,000 for it to the estate of the late Caroline Rhoads, but the offer was refused.

By the following spring Kahler's condition had worsened. Hoping that the pure mountain air of Pennsylvania would improve his health, he moved his family from New York City to his Harvey's Lake farm. It was not to be. He continued to suffer greatly up to the time of his death, which occurred in July of that year.

Though he had sunk about $15,000 in his Kahler Sanitarium and Mountain Village scheme, he still left a large estate to his heirs.

And to the end, he continued to relate with pride that he was Lincoln's shoemaker.

By the turn of the Century the Kahler shoe dynasty entered its final phase as Charles Otto's children began joining the firm. His daughter, Elizabeth, was a practicing surgeon-chiropodist by the time his son, Peter, completed his medical studies in 1901. Peter earned his degree of Doctor of Surgical Chiropody by working under the tuition of Sanford W. Adams, M.D., of the New York Post Graduate Hospital.

Proud of his son's academic achievements, Charles Otto shared joint leadership of the firm with him. Under their united direction, the Kahler shoe business flourished even more successfully.

In 1903 Charles Otto proceeded to create more historically-oriented mischief when he issued a company flyer bearing the family motto, "Tis A Great Feat to Fit Feet." It contained an altered facsimile of the original Abraham Lincoln foot autograph. To make the flyer more appealing, he made Lincoln's feet look narrower and more attractive than they actually were. Historians later reproduced the facsimile believing that it showed the true outline of Lincoln's feet.

On April 11, 1906, with his financial future looking bright, Dr. Peter Kahler married Elva Cora Goulding in Trenton, New Jersey. During their first year together they lived in a cottage in Ocean Grove, New Jersey. At this time little did Peter realize how close he was to assuming full leadership of the entire Kahler operation.

A handsome, even-tempered man with a happy-go-lucky outlook on life, he had a deep love for his family. When his father, Charles Otto, died suddenly the following year at age 58 in Mt. Vernon, New York, Peter was grief-stricken. Recognizing the burden thrust on him by the tragedy, Elizabeth and Charles Lincoln closed ranks to assist their brother in every way possible. This is particularly evident in an undated school prospectus that lists Peter as President, Elizabeth as Vice-President, and Charles Lincoln as treasurer.

After their life had settled back down, Peter and Elva began their own family in 1908. Their first daughter, Frances, was born that year. In 1914 she was followed by Helen, and in 1921 they had their last child, Barbara.

About the time of Frances' birth, Peter autographed the feet of the popular, energetic President, Theodore Roosevelt. When asked to comment on the experience, Kahler merely told reporters that Roosevelt wore a 9-C shoe.

Whether he did business with Roosevelt's successor, portly William Howard Taft, is not known. However, there is no doubt that he had President Woodrow Wilson as a client. Perhaps because Wilson was essentially a scholarly man, Kahler found that he had "the most tender feet" of any of the Presidents with whom he had dealt. He also remarked on one occasion, "President Wilson finds comfort in a size 8-1/2-B."

In 1915, mid-way through Wilson's first term, out of concern for Elva's health Kahler purchased a summer home in Bethlehem, New Hampshire. Elva was suffering from a debilitating asthmatic condition, and she found relief in Bethlehem's famous pollen-free environment. At this time she and the children spent only their summers there.

In 1918, as their wealth grew, the Kahlers moved into a palatial home in Montclair, New Jersey. Their old firm, Dr. Peter Kahler Sons, Inc., had just merged with the Lounsbury-Soule Company which was another venerable shoe firm. As a single organization they were renamed "The Kahler Shoe Company." Together they controlled the exclusive manufacturing rights for the famous Kahler-made shoes.

Following the merger, the Kahlers were now accepted members of New York's high society. Their affluent lifestyle permitted them to enjoy the services of a chauffeur, cook, maid, gardener, and nursemaid for the children.

It was at this time that World War I ended, peace was restored, and the United States stood as the greatest industrial force now existing in the world. Entering the 1920's, Americans went on an orgy of consumer spending. And the man sitting in the White House was affable, handsome Warren G. Harding.

A successful editor-publisher from Marion, Ohio, it was Harding's ambition to become our Country's "best loved" President. Unfortunately he was a man of mediocre intellect who had surrounded himself with untrustworthy friends.

During the two-and-a-half years that he was in office, he was another of Peter Kahler's noteworthy clients. In fact, it was in

August of 1922 that Kahler measured his feet. He found them to be the largest of any of the Presidents that he had fitted. According to his measurements, Harding took a 9-1/2-C shoe.

When Kahler wrote to Harding on September 5, 1922, to inform him that his shoes were completed, he added, "If it is Mrs. Harding's pleasure, I can at the same time make a sketch of her feet in the book in which my grandfather took the measurements of Mrs. Lincoln's feet."

Failing to get a response to this letter, on October 20 he wrote to Harding again: "You will recall that in August I came to Washington and took measurements of your feet for a pair of shoes. "I have been waiting to hear when it would be convenient for you to try them on, and when Mrs. Harding could be measured for shoes. I am anxious to take these measurements so that Mrs. Harding may have the shoes before going south.

"I am also anxious to see how your own shoes fit, and I am quite confident that they will add to your comfort in walking or standing. If you will let me know which day will be convenient for you, I shall arrange to come to Washington."

The outcome of this correspondence is not known, but the following year Kahler again wrote to Harding. This time he was trying to interest him in buying another pair of shoes. On February 16 he received the following response from Harding: "The President has received your letter of February 14th and he appreciated your kindness in this matter. However, he is not in need of any shoes just now."

In June of 1923, with his Presidential popularity falling, Harding set out on what he termed "A Voyage of Understanding" with the intent of bolstering his image. The trip took him to the West Coast and as far as Alaska. He gave speech after speech. The strain took its toll. Suffering from a heart condition, he collapsed during his return and died suddenly on August 2, 1923, in San Francisco. He was 57. Tragically, the corruption that was festering in his Administration was soon exposed.

Three hours and seventeen minutes after Harding died, Vice-President Calvin Coolidge was sworn in as President by his own father in the family homestead in Plymouth Notch, Vermont. Beginning at 2:47 a.m., the ceremony was performed near the flick-

The Kahlers of Bethlehem

(Photo permission of The Bettman Archives)

Pictured are two of the Presidents who enjoyed the services of the Kahlers. President Warren G. Harding, left, is standing next to his wife, Florence. Because she was excessively domineering, he called her "the Duchess." With them are Vice-President Calvin Coolidge and his wife, Grace. Following Harding's death, "Silent Cal" successfully established a more efficient and economically run government.

ering light of an oil lamp.

A shrewd, taciturn New Englander, Coolidge occupied the White House for the next six years while our Nation's prosperous and tumultuous "Roaring Twenties" ran their course. Because Coolidge was shy by nature, he seldom smiled. For this reason, it was rumored in Washington that he had been "weaned on a pickle."

While Coolidge expounded on his belief that "the business of America is business," the Kahler Shoe Company reflected this philosophy. It had now become so large that it had a chain of twenty-four exclusive stores which were in turn supplemented by more than two hundred department stores and specialty shops.

Because of this growth, Peter Kahler found the business demanding more and more of his time. Due to this fact, in 1925 he made the difficult decision to move his wife and daughters to

Bethlehem, New Hampshire, on a year-round basis. He particularly felt that such a move was in the best interest of his wife's health. Remaining behind in New York, with the exception of occasional vacations and holidays, for the next twenty years he only saw his family on weekends.

In 1926 the Kahler Shoe Company finally took a serious misstep. It negotiated a $350,000 loan with the Irving Bank and Trust Company so that it could open six more stores in key locations. In order to secure the loan on a long-term basis, it advertised the sale of "Three-Year 6% Sinking Fund Gold Notes" in $1000 denominations to interested investors.

To attract the investors, a circular was issued on September 1, 1926, which emphasized that the Company's yearly earnings from 1922 to 1925 averaged $93,774.44. It also stated, "It is interesting to note that since the establishment of Dr. Peter Kahler Sons, Inc., in 1853, the Company has never had an unprofitable year nor has it, at any time, shown an operating loss."

With hard times lurking just around the corner, the timing of the loan was disastrous. In the meantime, though, it was business as usual.

Having written to President Coolidge earlier that year concerning a new pair of shoes, Kahler received the following reply from the White House: "The President has asked me to say that he greatly appreciated your kind thought of him and that he will, if possible, give you an opportunity to make the measurements of his foot when you are next in Washington."

That opportunity came a few weeks later as evidenced by an unusual "Special Dispatch" sent from Washington to the Boston Herald on April 8 which said, "Dr. Peter Kahler of New York City took measurements for shoes for President and Mrs. Coolidge.

"Dr. Kahler said that President Coolidge wore number eight shoes and that his foot was 'almost perfect. A good walking foot that anyone ought to be proud of.'

"As to Mrs. Coolidge, he was not exact, saying that she wore about a 4-1/2 shoe. 'Her feet,' he said, 'were well-formed.'"

In the months ahead, the Coolidges continued to do business with Kahler. The following year, however, President Coolidge surprised the nation when he announced, "I do not choose to run in

Elva Kahler is seen sitting in the conservatory of her Montclair, New Jersey home with two of her daughters, Frances and Helen. Born in Trenton, New Jersey, on August 5, 1884, she was the daughter of Moses and Melinda Goulding. Moving to Bethlehem, New Hampshire, on a permanent basis in 1925 for reasons of health, she is buried next to Frances in the Maple Street Cemetery there.

1928." Those nearest him knew that ill health was the reason.

After leaving the White House, and returning home to Northampton, Massachusetts, Coolidge's health declined rapidly. He died a few years later.

In 1929 Herbert Hoover entered the White House. Because business had never been better, his Administration began on an optimistic note. The stock market continued to climb, and easy credit continued the free flow of goods, jobs, and money. That is, until the following October.

Unexpectedly, in October the stock market began giving off danger signals. When it did, economic nervousness seemed to grip the country. When prices on Wall Street plummeted, speculators started a wild sell-off. Then on "Black Thursday," October 24, thirteen million shares of stock were unloaded. On the following Tuesday, October 29, the stock market collapsed completely. The "Great

Depression" had now begun.

In the years ahead banks closed, businesses failed, mortgages were foreclosed, industrial production fell fifty percent, and twelve million people became unemployed. Throughout this period hunger and homelessness stalked the land.

Though President Hoover tried to calm fears by telling the American people that "Prosperity is just around the corner," they felt he had done too little too late. In 1932 the voters turned him out of office. Their new President, Franklin Delano Roosevelt, moved quickly to create what he called "A New Deal for the American people."

Through these dark years Peter Kahler struggled to hold the Kahler Shoe Company together. Using every available resource, he was barely able to keep the business going. As for his own family, he sustained it by primarily working as a surgeon-chiropodist. Despite his best efforts, however, life for the Kahlers was never the same. Their pursuit of the American Dream had run its course.

In 1945, after dissolving his end of the Kahler Shoe Company, a tired Peter Kahler joined his family in Bethlehem. Their twenty-year separation had finally ended. Tragically, it was at this time that Kahler's middle daughter, Helen, died from peritonitis at the age of 31. She had been a secretary to the President of the Bickford Restaurant Corporation in New York. Earlier she had been a nurse at the Littleton Hospital in Littleton, New Hampshire. She was laid to rest at the Woodlawn Cemetery in New York City. Her Aunt Elizabeth and her father would be the last members of the Kahler family to be buried there.

Blessed with longevity, Elva Kahler outlived her husband by twenty-two years. When she died on June 30, 1977, she was ninety-two years old. Both she and her daughter, Frances, are buried in the Maple Street Cemetery in Bethlehem.

Like his famous grandfather, Peter Kahler enjoyed only a short retirement. Diagnosed as having a leaky heart valve, he died on January 30, 1951, after helping his daughter, Barbara Newcombe, carry groceries into her Whitefield Road home. Deeply affected by his passing, a week later she gave premature birth to a baby boy who lived for only a few hours. However, she has three other children. They are twin daughters named Diana and Carol, and a son,

THE KAHLERS OF BETHLEHEM

Gary.

When Barbara's husband, James, died in May of 1972, she continued to earn a living by working as a secretary in the Guidance Department at Whitefield Regional High School. Now semi-retired, she continues to administer educational tests locally for the State Department of Education.

Interestingly enough, the Kahler story does not end here. Sometime during this Century a fire gutted the main office of the Kahler Shoe Company. Among the invaluable historical documents lost in the fire was the book containing the foot autographs of the Presidents. Then, in November of 1988, Professor Gabor Boritt of Gettysburg College in Gettysburg, Pennsylvania, made a surprising announcement. He stated that he had the authentic Abraham Lincoln foot autograph done by Peter Kahler, Sr.

(Photo courtesy of Barbara Kahler Newcombe)

Dr. Peter Kahler's three daughters posed for this photo in November of 1922 while they were still living in Montclair, New Jersey. From the left, they are Helen, 8, Barbara, 9 months, and Frances, 13. Of the three, only Barbara is still alive. Semi-retired, she continues to administer educational tests locally for the State Department of Education.

Ten years earlier Boritt's interest in Lincoln's feet was fueled by the revival of medical journal arguments that the President had Marfan's Syndrome. This is a rare genetic disorder often characterized by long limbs, elongated big toes, and superior intelligence. Remembering that he had seen a shoemaker's outline of Lincoln's feet in a history book, Boritt wanted to prove his belief that the President had normal feet.

At first his search for the source of the outline led him to Charles Otto's altered facsimile. Since the facsimile served no purpose, the search continued. Then, three years after his search began, he learned from a Lincoln file kept in an Indiana library that Mr. and Mrs. Edward A. Blumenstine of Harrisburg, Pennsylvania, had allowed a sketch of Lincoln's feet to be put on public display in 1945.

Eventually establishing contact with Mrs. Blumenstine, who was now an aged widow, Boritt gained possession of the ancient brown paper bearing the famous Kahler sketch which the Blumenstines had gotten from a former Kahler employee. However, seven more years were to pass before historians and foot experts pronounced both the sketch and Lincoln's signature on it as genuine. When they did, it confirmed Boritt's belief that Lincoln's feet were normal.

Beyond a doubt, Dr. Peter Kahler also knew this. Years earlier, after studying this same sketch done by his grandfather, he wrote: "The autographed sketched lines and diagnosis show a pair of healthy feet, large in size, but well proportioned to the great Executor's stature."

Today the Kahler-made boots that President Lincoln wore on the night of his assassination are on display at Ford's Theatre in Washington, D.C. They serve as silent reminders of how a little German immigrant rose from relative obscurity to carve a niche for himself and his family in our Nation's history.

And not to be forgotten, there is that other silent reminder which was found in Bethlehem, New Hampshire. It is the card that reads, "Let this man come right in." After all, it not only opened the door to the White House for the Kahlers, but it also served as the key that opened the door to their family history as well.

Franconia's Famous Murder:
The Hanging of Samuel Mills

JUST BEFORE he was hanged at the County Jail in Haverhill, New Hampshire, on May 6, 1868, Samuel Mills scribbled the following obscure message on one of his cell walls. It read: "Samma Mills murder, going to be 'ung today of May — good fellow but no man dont know it."

Unfortunately Samuel Mills is principally remembered today both for his cold-blooded murder of George Maxwell in Franconia, and for being the last man to be publicly hanged in Grafton County. At the time of his execution, however, it is apparent that he wanted to be remembered for something other than these two facts.

In that respect, this is the strange and twisted journey that he took in life that not only led to the brutal death that awaited him at the age of twenty-five, but also how he seized the moment and left this world a better man.

From what little we know of him, he was born in the District of Phillack, in the County of Cornwell, England, on February 13, 1843, to Thomas and Mary Mills. When he left England for this country in the early spring of 1863 he not only said goodbye to his parents, but also to his wife, Elizabeth Ann, and to his young children. It was to be the last time that he would ever see them. A miner by trade, it is presumed that he came to New Hampshire to make a fresh start. Especially since he had already run afoul of the

(Floyd W. Ramsey, Private Collection)

A miner by profession, Samuel Mills came to Franconia, NH, from Cornwell, England, to make a fresh start. Instead he became known as "the mean-looking customer" who brutally murdered George Maxwell. Because of his muscular neck, his spinal cord was not severed at the time of his hanging. Instead he slowly strangled to death.

law in England, as he was later to admit in his cell just before his hanging.

He landed in New York City about the middle of April, where he remained until the first of May. From there he went directly to Franconia, New Hampshire, to work in the Franconia copper mine. This was just a short distance from where he would eventually commit the crime that cost him his own life.

Following his arrival, for whatever reason he remained in Franconia for only a few weeks before he left for Michigan to work in the copper mines near Lake Superior. From there he again moved on, and worked in the mines at Galena, Illinois. Following another short stay, he then went to Rockaway, New Jersey, where he remained for some time.

Unable to settle down, he returned to Franconia in July of 1866. In the months ahead he first worked at the Franconia copper mine, and then at the Dodge gold mine in Lisbon. While he was working at the Franconia mine, he boarded just up the road from George Maxwell's farmhouse. At some point the two men met, and since Maxwell was an elderly bachelor who lived a somewhat lonely life they often played cards in his kitchen.

It was while Mills was boarding at Obed Quimby's boardinghouse in Lisbon that his criminal tendencies finally resurfaced. Over time, having grown desperate for the type of money that he could not seem to earn honestly, on the night of December 7, 1866, he broke into a trunk at the boardinghouse and stole a gold watch and about eighty dollars from a fellow miner.

Early the next morning, before the theft was discovered, he told friends that he was going to Landaff for the day. In reality, he was heading for George Maxwell's farmhouse in Franconia. Recently he had heard that Maxwell had sold property to a neighbor named Charles Brooks. Upon hearing this, Mills immediately was curious to know if Maxwell got his pay in money. When he was told that part was in money and part in notes, he thought the term referred to paper money rather than promissory notes. No matter, whatever money had changed hands he had plans for it.

Sustained by his greed, Mills trudged the long miles that lay between Lisbon and Franconia. Along the way he struggled to keep warm as he became soaked through by a freezing rain. As he pulled

Franconia's Famous Murder

(Floyd W. Ramsey, Private Collection)

On Saturday, December 8, 1866, which was to be the last day of his life, George Maxwell attended an auction being held in Franconia village by his friend, Alex Jesseman. When the weather turned to freezing rain, Mrs. Jesseman invited him to supper and to spend the night. When he declined the offer, he entered Franconia's history that night as the victim of a brutal murder.

up the collar of his short black coat, he passed several men on the road who would later provide the authorities with his description. Though they could not identify him by name, they agreed that he was an ugly-looking customer of medium height with dark whiskers and a mustache. They also said he was wearing a low black hat, gray pants, and eleven-inch-high boots.

By the time Mills arrived at Maxwell's, it was well past dark and the temperature had fallen. While the cold December wind howled down off the mountains, he impatiently banged on Maxwell's front door. A few minutes later Maxwell angrily left his supper table to answer the knock. In a subsequent confession Mills described what happened next:

"He came and opened the door and I walked in. He acted as though he was afraid of me. I said to him, 'Don't you know me?'

"I saw there were some things on the table. He stooped down and picked up a stick of wood and held it up. He then ordered me to leave. I then pitched into him.

"I did not mean to kill him when I went there. I threw him down two or three times. I did not knock him down with my fists. I then struck him with a stick of wood. He run into the pantry and I run in after him. I didn't know what he was going to do. I thought he might be after a gun to shoot me.

"The candle went out and we were in the dark. I did not stab him until after we went in the pantry. Then I stabbed him several times with my jackknife. It was a hard fight. He fought for his life, and I fought for my life. He hit me several times with the steelyards and sticks of wood. In the fracas I cut my finger, and he hit me on the shoulder and in other places.

"I knocked him down in the pantry with sticks of wood. I think the stove door was open, and light from the stove shone in and I saw he was rising. I took the ax and knocked him back to the floor, and that finished him. He died hard.

"I didn't stay in the house long. I went out to the barn and tried to get in, but I couldn't find the way into the barn. I was gone a spell. I don't know how long. I went back into the house and found the candle. I put down the curtains and then lit it. I looked in the pantry upon the poor man, and then turned away. I didn't look long. I then took up the teapot and drank some tea.

"I went into the bedroom and broke open the chest and trunk. I saw his deed, some notes, and some things but there was no money. Though I did steal the man's money in Lisbon, and his watch, I did not get any money off Maxwell. Also, I did not look in his pockets for money.

"Next I took the candle and went back to the barn. I lit the candle and got into the barn and harnessed the horse. I was about the barn this time half or three-quarters of an hour. I was not in the house long, but was about the barn some time because I couldn't find the way into the barn at first.

"I was about the place an hour and a half I should think. I can't say for sure. It seemed long to me. I felt bad after I killed him. Next I drove out on the road, and down through Franconia Village. When I got near Henry Spooner's the horse took fright and turned clear around. It was dark and I couldn't guide him."

Years later, when the author, Ella Shannon Bowles asked Elmore Whipple about this incident, he said, "When Mills reached the hill back of the Franconia Baptist Church, he got out of the wagon and walked to spare the horse and that was where he left one clue. One turned-over shoe left a definite track in the mud."

Overlooked was the fact that following his capture Mills took exception to this particular bit of evidence, stating, "They were mistaken about my boots. One of them was worn down a little on the heel, but not much."

When asked how he got away, Mills said, "I went to Littleton. I guess it was about nine o'clock when I was there. They were all up. There was a light on in every house. I turned to the right, and went

Franconia's Famous Murder

(Floyd W. Ramsey, Private Collection)

This is the house in which George Maxwell was cold-bloodedly axed to death in his pantry. It is located exactly one-half mile south of the Willow Cemetery on the Easton Road where he was laid to rest. Though it has changed ownership and undergone extensive renovations since this photo was taken, it is still easily recognizable.

right up the river. I did not know the road to Gorham, but went just where the horse led me.

"When it got to be daylight I saw I was all covered with blood. I stopped the horse in the road and got out and washed the blood from my coat. It was in a pond that was there. I then went to the hotel in Gorham and told them to feed my horse four to six quarts of oats."

About the time that Mills was sitting down to a late breakfast at the hotel, Nathan Brooks was driving through Franconia Village with Mrs. Lucy Grimes Priest. They were on their way to the East Landaff church where Mrs. Priest was scheduled to sing that morning. Knowing this, the storekeeper at Parker's Store stopped Brooks and asked him to tell George Maxwell that there was a crate of hens waiting for him and he should see about taking care of them.

Arriving at Maxwell's farm, which was just a little over two miles from the Village, Brooks went to the back door. After receiving no response to his knocks, he pushed open the door and quietly entered the house. He was not prepared for the grisly scene that awaited him.

As his eyes adjusted to the poor light, he found Maxwell's body lying in a pool of blood on the pantry floor just inside the open door. Not only was his head badly mangled, but worse still, the whole blade of an axe was buried in his neck. Blood covered the walls, ceilings, doors, and window curtains. Brooks could also see it floating in nearby pans of milk.

It was a scene that would haunt him for the rest of his life.

Still in shock, Brooks fled through the house and exited by the front door. When Mrs. Priest saw him, she immediately noticed that all of the color was drained from his face. He screamed at her, "Maxwell is killed, by God! Get help as quick as you can, Lucy!"

(Floyd W. Ramsey, Private Collection)

This is Moses Sargent, the Boston detective who eventually proved worthy of his hire. Sent for by Franconia Selectmen Joel Spooner, Henry Noyes, and David Appleby, his plodding and persistent investigation finally led to Mill's apprehension in Galena, Illinois.

That day passed quietly for Mills, and that night he sneaked over to the early freight train on which he planned to make his escape from Gorham. Finding that there were several empty boxcars, he hid in one of them and slept there to avoid anyone who might be pursuing him.

Arriving safely at the Groveton depot that morning, while the train was being made up and freight taken on, he again went to a hotel where he had breakfast and a glass of whiskey. Overhearing that there were men in town tracking a murderer, he downed his whiskey and slipped back to the boxcar unobserved.

Having no way of knowing that Mills was nearby, Mr. W.C.

Franconia's Famous Murder

This graphic inscription on the back of George Maxwell's headstone preserves the memory of the violent death he suffered at the hands of Samuel Mills on the night of December 8, 1866. The headstone can be seen at the entrance to Willow Cemetery, which is near the Franconia Inn on the Easton Road.

(Floyd W. Ramsey, Private Collection)

Goodwin of Bethlehem, New Hampshire, got aboard the train and asked the conductor if he noticed any passengers who were acting suspiciously. The conductor informed him that there were only three passengers aboard, and that they were all well known locally. Consequently, Goodwin did not entertain any further thoughts that the murderer was on the train.

At Island Pond, Vermont, Mills left the boxcar and went to a nearby grocery store. He told the proprietor that he was tired and needed a place to sleep. The storekeeper directed him to an upstairs bedroom. That night, when he went upstairs to tell Mills that he was closing shop while he went to supper, Mills became frightened when he heard him enter the room. Instantly he sprang out of the bed and wildly asked the startled storekeeper what he wanted.

An hour later, when the storekeeper returned for his evening hours, Mills was outside waiting for him. Following him into the store, Mills asked him if there was a night train to Montreal. Told that there was, he then went back upstairs and remained there until the train was due in.

Just before leaving Island Pond, he purchased a steel watch chain from the storekeeper. Taking out a gold watch, he detached a silver chain from it and substituted the steel chain for it. Examining the silver chain, the storekeeper asked Mills why he preferred the steel chain. Mills informed him that he sold the silver chain and wanted the steel one to take its place.

When the train came in on schedule, Mills left the store and headed back to the depot. Due to his peculiar behavior the storekeeper started to follow him, but returned to the store after he lost sight of him in the crowd. Inside the station Mills bought a through ticket to Detroit. When the train departed at 10 p.m. for Montreal he was aboard.

The next day, when news of the murder reached the storekeeper, he immediately suspected his strange visitor of being the wanted man. When he met with Mill's pursuers, the watch chain that he described for them fit the exact description of the one stolen at Lisbon. For the moment this was the last positive trace of Mills.

When sharing this fact with the readers of the December 15th issue of the Littleton Gazette, the reporter lamented, "Mills' escape has been very mysterious. Not having shown a spark of shrewdness from the beginning, it has been all luck with him."

After arriving in Montreal, Mills was only there for an hour or two when his train departed for Detroit. Following his arrival there, he remained in Detroit for two days. During this time he carefully searched the newspapers for any mention of the murder. Seeing none, he then traveled to Chicago by way of the Michigan Central Railroad. He stayed in Chicago for one night, and then went on to Galena, Illinois, where he had previously worked. He now felt comfortable in the fact that he had made a successful escape.

Back in Franconia, every effort was being made on the part of the selectmen and the local citizenry to bring Mills to justice. Over the next few weeks posses made up of men and boys scoured the woods searching for him. When these efforts proved fruitless, the selectmen sent to Boston for a detective named Moses Sargent.

Arriving in Franconia, at first Sargent traveled between there and Lisbon pursuing one lead after another. Next he seemed to sit around Parker's Store a lot just visiting. Locally, people began to express their disgust with him. Finally, however, when he was satisfied beyond all doubt that Mills was the man he was looking for he went to see Obed Quimby in Lisbon.

With Quimby's help, Sargent made a drawing of Mills' face and then sent copies of it to newspapers throughout the United States. Accompanying each drawing was the warning that Mills was sus-

Franconia's Famous Murder

The late Clayton Bailwitz proudly looks up at the signs attached to his home located on Court Street in Haverhill where New Hampshire's famous "Last Public Hanging" took place. Profoundly aware of the role his house played in our State's history, he kept his door open to visitors from all walks of life while he was alive.

pected of being a murderer, and that information was being sought from anyone who might know of a person who resembled him. It was a long shot, but before long it paid off.

On the first of February a message was received from Galena, Illinois, expressing the belief that they had the man being sought already in custody. Immediately Sargent and Captain Goodwin of the Littleton Police Department left for Galena. Goodwin had in his possession a requisition from Governor Smith which authorized him to bring Mills back to New Hampshire.

When the two men arrived in Galena, they were surprised to see that Mills was still wearing the same clothes he had on at the time of the murder. When he protested to them that he was an innocent man being held unjustly, they threw facts at him that he couldn't refute. Losing his self-assurance, he grew pale and asked for a drink of water. Having no other choice, he finally gave himself over to the law.

It was close to the middle of February when the train carrying Mills pulled into the station at Littleton. Standing on the platform, a large crowd had gathered to get a look at him. Toward their outer edge, Alex Jesseman sat patiently in his carriage waiting to drive the returning party to Franconia. As a former Franconia selectman and friend of George Maxwell, he looked forward to the day when Mills would be brought to justice.

Understandably nervous, Mills sat quietly between Sargent and Goodwin during the nine-mile journey. Then, when he spotted lighted lanterns off in the distance toward Franconia Village, he became badly frightened. He thought they belonged to angry villagers who were waiting to lynch him. He calmed down after Jesseman explained that Gale River was flooding the road, and that the lanterns were strung up through the fields to act as guideposts.

Following a preliminary hearing in the town hall, Mills was then taken to the old tavern where he was locked in chains. The next day the school was closed so that the children could all go to the tavern to see what a murderer looked like. Even though Mills was confined to a corner room and his legs were shackled, his appearance alone frightened some of the girls. Nevertheless, he spoke to a lot of the children as well as to some of the older people who dropped by to look at him.

On Tuesday evening, February 12, he was taken back to Littleton for a preliminary trial before the Honorable Harry Bingham. After a few witnesses had been examined, he waived further trial. He then signed a brief confession, and was taken to the old Haverhill County Jail to await his full trial.

It was only two weeks later that he attempted his first escape. Because he played a shrewd game, he came close to succeeding. There was a trustee at the jail who was given the liberty of going in and out of the jail at his leisure. From time to time he entered Mills' cell. On this occasion, as he left the cell, Mills quietly threw a small stick of wood on the threshold. It was just large enough to prevent the door from closing tightly, and it caused the bolts to pass outside the sockets.

Once it seemed safe, Mills opened the door and descended the stairs. He was about to jump the outside fence when he was seen by the trustee. The man immediately sprang for him, and struggled to hold him until help came. During the tussle they both made a lot of noise. This aroused the jailor. He ran to the scene and put irons on Mills. Once secured, Mills was then confined to one of the first-floor cells until he could be safely returned to his regular cell.

Mill's trial finally began on Monday afternoon, April 1, 1867, at the courthouse in Haverhill. At five o'clock he was brought into the courtroom, and on motion of Attorney General Clarke, he was formally arraigned. When asked how he pleaded to the charge of murder in the first degree, in a clear and distinct voice he said, "Not guilty!" Seventy-five men were then called, and each answered to his name. From them a panel of twelve was readily drawn to act as the jury.

Franconia's Famous Murder

(Floyd W. Ramsey Photo)

Samuel Mills' cell in the old County Jail at Haverhill, New Hampshire, is much the same today as it was when he was hanged in 1868. In his last hours here, having a guard constantly near him apparently baffled whatever his last plan was to escape.

The next morning the court convened at nine o'clock. Richard Calley of Hill was appointed foreman of the jury for the trial. Next, Mills was brought to the box. He appeared to be calm and self-possessed, and spoke of objecting or accepting each of the jurors in the same clear and distinct voice that he used previously to proclaim his innocence. To the reporters present he seemed less affected by the proceedings than did many of the jurors.

Due to the great interest in the trial, each day the courtroom was crowded. Especially noticeable was the large number of women present.

By Friday morning, April 5, the State concluded its evidence against Mills. The next day the trial ended. Mills was pronounced guilty, and he was sentenced to be hanged on the first Wednesday in May of 1868. He was then ordered to remain confined at the old County Jail until the time of his execution. This meant that he had a whole year in which to create mischief.

Needless to say, he wasted little time in that respect. On Sunday, April 21, he escaped from the jail at about two a.m. by sawing off the iron grates in his cell window with a knife he had hidden previous to his trial. His absence was not discovered until six a.m., which was the time when the jailor made his scheduled visit to Mills' cell. Within minutes after the alarm was sounded, all of Haverhill responded to the excitement.

Men went off in all directions to search the woods, and to guard the roads, while Sheriff Grove Stevens busied himself preparing a poster which not only described Mills but also made known the offer of a $500 reward for any information leading to his capture.

Within a short time it was found where Mills had walked over plowed ground, and where he had stopped and broken off one of his shackles. Some distance from that spot the other shackle was found. This meant that he had the full use of his feet and legs.

Once he was completely free of the shackles, Mills headed for the woods. As much as he could, he stayed off the main road until he reached the town of Bath. After arriving there, he took to the road and headed for Lisbon. It was not until Tuesday morning, at about 5:30, that he was spotted by Darius George at the lower end of Lisbon Village.

Shortly after being seen by George, Mills called at the house of Charley Chase. He not only asked Mrs. Chase where Obed Quimby lived from there, but he also asked her for breakfast. After telling him what he wanted to know, and that she did not quite have breakfast ready, Mrs. Chase returned to her kitchen for a moment. When she returned, Mills was gone. She could see him running across the fields in the direction of the Atwood Mines.

Later that day Mills' luck began to run out. He got lost and wandered around in the woods for hours without gaining badly needed distance. That night he slept in a wagon in the lower part of Littleton on the Theron Allen property. The next morning he stole one of Allen's hens, and left before the family got out of bed. Once out of sight he roasted the hen, ate a portion of it, and jammed the rest in a pocket.

Before noon that day he appeared in the northern part of Littleton where he had a meal at the home of James Merrill. He was next seen heading for Dalton. As he passed by the sawmill there, young C.M. Cushman recognized him even though news of his escape had not reached that area. When Cushman told his father that he had just seen Samuel Mills, the murderer, his father refused to believe him.

Young Cushman was so confident that it was Mills that he harnessed up the family horse and drove past him for a closer look. He then quickly drove to Ruggles' store, which was some miles farther on, and asked for help in apprehending him. In the meantime another man overtook Mills and offered him a ride. Mills rode to the store, but said later, "When I got out of the wagon I smelt a

Franconia's Famous Murder

(Floyd W. Ramsey Photo)

The upper last window to the right is the one that Samuel Mills had to step through on his way to the gallows. The window of his second-floor cell can be seen directly behind the large tree. On the day of his hanging a rough hemlock joist projected from this window, and the hanging rope was suspended from it.

mice."

With his suspicions aroused by the sight of the men standing on the store porch, Mills bolted and ran in the direction of Lancaster. However, the men soon caught up with him and forced him to return to the store. Despite angry protests on his part, he was carefully guarded while an effort was made to identify him. Chester Fiske of Littleton, who worked nearby, was sent for. As Fiske approached the store he called Mills by name. Mills lost his composure and acknowledged that he was "Sammy Mills and no one else."

After Mills was handcuffed and chained, Cushman and Fiske put him into a wagon for the return trip to Littleton. During the ride Mills referred to himself as "an unfortunate devil." When questioned about his escape, he told them that no one helped him. He explained that he sawed off the grates with the knife which he was still carrying, and that it took him nine nights to do it.

Following Mills return to Haverhill the next day, a blacksmith was called in to fasten a heavy chain about his ankle. Once the chain was in place, it was attached to a steel staple. The staple was then driven into a beam located in the middle of his cell. Ironically, if Mills had left this chain alone he might have carried off another escape during the last full week of his life.

As the months passed, and his execution date loomed uncomfortably close, Mills received a letter from his mother which was to eventually play an important part in the way he went to his death. In the portion that was written on March 18, 1868, Mary Mills wrote:

"My dear son, we are all glad to hear you are still well in health, but very sorry to hear that you have not given your heart to Christ, the Redeemer of the world. My dear son, it is quite true what you wrote when you said a letter is not like the face of a friend. We can't tell nor convey our feelings by writing like we can when face to face.

"Oh, my dear son, if I could but look on you once more, which I must give up all hope of doing in this world—and worse than that, you tell me you are not prepared to die. My dear son, give up this world and give your heart to Christ, then you will find comfort and rest. There will be no more sorrow there.

"My dear son, your poor old mother is still spared, but in a very, very weak state, almost broken-hearted. You said you had but a short time to live. God only knows—my time may be shorter than yours. But oh, my dear son, what an end! You said you would like to see someone of the family come over. Your poor mother is barely able to move up and down. If I was able to undertake the journey, I would be there before now even if I begged my way over. I am very sorry to acquaint you, but we are so situated that neither one of the family will be able to go over to see you. Father and Thomas say it would be more than they could do to go over there and see you where you are, and then to have to leave you behind them for that awful doom."

Due to the length of the letter, Mrs. Mills did not complete writing it until the following day. At this time she wrote:

"My dear son, your poor wife has been down here today and is like myself in great trouble. Your dear children are well.

"My dear son, your poor father is very unwell with his complaint as well as trouble. The two combined are taking great effect on me, but thank God I am able to pray, and do pray for you night and day, and also pray for them that have the keeping of you. May the Lord bless you together.

"My dear son, we can't expect many more letters from you, but we shall be relieved in our trouble if you can tell us you have Christ in your heart. My dear, dear son, we hope to hear from you again and again before you leave this world. Oh Lord, have mercy on my dear Samuel.

"I can't say more, my dear, for I am almost exhausted. All the family are most broken hearted for you. The time we have to live will be in lamentation. No tongue can express our feelings. My dear son, we must come to the goodbye, for the present, hoping to meet in Heaven.

"From your ever loving parents, Thomas and Mary Mills."

Under the date of March 19, Mills also received a letter from his brother, Thomas, and learned of more grief in the family. Particularly for his mother. Thomas said, in part:

"My dear brother, in writing this to you I must privately inform you about our poor brother Henry. Mother is not aware of it. We intend to keep it from her, for if she becomes acquainted with it, and with all the trouble about you, she will never stand it for she is almost crushed to the earth as it is. Our poor brother Henry sailed from Hong Kong, bound to another port in China on the 10th of May last, and has not since been heard of. So poor Henry must have been drowned before we received his last letter, I think in July."

Following receipt of these letters, on April 29 Mills wrote his last letter to his parents. In it he quoted at length from Scripture, and he urged them not to grieve for him because he felt he would soon be better off. He closed by saying that he hoped to meet them all in Heaven. On the same day he also wrote the following excerpted letter to his wife. He said to her:

"My dear Elizabeth Ann, I once more write you a few lines as it is my last opportunity I have to address you in this world. I little thought when I left you that we should be separated forever, and by this form of punishment which I cannot fully describe. I acknowledge that it is on account of my transgressions that I am thus called upon. I want to inform you that although I have been a bad sinner I love Jesus Christ the Savior of sinners. I trust he has pardoned me and taken away my fear of death.

"I want you to bring my children up in the nurture and admonition of the Lord. Oh, that I had given my heart to God in my youth, I might have been saved from this ignominious death and saw my wife.

"Elizabeth Ann, you state in your letter that you have a good home with your father and mother. Yes, I know there is a home for you and the children, thank God.

"Elizabeth Ann, I come to my well wishes, wishing your father and mother, brothers and sisters, the joyful mercies of God and you and my Dear little children the same, rejoicing in hope, patient in tribulation, continuing constant in prayer.

"From your well wisher, Samuel Mills. Kiss my children for me.

"I have wrote to father."

Despite the pious tone in these letters, Mills still held out hope that he would outwit the law and escape the hangman's noose. His final attempt to escape was made during the last full week of his confinement. To that end he extracted a rod from the stove in his cell, and somehow he also destroyed the rivet which fastened the chain to his ankle so that he was free in his movements. Once this problem was out of the way, he set about removing the plaster from the ceiling in one corner of his cell. Once he had exposed the large timbers, he hoped to burn through them by heating the rod. He was trying to exit through the ceiling because an alarm had been recently connected to his cell window. It was set to go off the moment a bar in the window was severed.

He might have succeeded in this effort if he had ignored the chain until after he had completed making the hole in the ceiling. As it was, he had not progressed very far when it was seen that he had slipped out of it. Commenting on this fact, a reporter wrote: "It was characteristic of the man. Again, showing his cunning and ingenuity, but still his want of brains."

Tuesday, May 5, was Mills' last full day of life. Early that morning he was temporarily removed from his cell and placed in the one adjoining it so beams could be extended from his window and out over the scaffold. These were the support beams for the one from

FRANCONIA'S FAMOUS MURDER   219

(Floyd W. Ramsey Private Collection)

This dramatic photograph was taken just seconds before Samuel Mills was hanged at the old County Jail on May 6, 1868. He stands out clearly because of the white canvas bag that he is wearing. This was the last public hanging held in Grafton County. Future executions took place at the State Prison in Concord as established by authority of the General Statutes of New Hampshire which went into effect on January 1, 1868.

which he would be hanged. In order to allow the transfer, the heavy chain which he had worn for months was removed and fetters less burdensome were put around his ankles. During the removal, Mills laughed at the blacksmith when he made a mistake in striking the metal.

Once the beams were secured, he was returned to his cell. Throughout the day he could plainly hear the sounds made by the tools during the construction of the scaffold. Though he appeared to show little concern, at one point he asked the guard how they were going to get from his cell to the scaffold. When told that stairs would be built for that purpose, he said lightheartedly, "I suppose that means I must walk out there tomorrow."

Following the completion of the scaffold, the half-inch manila rope that was going to be used was then tested. It successfully bore the strain of a two-hundred-pound rock falling a distance of six feet.

The platform, which was no more than a floor of rough boards thrown across the jailyard walls, was three feet lower than Mills' cell window. The trap was placed near the center of it, and beneath the trap the earth was removed so that Mills would fall nine feet.

For the most part, Mills passed that day as he did other days. He ate heartily, smoked his pipe, chewed tobacco, and he read and walked in his cell. He was curious to see visitors, but only members of the press were allowed to converse with him. However, because he had a wild, restless look in his dark eyes, they felt uncomfortable in his presence. The only reference he made to the murder that day occurred when he questioned the reporter who found Maxwell's horse in Gorham. Laughing, Mills asked him what he did with it.

Toward sunset he began to show signs of restlessness beyond just the look in his eyes. For a brief period he walked his cell clanking his chain like a maniac. Attempts on the part of his guards to draw him into conversation utterly failed. Finally, remembering his mother's letter, he decided to make his peace with God. For that purpose, Reverend Gowen, pastor of the Methodist Church, was admitted to his cell along with a gentleman named Edward Page who had won his confidence by different acts of kindness.

Surprisingly, shortly after the two men had entered his cell, Mills handed some tools to Page which he had kept hidden. As he did, he said, "Under favorable circumstances I could have made my escape in an hour and a half by using these." Following this admission he had a long talk with Reverend Gowen.

Later that night Mills told the guard on duty that he was going to die like a man. For the remainder of his waking hours he devoted most of his time to a study of the Bible. Near midnight he fell asleep, and from then until dawn he slept fitfully. Tossing and turning, he often muttered, "Oh, God!" and Oh, Heaven!" When he awakened that morning, he started his last day off with a good breakfast but omitted his usual smoke.

As the town clock struck the hours with relentless progress, he appeared to grow more and more serious. On request, Reverend Gowen was sent for again and Mills spent more time with him. Next he visited with one or two friends, and requested that no strangers be allowed to look into his cell.

Outside, the morning weather remained dark and gloomy and

Overcome by the excitement accompanying the hanging of Samuel Mills, Wilbur F. Parker, 19, of Franconia became sick to his stomach moments before the trap was sprung. Consequently he failed to witness the execution. Following his graduation from Newbury Academy, he owned and operated a store in Franconia which is now an apartment building just across the highway from the old stone stack.

(Photo courtesy of Betty and Robert Sweet)

showed signs of rain. Despite this threat, beginning at 8:00 a.m. a large crowd assembled on the grounds to witness the execution. By 10:00 it was estimated that 3000 people were there. In addition, a crowded excursion train from Littleton was also expected later based on the understanding that the hanging would take place between 11:00 a.m. and 2:00 p.m.

Despite this fact, at 10 o'clock Sheriff Stevens, his deputies, legal advisors, and newspaper reporters ascended the platform. Assured by the hangman that everything was ready, Sheriff Stevens and his assistants then walked up the short stairway to the window leading into the jail. Seeing what was happening, Mills hurriedly scribbled on his cell wall: "Samma Mills murder, going to be 'ung today of May — good fellow but no man dont know it."

After his hands were handcuffed behind him, Mills appeared at the window at 10:07. He was bareheaded, his woolen shirt was open at the neck, and his face was extremely pale from his long confinement. While attempting to follow Sheriff Stevens through the opening, he banged his head quite hard. After he stepped on to the stairs, he was followed by Sheriffs Morrison and Ticknor.

After descending the stairs, he took his place over the drop. His teeth were firmly set as if he were nerving himself for what was to come. While positioning himself, he nodded to a friend that he saw in the crowd. Then, as his eyes wandered over the upturned faces before him, one man shouted, "How are you, Sammy?"

While Sheriff Stevens adjusted the noose about his neck, Mills spoke a word or two to him. After the death warrant was read, Reverend Gowen stepped forward and offered up a prayer. Mills did not bow his head, but stood there calmly gazing at the crowd. Occasionally he would shake his head and twist his neck as though the rope felt uncomfortable. Determined to die fearlessly, this was the only sign of feeling that he showed.

Standing there looking at his watch, as soon as the prayer ended Sheriff Stevens said, "Mr. Mills, you now have fifteen minutes more to live. If you have anything to say you now have the chance."

Earlier that morning Mills asked Sheriff Stevens for permission to address the crowd. Now he looked at him and replied, "I don't know as I have anything to say."

The sheriff repeated the offer. This time Mills said, "I don't know as I can make any further confessions."

Nodding his head, the sheriff told him that he could say anything he wished. Mills then turned to the crowd and spoke out in a loud, clear voice. He said, "Gentlemen, I am guilty. Samuel Mills is guilty now, but I think I have made my peace with God. Samuel Mills has lived like a man, and he is going to die like a man. If I have done anything wrong I hope you will forgive me."

Following a slight pause, he added, "I bid farewell to this world and hope that we shall meet in Heaven. You will tell folks around, gentlemen, that Sammy Mills died like a man and is guilty of his crime."

At 10:20, while the white canvas body bag was being adjusted about him, he turned to Reverend Gowen and said, "I have nothing against any man, and I am at peace with all the world."

Just before 10:29 the sheriff stepped forward and informed Mills that he had one more minute to live. A last adjustment was quickly made on the rope, and then the black cap was drawn over his face. Just before it covered his mouth, he cried out, "Goodbye, gentlemen! Luck to you!"

Looking at his watch, at exactly 10:30 Sheriff Stevens exclaimed, "Samuel Mills, your time is up! May God have mercy on your soul!"

The drop fell and Mills instantly disappeared beneath the platform. When he hit the end of the rope, a heavy thug could be heard by the men standing near the drop. As the sheriff and his deputies looked down on him, he remained nearly motionless for three to four minutes. Then his lower extremities could be seen trembling. This was followed by one final tremor as his heart made its final beat.

A few minutes before eleven he was taken down, his body was placed in a plain wooden coffin, and he was carried out to the street where he was put on public display. He remained there until shortly after noon. After his coffin was sealed, he was carried off to a pauper's grave at the nearby burial ground.

True to his word, Samuel Mills had died like a man. But, more importantly, thanks to his mother's love he also left this world a better man.

The Night the Bomber Crashed

(Photo courtesy of Charles Harrington)

Not knowing that he was in the heart of the White Mountains, on the night of January 14, 1942, 1st Lt. Anthony Benvenuto brought his B-18 down to 3800 feet in an attempt to lessen an icing problem. By doing so, he put the plane on a collision course with Mt. Waternomee in the North Woodstock, NH, area. Built at a cost of $80,000, the bomber was primarily used for supporting ground forces and defending our coastline against enemy attacks.

DURING THE EARLY EVENING hours of Wednesday, January 14, 1942, a singular tragedy occurred near the Mt. Moosilauke area of North Woodstock, New Hampshire, that caused many of the local residents to believe that they were being bombed by Japanese warplanes. Their fear was triggered by Japan's sneak attack on United States military installations at Pearl Harbor in Hawaii on December 7, 1941. This attack left our Pacific Fleet severely crippled, and 2,330 dead and 1,145 wounded.

The problem was compounded three days later when Japan's Axis partners, Germany and Italy, also declared war on us so that our Country was completely drawn into World War II. Militarily unprepared for such an undertaking, and extremely vulnerable to further Japanese air strikes, alarmed Americans developed a bad case of war jitters.

These jitters were momentarily unleashed locally when three tremendous explosions occurred on Mt. Waternomee exactly five weeks after Pearl Harbor. The houses in both Lincoln and North Woodstock shook, windows rattled, and cups and saucers danced on kitchen shelves. As a matter or record, the shock waves from the blasts were so powerful that they were actually felt twenty-two miles to the south in the small college town of Plymouth.

This frightening experience was set in motion eight hours earlier when a B-18 twin-engine bomber took off from Westover Field in Chicopee Falls, Massachusetts. With a flying range of 2100 miles, the bomb-laden aircraft headed out over the Atlantic Ocean on an anti-submarine patrol that would bring it just off the coast of Newfoundland. German submarines were known to frequent the shipping lanes there with the intent of torpedoing Allied convoys carrying badly needed war materials to the British Isles and Russia.

It was while on the return flight that the aircraft first encountered the blinding snow squalls and drastic wind changes just off the New Jersey coast that were to throw it so far off course. Part of the dilemma was also caused by the navigator's inability to compute the drift factor. Added to this was the fact that the officers aboard the plane were not experienced in handling a B-18. Actually, they were trained B-24 personnel. In the final analysis, all seven men aboard the plane were a "borrowed" crew thrown together for this one particular assignment.

1st Lt. Anthony Benvenuto of Brooklyn, New York, was the pilot, 2nd Lt. Woodrow Kantner of Crawford, New Jersey, was co-pilot, and 2nd Lt. Fletcher Craig of Gridley, California, was the navigator. Backing them as "fill-ins," PFC Robert Picard of Springfield, Massachusetts, was a machine gunner, Pvt. Richard Chubb of North Billerica, Massachusetts, was the aircraft mechanic, Pvt. Raymond Lawrence of Worcester, Massachusetts, was another gunner, and Pvt. Noah Philipps of Fayetteville, Arkansas, was bombardier.

Though the plane was completely enveloped by snow squalls, Lt. Benvenuto continued to maintain a surveillance altitude of 4,000 feet. It was his belief that they were still over the Atlantic Ocean. With each passing minute, however, Lt. Craig grew more and more uncertain as to just where they were. When a momentary break in the clouds revealed the lights of a city below them, all three men believed they were passing over Providence, Rhode Island. Acting on that assumption, Craig handed Benvenuto the coordinates that would bring them over Westover Field.

Now flying a northwesterly course, the plane grew harder to han-

The Night the Bomber Crashed   227

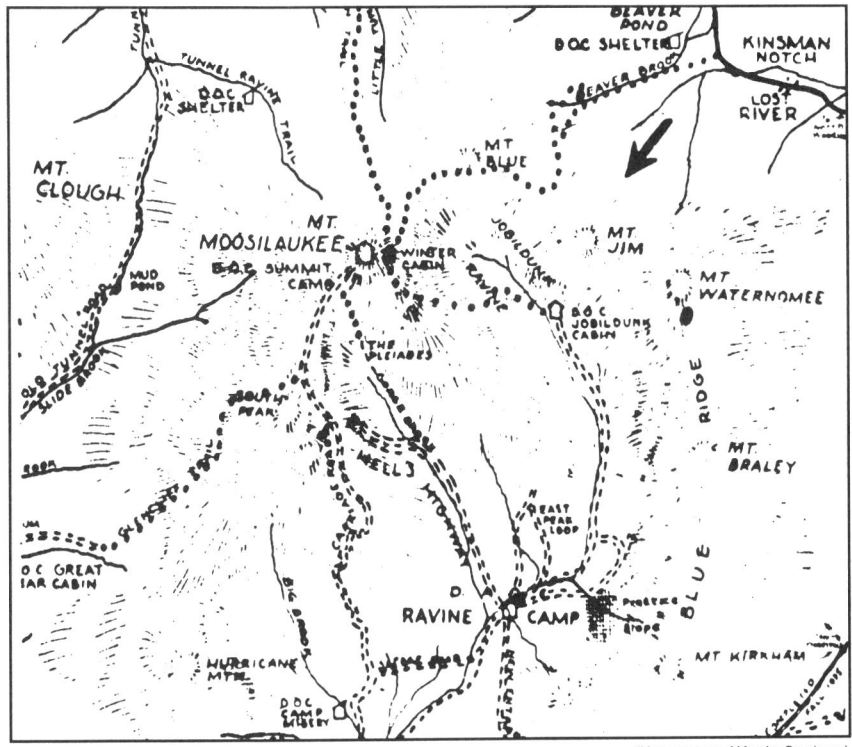

(Map courtesy of Marsha Cousineau)

This map of the rugged region near North Woodstock, N.H., showing where the B-18 crashed, was run on the front page of the Manchester Union on Thursday morning, January 15, 1942. The arrow erroneously points to Mt. Jim, the third highest peak of the Mt. Moosilauke group where the accident was originally thought to have occurred. The black dot beneath Mt. Watemomee shows the true location of the tragedy.

dle as the wind turbulence became more severe and the outside temperature plummeted. When ice began forming on the wings, Lt. Kantner noticed that the cockpit temperature was only 14 degrees.

As the aircraft became more unstable, both men had to fight the controls. Before long, drenched with sweat and fighting fatigue, Lt. Kantner desperately began twisting the overhead radio dial in an attempt to establish a fix on their location. Not knowing how far off course they were, he was dialing the wrong frequency.

With the ice buildup growing worse, airspeed dropped to 160 miles per hour. Only the carburetor heat control kept the two 1000-horsepower engines running. In an attempt to lessen the icing problem, Lt. Benvenuto dropped the plane to 3800 feet. By doing so, he put them on a collision course with the mountains that lay directly ahead.

As it turned out, the city they had seen earlier was not Providence, Rhode Island. It was Concord, New Hampshire!

Minutes before the crash, Lt. Craig stepped into the cockpit. Bent over between Benvenuto and Kantner, he nervously stared out the windshield for signs of a landmark. Distracted by his presence, Kantner snapped at him, "For God's sake, Craig, go back and sit down!"

No sooner had Kantner given the order when he spotted a white, tree-studded landscape coming at them fast. "My God," he thought, "it's a mountain." Instantly he yanked back on the control column and kicked right rudder. As the ice-laden aircraft lifted its nose and turned, it hit a downdraft. Instantly it fell into a stall.

Shearing off treetops, the 27,000-pound airplane pancaked its way through deep snow. As it smashed through a thick growth of trees, one wing was ripped off by a yellow birch. Part of the other wing also disappeared. Traveling over a distance of seventy yards, the body of the aircraft split open before it finally ground to a stop and settled in the snow.

While the wind howled furiously over and through the wreckage, high octane fuel began dripping on the one remaining engine. Minutes later a fire erupted, and it rapidly worked its way through the fuselage. Seemed possessed of a deadly intent, it headed straight toward the 300-pound bombs!

Minutes before the crash occurred, ten miles down in the Pemigewasset Valley in the small papermill town of Lincoln, Dr. Allan Handy was sitting in the lobby of the Lincoln Hotel playing bridge with friends. Downstairs in the local beer parlor, "Slim" Rogers, a Parker-Young Company mill worker, had just punched in "Good Night, Irene" six times on the 5-cent jukebox to get back at the ill-tempered bartender. Returning to his table, Rogers chuckled and told his companions, "There, that'll give the old Coot somethin' to really hollar about."

As the song repeated itself, the beer drinkers began stomping their feet in time with the music. Shortly after 7:45 p.m. the large three-story building began trembling. Thinking the disturbance was

The Night the Bomber Crashed

The B-18 co-pilot, Woodrow Kantner, is seen third from left. His navigator, Fletcher Craig, is sitting next to him wearing sunglasses. They are pictured on a fishing trip in Los Angeles, California, on November 28, 1941. As late as March of 1989 Kantner was unsuccessful in determining why Craig was no longer corresponding with him.

caused by the foot stomping, the bartender hollered over the shaking beer mugs, "If you Ya Hoos don't knock it off I'll pull the plug on the jukebox!"

His anger soon turned to amazement as his customers hurried outdoors to track down the cause of the tremor.

Upstairs the card game broke up when a glowing fire on a mountaintop to the west drew the players to the lobby's front window. Dr. Handy was still looking at it when a telephone call brought word that an Army bomber had crashed near Mt. Moosilauke.

Excusing himself, the young physician drove to his house and hurriedly changed into ski clothes. Before heading out to his car, he stuffed bandages into his parka and checked the painkillers in his black bag. He had a feeling that it was going to be a very long night.

Shortly after 7:40 Sherman Adams left his Pollard Road home to attend neglected duties at his office on Main Street. As the town's Representative to the New Hampshire Legislature, and head of the Parker-Young Company's Timberland Department, he often found himself juggling his workload. While driving down Main Street through the lightly falling snow, he spotted the glow of a fire in the vicinity of the Dartmouth Outing Club Summit Camp on

The day following his heroic participation in the rescue of the five injured airmen on Mt. Waternomee, Paul Dovholuk left for military service. Following rigorous training at Jump School at Fort Benning, Georgia, he was assigned to the 502nd Parachute Regiment of the 101st Airborne Division. For outstanding bravery, he was promoted on the battlefield to second lieutenant. He was awarded the Bronze Star with cluster for bravery, the French Croix de Guerre, Belgian Crois de Guerre and Dutch Lanyard. Severely wounded, he was discharged in 1948 with the rank of captain.

(Photo courtesy of Paul Dovholuk)

Mt. Moosilauke.

Upon arriving at his office he immediately telephoned Hans Paschen, General Manager of the Club. After reporting the fire to him, Adams drove to the home of Charles Doherty, a Lincoln selectman. Together they rode to the Sawyer Highway off Lost River Road to investigate the situation.

In the meantime, from Hanover Paschen telephoned the Dartmouth Outing Club Ravine Camp which was located near the Summit Camp. He learned that the fire was a short distance off to the east, possibly on desolate Mt. Waternomee. His curiosity aroused, he next telephoned the North Woodstock Fire Department. The dispatcher told him that there was not only a fire on Mt. Waternomee, but that explosions had also taken place.

Acting on this information, Paschen contacted his Assistant Manager, John Rand, and arranged to meet him in North Woodstock no later than 11:15. He also enlisted the help of three undergraduate students—David Sills '42, Robert White '42, and Richard Backus '44, who were experienced mountain climbers.

(Photo courtesy of Charles Harrington)

This is a rare photo of the fire-destroyed engine. It was taken in the debris field only days after the crash occurred. The flames started when fuel leaked on to the hot engine. They then spread quickly to the bombs. In the explosions that followed, the aircraft was blown apart.

He hoped that he wasn't initiating a wild goose chase.

Back in Lincoln, a short distance from the hotel, a social was being held at the high school for the benefit of the Senior Play ticket selling winners. The students in attendance were enjoying a mock wedding in the gymnasium when the building began shaking. Several of them rushed outside accompanied by Miss Esther Cooper, the domestic science teacher. Seeing a brilliant flash of light in the night sky, she pointed it out to them. In the group, Murray Clark, 14, looked on with more than just idle curiosity.

In North Woodstock, just before the tragedy occurred, Mrs. Francianna Huot stepped off her porch to drive uptown when she was suddenly startled by the roar of a low-flying aircraft. Looking up through the snowy overcast, she saw a large American twin-engine bomber passing directly over her house. A feeling of dread seized her as she realized that it was on a collision course with the mountains just ahead. Minutes later she felt the concussions from a tremendous explosion. Shaking nervously, she quickly drove to Police Chief William Ward's house. Wiping tears from her eyes, she reported the cause of the explosion to him.

Before she was finished, another explosion followed.

At North Woodstock's community building known as "Donna Ross Hall," a basketball game was in progress. As word of Mrs. Huot's experience traveled through the crowd, Paul Curtis, a Laconia Evening Citizen newspaper boy, learned why the building had just shook. Leaving the game, he ran home to tell his parents. On hearing the news, his father, Wilfred Curtis, immediately went upstairs to change into winter clothes.

With his mother's permission, young Curtis telephoned the night editor of the Laconia newspaper. When he answered the phone, Curtis exclaimed, "I thought you should know a bomber crashed into a mountain here! I heard there were three explosions. Honest, they rocked the whole town!"

At that moment Russell Hilliard, State Director of Aeronautics, was in Laconia attending a Civil Air Patrol meeting. Partly as a result of Curtis' call, State Police officers were sent to notify him of the accident which had also been corroborated by other sources. As soon as he could, Hilliard broke away from the meeting and departed for North Woodstock accompanied by Gardner Mills, a local pilot.

Just prior to Curtis' call, State Police and the U.S. Forest Service had been alerted to the possibility of such a crash by "Army Flash" messages recorded at 7:43 and 7:45 p.m. at the Regional Filter Center in Boston. The Campton Observation Post manned by Fred Nowe was credited with being the first to report spotting the errant aircraft and the subsequent crash. It was not until fifteen minutes later that "Cy" Stewart, who was in charge of the Lincoln Post, sent in his Army Flash message which verified explosions had occurred in the North Woodstock area.

After dropping Doherty off where a small crowd had already gathered along the Sawyer Highway, Sherman Adams returned to his office. Minutes after talking with Cy Stewart, he got a call from Charles Mead, District Ranger for the White Mountain National Forest. Calling from Plymouth, Mead asked, "Mr. Adams, what can be done by way of organizing a search party to assist possible survivors?"

Adams replied, "Chet, I'm afraid the chance of anyone remaining alive following those explosions is very remote."

Despite this observation the two men began formulating rescue

(Photo courtesy of Dr. Robert Averill, Dartmouth '72)

Despite the long passage of time since the crash occurred in the early evening of January 14, 1942, much of the aircraft debris on Mt. Waternomee makes it look as though the tragedy happened only yesterday. Seen are the remains of an almost complete wing and a mangled portion of the cockpit.

plans. Mead told Adams he'd meet him on the Sawyer Highway at 10:00 with other forestry personnel, toboggans, first aid equipment, and two-way radios. He assured him that Forest Supervisor C.L. Graham had authorized full forestry participation in the undertaking that lay ahead.

Back at the Sawyer Highway, over the objections of state police officers sent there to prevent unauthorized entry to the crash site, twelve members of a local search party entered the woods at 8:15. Among them were Neil McInnis, Paul Dovholuk, Robert Kelley, Everett Kinne and Charles Doherty.

As McInnis' group progressed up the mountain, each of the men took turns breaking trail. During the ascent blowdown caused by the 1938 hurricane proved to be a chronic problem. At one point a member of the party found himself chest deep in snow when he dropped down between two fallen trees.

With the ascent growing steeper, and the snow depth increasing, exhaustion began to affect the older men. Rest stops became more frequent. Going into the third mile the group began shouting "Hello! Hello!" hoping for a return response. Periodically they stopped and listened for any replies that might be heard over the roaring mountain winds.

Finally, a mile from the crash site their efforts unexpectedly produced a distant shout. The plaintive cry of "Help! Help!" drifted down to them. Due to the wind-whipped snow, however, their flashlights and oil lanterns lacked distance. Not knowing what they were about to face, they stopped in their tracks. In nervous silence they listened. Finally one of the men asked, "Did any of you guys bring a gun?" Uneasy laughter broke the tension and they moved on.

After the group traversed a snow-filled gully, the cries reaching them grew louder. Then, like ghostly apparitions, three airmen in blood-stained flying gear staggered into sight. As they stumbled nearer, one behind the other, it was evident that they were in deep shock. The lead airman, Lt. Fletcher Craig, the navigator, appeared to be the least seriously injured. He had only facial lacerations and bruises, while the co-pilot, Lt. Woodrow Kantner, not only had similar cuts but also a broken forearm and ankle. Private Richard Chubb, the mechanic, had an ugly cut over his left eye, his front teeth were missing, and his jaw was badly fractured.

Thinking that he was the sole survivor, Chubb was completely unaware that Craig and Kantner were ahead of him during his trek down the mountain. All that kept him going was the thought that he had to get help for his fellow crew members.

While one party member tied a bandanna over Chubb's eye wound, McInnis sat down in the snow and removed his boots and socks. He then pulled the heavy socks over the young airman's cold feet.

As members of the rescue party examined Kantner, he told them, "From the crash site Craig and I could see lights down in the valley. We struck off toward them, hoping to get help for the rest of the crew. When I was walking away from the plane, it blew up and a large piece hit me in the shoulder blade. Maybe that's when my arm got broken."

Shaking his head, he added, "After the plane blew up, I doubt that anyone up there could still be alive." Then, looking around at the hostile environment surrounding him, he asked, "Where are we, anyway?"

Told that he was in North Woodstock, New Hampshire, he said, "Until I saw the mountain I thought we were out over the ocean

Sweat-soaked following the rugged climb up Mt. Waternomee, Woodrow Kantner and his wife Barbara examine the engine that escaped the explosions. This photo, taken in mid-August of 1981, shows how well preserved the engine looked nearly forty years after the tragic incident.

near Boston on an anti-submarine patrol. We were all right until we hit the blizzard off the New Jersey coast. I guess our compasses got messed up. Turning to Craig, he said, "Do you realize we were at least 150 miles off course?"

Now anxious to continue on, Dovholuk, Kelley, and Kinne separated from the group and continued the climb by themselves. Not long after their departure, Dr. Handy arrived and administered first aid to the three airmen. He gave each of them painkillers, and he adjusted Chubb's makeshift bandage which had fallen over both eyes. He also advised McInnis to put Kantner on a toboggan as soon as possible. He then moved on, hoping to catch up to the three men.

Though they were making good time, with only one flashlight and a kerosene lantern between them Dovholuk, Kelley and Kinne sometimes lost the trail made by the airmen. Increasing winds and the growing snow squall occasionally obliterated the trail altogether.

During the fifth mile of the ascent another cry for help reached them. Moving in the direction of the sound, they came across the pilot, Lt. Benvenuto. Having crawled two-hundred yards from the wreckage, he was lying there with a broken back. Then, unexpectedly, over the eerie creaking sounds coming from the remains of the bomber they heard another cry for help. Unbelievably, someone else was still alive at least seventy-five feet closer to the wreck.

In a weakened voice Lt. Benvenuto warned the men, "Don't get too near the wreckage. There's still plenty of hot stuff that hasn't gone off yet."

With Kelley and Kinne showing no signs of movement, Dovholuk made the decision to go to the injured man's assistance. Taking the flashlight, he carefully walked around splintered trees and smoldering metal. Arriving at the site where the young man was lying, Dovholuk could see that he was in deep pain and nearly frozen to death. Even worse, his left leg was wrapped around a small tree.

Bending over him, Dovholuk said in a gentle voice, "I'm here to help you. My name's Paul Dovholuk. I'm going to try to straighten your leg out so you'll be more comfortable."

As the young man nodded feebly, Dovholuk knelt down and very slowly worked the leg into a normal position. When he was finished, he said, "I know that hurt, but it looks to me like you've got what it takes to make it."

Attempting a smile as he agreed the airman said quietly, "I'm PFC Robert Picard, a gunner. After I crawled out of the burning plane, I dragged myself as far as here when it exploded. I don't know why, but my head hurts worse than my leg."

Wincing, Dovholuk wondered what else he could do for Picard. Noticing the he had lost his hat and gloves, he took off his own hat and mittens and gave them to him to put on. Minutes later Ralph Goodwin, a Parker-Young acid plant worker, appeared out of nowhere.

Recognizing that the injured men needed protection from the cold, he soon had two fires roaring. One beside each of them. Working with him, Dovholuk was amazed by the man's efficiency in getting them started. Especially against such a strong wind.

Satisfied that his purpose there was finished, Goodwin said good-bye and headed back down the mountain to let ascending rescue parties know what to expect.

Some time after Goodwin's departure, Dr. Handy came up over the rise. While Dovholuk, Kelley, and Kinne fanned smoke and flying sparks away from the airmen's faces, he gave them badly needed medical help. After finishing with Benvenuto, he improvised splints for Picard's leg. When he was done he stayed close to the heat, periodically checking on each of them.

Before long he had to supply Dovholuk, Kelley, and Kinne with bandages so they could wipe their smoked-filled eyes and noses.

While this was going on, halfway down the mountain Sherman Adams' group encountered the men assisting Kantner, Craig, and Chubb. They were first alerted to their approach when they heard a voice above them ask, "How much further?"

It was now 12:30 a.m.

Ralph Goodwin, who was in the process of passing the slow-moving group, apprised Adams of the situation on the mountain. He also noted that two of the crewmen were missing and believed to be dead.

Now having definite information to work with, Adams and the forestry personnel revised rescue plans accordingly. Using one of the portable radios, Ranger Mead relayed an updated report to Ranger Tom McConkey at the base station. At Adam's request, he asked to have state police dispatched to a nearby lumber camp to get at least thirty woodsmen for the purpose of clearing the trail of brush and blowdown. Though it would be time consuming, it was felt this was the only way the two airmen could be tobogganed out.

Adams also requested that his wife Rachel organize the members of her local Red Cross chapter so they would be at the base to serve lunch and coffee as the rescue crews returned.

Hans Paschen, noticing that some of the men in the descending group were close to exhaustion, assigned his Dartmouth Outing Club assistant, John Rand, to the task of helping get Kantner down the mountain. Rand himself was later relieved of the duty by the arrival of Henry Cousineau, a Parker-Young employee who had once worked on the mountain as a member of the Civilian Conservation Corps during the '30s. Having just come off the night shift, Cousineau rushed to the scene to be of assistance.

This group never reached the highway until 2:00. A half-mile from their destination, Kantner's shock began wearing off. As the pain from his broken limbs became unbearable, he asked to be set down in the snow. While sitting there, he expressed his frustrations by saying, "To hell with it."

Understandably, he completed the last half mile on a toboggan.

Meanwhile, Adams decided to break away from the crew pulling the heavily loaded toboggan. Needing several men to help him backpack badly needed supplies to the crash site, he selected Rangers Mead and Chester Kinney of Littleton, Parker-Young forester Robert Sinclair, and a small handful of locals for the undertaking.

Once underway, they moved at a pace more to his liking.

During the difficult ascent, Ranger Mead radioed their progress to the base every half hour. At 3:00 he finally reported that they had reached the scene.

After visiting with the airmen, Adams conferred with Dr. Handy about removing them. While waiting for the toboggans, he assisted Handy in treating them with chemical heating packs which his group had carried in.

As Lt. Benvenuto was being covered with U.S. Forest Service blankets, he again issued the warning about unexploded bombs. Radioing the base, Mead passed on the warning. "Under no circumstances," he emphasized, "are any unauthorized personnel to be allowed near the wreckage."

Adams' group now decided that the search for the missing men would be left strictly up to the Army.

By the time the forest guards and the Dartmouth Outing Club members had arrived with both the supplies and the toboggans, the Parker-Young woodsmen had almost completed swamping the trail. Dr. Handy supervised the slightest movement of the two airmen. He had Picard positioned headfirst to keep tension off his leg during the descent. At 4:00 the rescuers prepared to leave the mountain.

It would take them six hours to reach the ambulances waiting at the base.

Due to the treacherous terrain, it was sometimes impossible to proceed at more than a quarter-of-a-mile an hour. The entire five-mile descent was extremely painful for both men. Throughout the ordeal, Paul Dovholuk remained at Picard's side comforting him.

Staying behind, Rangers Mead and Kinney remained at the

The Night the Bomber Crashed 239

(Photo courtesy of Gary Remal)

The co-pilot at the time of the B-18 crash, Woodrow Kantner, left, examines the remains of the cockpit with his host, North Woodstock resident Charles Harrington who was responsible for his return to the crash site.

crash site with a Parker-Young crew. They stood guard over the wreckage until Army authorities relieved them that afternoon.

Dr. Handy, delayed by woodsmen needing medical help, did not reach his car until after the ambulances had taken Benvenuto and Picard to the Lincoln Hospital rather than to the larger one at Plymouth where he planned to set up their treatment.

Arriving at the highway around 10:00, the airmen and the toboggan crews were greeted by Army personnel, state police, Foresters, reporters, and interested onlookers. On duty since 3:30, Mrs. Adams' group had coffee and sandwiches waiting for them.

As Miss Mina Kelley served a toboggan crew member a cup of coffee, she asked him how badly damaged the plane was. Without mincing words, he replied, "I'm sorry to say, it's scattered all over hell."

The youngest volunteer coming out of the woods that morning was Murray Clark, 14, the boy who had been at the high school social the night before. He was the son of Florence and Edward Clark, owners of Clark's Trading Post in Lincoln. Ironically, ten years to the day, his mother had ascended Mt. Washington with a sled-dog team and still held the record for being the only woman to do so.

Just before the ambulances departed, Lt. Benvenuto sadly told Army officers, "I know I plotted a course in which there were no mountains."

Sometime later an exhausted Dr. Handy drove down Route 3 toward Plymouth. Along the way he fell asleep at the wheel. Fortunately a large snowbank blunted the impact when his car left the road. Unhurt, he backed out to the highway and continued on to the hospital.

Arriving in a disheveled condition, he was shocked to learn none of the injured men were there. Hurrying back to Lincoln, he found all five in the small upstairs hospital rooms ordinarily occupied by lumberjacks and papermill workers.

Back at the Sawyer Highway the next stage of the drama had already begun. The Army contingent carrying heavy equipment up the mountain was followed by a bomb expert named Howard Schlansker. He was a lieutenant from the Ordnance Unit at Grenier Field in Manchester. His group handled the dynamite that was to be used in exploding any remaining bombs.

After relieving the forestry personnel and the Parker-Young crew, the search was begun for the missing airmen and live ordnance. Unexpectedly, a mill worker named Don Osgood was caught taking pictures at the crash site. From North Woodstock, he was just an amateur photographer influenced by the excitement. He had sneaked into the area knowing that it was "off limits." The adventure temporarily cost him his camera. Several months later he got it back.

Following Osgood's removal, the search continued under the direction of Major Clayton E. Hughes, a member of the Army Board of Inquiry. Assisting him was Lt. Harry Swan of the Accident Classification Committee.

Late that afternoon, while working through the wreck area

which covered over 250 yards, the badly charred remains of the airmen were found in a section of the bomber that had been blown away from the fuselage during the explosions.

Radioing the base, Hughes reported the find and requested civilian assistance for the removal of the bodies. Among the local volunteers helping with the grisly task were Joe Mulleavey, Clifford Gagnon, and James Walsh.

That same afternoon Captain Frank R. Fleming, who was in charge of a convoy of ambulances from Grenier Field, parked his vehicles in front of the Lincoln Hospital. Conferring with Dr. Handy, and also with Dr. Betts Copenhaver of North Woodstock, he made the decision to transfer four of the airmen to the base hospital. Only PFC Picard was left behind due to his extremely unstable condition.

Prior to leaving, Fleming sent an ambulance to the Sawyer Highway to await the arrival of the bodies.

After the remains of the airmen were brought out at 9:30 p.m., they were examined by Dr. Leon Orton, Grafton County Medical Referee. When he was finished, the bodies were driven straight to their home base at Chicopee Falls, Massachusetts.

That night Major Hughes, Lt. Swan, and Lt. Schlansker, along with the Ordnance Unit, spent an uncomfortable night on the mountain. With the temperature dropping to 25 degrees below zero, many of the soldiers later complained that it was the worst experience they ever had.

The next morning a 300-pound demolition bomb was found. Since it was buried deep in the snow, Lt. Schlansker supervised the shoveling. He knew the bomb could explode without warning.

Once the bomb was fully exposed, Schlansker carefully packed dynamite around it. Ordering all the men to hide at a safe distance behind trees, he set the charge off. To his dismay it only split the bomb casing. He then had the very dangerous job of packing more dynamite.

This time the bomb exploded with a cataclysmic roar, sending pieces of flying metal dangerously close to several of the concealed men.

In addition to destroying the bomb, the group had another top priority assignment on the mountain. It was to find the Norden

Bombsight and to retrieve any of it that was left.

Developed in the United States in 1930 by Carl L. Norden and Theodore H. Barth, this highly sophisticated instrument was sought after by the enemy powers. It was so top secret that it was not patented until two years after the war ended.

Following the retrieval of the bombsight that afternoon, Major Hughes officially abandoned the crash area. Withdrawing all military personnel, he later met with the reporters waiting for him at the highway. Asked to describe the crash, he said, "It was the worst I have ever investigated. With the plane blown up beyond all recognition, the wreckage gave absolutely no indication it once had been a bomber."

Concerning the location of the tragedy, he observed, "It is without a doubt one of the most inaccessible and rugged spots where it could ever have happened."

Addressing the finding of the bomb, he also stated that live hand grenades had been found. Emphasizing that there really was nothing of value left up there, he warned, "The curious might pay a horrible price if they prowl around the wreckage."

Concluding the interview, he confessed he was baffled by the 'miracle' of the five men escaping death. Not only during the crash itself, but also from the fire and explosions that quickly followed.

That same day PFC Picard's condition showed signs of stabilizing. When he learned that Paul Dovholuk was downstairs being debriefed by Army officers, he sent word that he wanted to see him.

During their brief visit, Picard expressed his gratitude to Dovholuk for saving his life. He also remarked, "I understand you're going in the service tomorrow." Dovholuk nodded that he was. Picard asked, "What branch?"

Smiling, Dovholuk told him, "The paratroopers."

"Oh, no," Picard exclaimed, "that's like committing suicide!"

After shaking hands with him, Dovholuk wished him well and left. That was the last time they ever saw one another.

The next day at the Grenier Field base hospital Lt. Kantner underwent another shock. He learned that the TWA Douglas Sky Club transport he was supposed to be on for a return to his home base in California had crashed thirty miles southwest of Las Vegas, Nevada, on Table Rock Mountain. Fifteen Ferry Command pilots

On July 3rd, 1992, a Fiftieth Anniversary Commemorative observance of the B-18 tragedy was held at the Town Park in Lincoln just across the street from the old Lincoln Hospital. Standing with his back to the camera, Dr. Allan Handy is seen sharing his special memories of the rescue with Richard Chubb, Paul Dovholuk, and Woodrow Kantner. Murray Clark, the youngest of the rescuers, served as the program's master of ceremonies. A beautifully prepared proclamation from Governor Judd Gregg and a congratulatory letter from President George Bush were among the highlights of the occasion.

(Floyd W. Ramsey Photo)

aboard it were killed. Other victims included the movie actress Carole Lombard, the wife of screen idol Clark Gable, her mother, and Otto Winkler, a Metro-Goldwyn-Mayer publicity agent.

The irony behind the tragedy didn't escape Kantner. He realized that if he hadn't been in the New Hampshire accident, he would have lost his life two days later.

The following week, since Picard now remained stable, he was also transferred to Grenier Field. As his ambulance pulled away from the Lincoln Hospital, one of the medics shouted to Dr. Handy, "You did O.K., Doc!"

Later Dr. Handy learned that many of Picard's baffling symptoms were part of a condition called "Bomb Blast Syndrome" which included multiple hemorrhages in many organs.

The years passed. World War II ended with the signing of a formal surrender document aboard the U.S. battleship Missouri on September 2, 1945, in Tokyo Bay. At its conclusion the war turned out to be the most destructive one in the world's history. It had cost the lives of 16 million military personnel and 18 million civilians. These numbers include more than 400,000 Americans who made the ultimate sacrifice after responding to their Nation's call.

Of the the three local men who spent that long exhausting night on Mt. Waternomee, in 1994 only Paul Dovholuk is still alive. Now living in Littleton, New Hampshire, he emerged from the war as a highly decorated hero who served with the 101st Airborne Division. He is a member of an exclusive group known as "The Screaming

Eagles." A semi-retired contractor, he spends his winters in Ruskin, Florida.

Among the five airmen who survived the crash, Woodrow Kantner and Richard Chubb are both living. Kantner is a successful real estate developer living in Stuart, Florida. He has a first class marina complex there which he has named "Lost River" after the area in which the crash occurred. Chubb recently retired as a maintenance foreman at L.G. Hanscom Field, in Bedford, Massachusetts, and he and his wife Florence now live in Lake Havasu City, Arizona.

Following the war Kantner kept in touch with Fletcher Craig, who became a dentist in San Francisco, California. In recent years, however, his Christmas cards to Craig have gone unanswered. Whether or not he is still alive remains an unanswered question.

Kantner's, Chubb's, and Dovholuk's efforts to locate Robert Picard have been unsuccessful. After trying to find him through a national Disabled Veterans magazine, both Kantner and Chubb received an anonymous letter filled with religious messages. The return address simply said "B-18, Air Force." On the envelope was a California postmark, the state where Picard is believed to be a member of a religious commune.

Anthony Benvenuto did not survive the war. After recovering from his back injury, he was returned to active duty. He died when his B-24 was shot down over Asia.

Nearly forty years later, on August 14, 1981, Kantner returned to North Woodstock accompanied by his wife Barbara. The trip resulted from a letter published in the August 1980 issue of Air Classics magazine, a letter which was written by Charles Harrington which contained a brief account of the Mt. Waternomee crash.

Harrington, a North Woodstock barber with a strong interest in local history and vintage aircraft, was eventually contacted by Kantner and agreed to help guide him to the crash site.

Following Kantner's arrival, that weekend a hiking party consisting of a dozen people made the ascent to the wreckage. Leading them was Alvin Lee, a local man who had made the trip innumerable times. On reaching the crash area, Kantner was sweat-soaked and tired from the difficult climb. Looking around, both he and his wife were amazed at how much of the wreckage still remained.

The Night the Bomber Crashed

(Floyd W. Ramsey Photo)

Peter Gould, right, an executive at the Millfront Marketplace in Lincoln, served as program chairman for the Fiftieth Anniversary Commemorative observance held there on July 3, 1992. He looks on as Paul Dovholuk, Woodrow Kantner, Dr. Allan Handy, and Richard Chubb discuss the B-18 tragedy that drew them all together fifty years earlier.

Staring at the engine, Kantner said, "When you see something like this you wonder how the hell you got out alive." Then, remembering the fiery death of the fifteen Ferry Command pilots and Carole Lombard, he added, "I'm a realist. When it's your time to die, you do. This is a part of my life, and it was an important part. And I feel I'm alive now because of it."

The next year Kantner returned to Harrington's house. This time for a reunion with Richard Chubb. Though they didn't climb the mountain, they were drawn back together by the strong bond which had grown between them from that singular night in which they had experienced survival against overwhelming odds.

War Hero Remembered

Following his heroic participation in the rescue of the five wounded airmen on Mt. Waternomee, Paul Dovholuk entered military service on January 16, 1942.

After rigorous training at Jump School at Fort Benning, Georgia, he was eventually assigned to the 502nd Parachute Regiment of the 101st Airborne Division. Over the next twelve months he was promoted from private to first sergeant. At 23 he was the youngest man in his regiment to hold this rank. His men affectionately called him "the Old Man."

Paul Dovholuk

Shipped to England, the 101st Airborne trained for the D-Day invasion of Normandy. At 1:00 a.m. on June 6, 1944, Dovholuk's outfit parachuted right on top of the German army in France.

On June 9, during fierce fighting, Dovholuk learned that German soldiers were hiding behind a nearby church. Positioning his men for a deadly crossfire, Dovholuk climbed into the church steeple. Seeing a German scurrying for cover, he opened fire with his submachine gun. His men also opened up. Soon a German shouted, "Stop firing!"

Following the surrender, Dovholuk and his men learned that they had just captured 88 members of Hitler's Elite German Paratrooper Corps. For his part, Dovholuk received a Bronze Star and a battlefield commission. He was now promoted to second lieutenant.

His exploits in the D-Day Invasion later appeared in the September 9, 1944 issue of Saturday Evening Post. The article was entitled, "The Paratroopers of Purple Heart Lane." In this battle, sixty-five percent of Dovholuk's outfit were either killed, wounded, or captured.

Beginning on September 17, 1944, Dovholuk saw seventy consecutive days of combat in Holland. In October he was promoted to first lieutenant.

While fighting in the famous Battle of the Bulge, on December 22, 1944, he was seriously wounded. Following years of reconstructive surgery, he was discharged from the service in 1948 with the rank of captain.

As a result of his outstanding heroism he has received international recognition. Today he lives quietly and modestly on the Old Franconia Road in Littleton.

The Short Adventurous Life of Dr. Benjamin Ball

DESCRIBED AS A MAN of unfaltering courage and singular coolness of head in the face of extreme difficulty, Dr. Benjamin Lincoln Ball of Boston, Massachusetts, was about to prove the truth of that description as he stepped from the train in Gorham, New Hampshire, on Wednesday morning, October 24, 1855.

Following his return from Europe more than a year earlier, he dreamed of making an excursion to the White Mountains to compare some of the finest American scenery with that which he had seen while abroad. However, various engagements interfered with his plans for such a trip, and the season passed when it was safe to make such a journey that year. Then, as the following summer advanced and passed as well, his time was further taken up by preparations for the publication of his book, *Rambles in Eastern Asia*.

(Photo courtesy of Jean Palm, Randolph librarian)
Dr. Benjamin Lincoln Ball's miraculous escape from death on the summit of Mount Washington in October of 1855 was due in large measure to his medical training. In describing Ball's hairbreadth escape, the author, F. Allen Burt, wrote, "In all the history of Mount Washington there is no record of anybody else living through sixty hours of exposure there without food, drink or sleep while battling a winter storm with no shelter but an umbrella."

Early that October, while conversing with friends who had visited the White Mountains, he learned that even though it was late in the season the scenery there was still worth the visit. Accordingly, he resolved to go as soon as he possibly could.

As fate would have it, on the evening of October 22 while he was visiting at the house of a friend, he met the Reverend Thomas Starr King. King, who was well known for his love of the White Mountains, spoke to him of the grandeur and beauty of the scenery to be seen from the summit of Mount Washington. He also remarked that he himself would most certainly like to see the surrounding mountains in their gray costume of late autumn as well as their white robe of winter.

Agreeably impressed by King's remarks, Dr. Ball was now determined to visit the White Mountains immediately.

The next afternoon the sun shone clear and warm in Boston, and it held out the promise of continued fair weather. This was all Dr. Ball needed to call on his friend, Dr. A.B. Hall, to see if he wished to join him on his trip to the White Mountains. Unfortunately Dr. Hall's engagements prevented him from leaving Boston at that time. Consequently, Dr. Ball returned home with the resolve to go alone.

Picking up a small valise which he had already packed, he made haste to reach the Eastern Railroad Station in order to catch the 2:30 p.m. train north. Following his arrival in Portland, Maine, a little after dark, he was disappointed to learn that there were no trains to Gorham, New Hampshire, before the next day. Since he had no other choice, he rented a room for the night at the Commercial House.

The following morning he arose early only to learn that the day was wet, gloomy, and cold. His first impulse was to return to Boston, but then he decided to proceed on to Gorham on the chance that the sun would come out.

As Dr. Ball disembarked from the train shortly after 11:00 a.m. the rain continued to fall in torrents, and since the area was shrouded in fog, there were no mountains to be seen. Following the conductor to the Alpine House, he asked him, "Could you please tell me, just where are the White Mountains?"

"Oh," the conductor replied, pointing toward the front of the hotel, "they are off there seven or eight miles. You will not be able to see them short of the Glen House unless the fog clears away."

"Very well," Dr. Ball said, "I will go to them and endeavor to get a view of them. I thought before this, that if I succeeded in seeing them from this place, and the weather continued stormy, that I should return home."

Hiring a horse, at noon he set off for the Glen House with his valise in front of him and with his umbrella raised to shield him from the continuing downpour. Little did he realize how important that umbrella would be to him in the days just ahead.

Arriving at the Glen House, he observed that the mountains were still concealed by the dense fog. While housing the horse at the stable, he decided to stop for only a half hour and then to return to Gorham for the trip back to Boston.

In the months ahead he had every reason to wish that he had stuck by that decision.

On entering the hotel, Dr. Ball met the proprietor, Colonel Joseph M. Thompson. While standing by the fire drying his clothes, he asked him, "The mountains are not now to be seen, I presume?"

Thompson answered, "No sir, you will not probably be able to see them today. At all events, not till after the weather has cleared up."

When Thompson mentioned that a new road was presently being constructed that Ball might walk up, his dwindling interest was immediately rekindled. "The new road," he asked, "what is that?"

Thompson answered, "It is the carriage road which is being built by a New York company so that people may ride all the way up Mount Washington on a smooth Macadamized road to the summit."

"I suppose I can follow the road easily enough?" Dr. Ball replied.

Thompson said, "Oh, yes. There is no difficulty about that. You can see it from the window there. It crosses the bridge, and enters the woods a little beyond. If there was no fog it could be seen to the Camp House and the Ledge, which is as far as it extends at present."

Dr. Ball then asked, "What am I to understand by the Camp House? The Ledge, I presume, is a ledge of rocks?"

THOMAS STARR KING
(Photo courtesy of Jean Palm, Randolph librarian)
It was the Reverend Thomas Starr King's chance meeting with Dr. Ball in Boston, and their subsequent discussion of the beautiful view from the summit of Mount Washington, that sent the young physician hurrying off to the White Mountains the next day for the misadventure that almost cost him his life. King's book, THE WHITE HILLS, *was considered the best book ever written about the White Mountains for more than fifty years.*

Thompson told him, "The Camp House is a small one-story building for the use of the workmen on the road. It is about four miles from here, or about halfway to the summit. It is situated at the foot of the Ledge. The Ledge is a kind of high bluff with a steep and somewhat precipitous face. At one point a path leads up and over the top. This is called the bridle path and is the one used by visitors in making the ascent to the summit either in walking or on horseback."

Dr. Ball replied, "I think I will take a walk up the carriage road, and be satisfied with a survey of that."

By way of warning, Thompson told him, "I would by no means attempt to go to the summit. It is too late in the day. Besides, you could see nothing for the clouds."

Because the wind had now started blowing, before leaving the Glen House Dr. Ball exchanged his top hat for a cloth cap which he saw hanging in the room. And, since it was still raining, he also took along his umbrella.

Shortly after crossing the bridge he came upon the new road. Though he found the walking wet and rough, the pure cold air invigorated him. Walking quickly, in less than two hours he reached the Camp House. Without stopping, he went past it and scrambled up the Ledge. Reaching the top without too much difficulty, he still found the view limited by the fog. However, not one to admit defeat, he headed for the higher ground that he could see before him.

As he climbed higher, the cold wind penetrated his clothes and the rain formed a crust on the snow that continuously broke under his weight. Walking for an hour, he found it very tiring to continue stepping on the collapsing snow which now measured a depth of twelve inches. Not seeming to gain any distance, he turned to retrace his steps. As darkness closed in on him, he panicked a little and began running downhill.

Falling frequently, the darkness made it difficult for him to see his tracks. He made his way by feeling the indentures in the broken crust. Just as he began to fear that he had lost his way, the Ledge suddenly appeared beneath his feet.

Virtually sliding from one rock to another, he arrived at the Camp House completely encased in ice and chilled through from the cold. Admitted into the building by Mr. J.D. Myers, his coat was

The Short Adventurous Life of Dr. Benjamin Ball

(Photo courtesy of Jean Palm, Randolph librarian)

At the time that Dr. Ball arrived at the Glen House in October of 1855, Dolly Copp was selling her homespun linens and delicious homemade delicacies to Colonel Thompson for the comfort of his guests. Her two sons, Jeremiah and Nathaniel, also left the family farm that year to work as laborers on the construction of the Carriage Road.

immediately hung up to dry and his shoes were taken off and his stockings rung out. Given a dry pair, he then sat down and enjoyed the warmth of a blazing fire.

Following a welcome cup of hot coffee and a hearty supper, he accepted Mr. Myers' invitation to spend the night. However, as tired as he was, because his mind was so full of thoughts he spent the entire night listening to the wind howl and the rain pelt the roof. When the morning light appeared, he was still wide awake.

That morning, as he stood outside the Camp House with Mr. Myers, he saw that the rain had freed the bridle path of snow. Unfortunately this led him to believe that if nothing stood in his way he could easily reach the summit and be back at the Glen House by noon. In addition, he also thought he could then take the night train to Portland and be back in Boston no later than noon of the next day.

When he shared these thoughts with Mr. Myers, Myers proceeded to tell him of the tragedy that had occurred there just a month earlier.

Dr. Ball interrupted him asking, "I presume you are referring to Miss Lizzie Bourne?"

Myers replied, "Yes, Miss Bourne from Kennebunk. She was a beautiful lady. I saw the party when they passed here. They were all in such good spirits. I knew it was too late in the afternoon for them to go. I tried to prevail upon them to stop here overnight, but they were determined to go on. It was a sad sight when they brought her over the Ledge. To see her form so lifeless, and all so changed and sorrowful. I pitied the whole party from the bottom of my heart."

He concluded, "I later learned that she did not die from the cold, but from fatigue and general exhaustion. I believe they also said she had some difficulty of the chest. It seemed hard that they could not find the Summit House when they were so near to it."

In preparation for the ascent, Dr. Ball drank a bowl of coffee and ate lightly since he had little appetite. He also exchanged his shoes for a pair of Myers' stout thick boots which were much too large for him. And, since it continued to sprinkle, he took his umbrella along with a cane that Myers gave him as a present.

As he departed, Myers told him, "Should you see any bears in your way let me know and I will come up with my gun."

Ascending the Ledge with little fatigue, Dr. Ball reached the top of it within a half hour. From there he could see that the ground climbed gradually. Beyond a quarter of a mile, however, the landscape was obscured by misty clouds.

Starting upward, he was soon surprised to find the large footprints of a bear. The animal had apparently followed behind him during his descent the night before. Returning to the Ledge, he shouted this information down to Mr. Myers.

Returning to the climb, a mile further on he lost the path altogether as the snow depth mounted up to ten inches. He then recalled that he had heard that the mountain between the Camp House and the summit was made up of four peaks, and that Mount Washington constituted the fourth and last peak.

As he passed the first peak, his trek became more difficult. His feet broke through the crust at each step, and this caused a great deal of pain to his ankles. Occasionally his feet got caught between hidden rocks, and he sometimes experienced rough going in extricating them.

Whenever the way of his climb became too difficult he would retrace his steps or make a circuit until he found a way around the obstacle. At times, when the clouds broke away, he saw blue sky.

The Short Adventurous Life of Dr. Benjamin Ball

(Photo courtesy of Jean Palm, Randolph librarian)

In order to make the summit of Mount Washington safe and comfortable for the increasing numbers of tourists coming up the mountain, the first Summit House was built there in 1852 by Joseph S. Hall and Lucius M. Rosebrook. Hall later played a role in rescuing Dr. Benjamin Ball of Boston after he became lost there in a snowstorm in the late autumn of 1855.

Tragically, he allowed this encouragement to lure him on.

Somewhere between the second and third peaks the air turned disagreeably cold. The rain then turned from sleet to hail, and finally to heavy snow. When the wind increased, he closed his umbrella and used it as a walking stick along with the cane. Once, while disengaging his feet from among the rocks, he thought of turning back but at that moment the clouds opened again and drew him on.

As the landscape quickly became obscured once more by the clouds, he thought, "There is the third peak, and not more than fifteen minutes walk from here. I will keep along yet and reach it."

Struggling in that direction through the heavily falling snow, he again found that he could not travel in a straight line due to the rise and fall of the rocks. This misled him into believing that he was at least three-fourths of the way to the summit of Mount Washington. Whatever the situation, he felt certain that he could follow his footsteps back when he chose to return. He was pleased that he had taken the extra precaution of occasionally placing two stones together upon the tops of large rocks in the event that he had to use them as guide marks.

Leaving the top of the third peak, he made his way down a gradual slope. During the descent he noticed once again that the air was piercing cold. As the wind grew more violent, the snow whirled around him like a thick blanket. Convincing himself that the storm would dissipate within a half hour, he also believed that within that time he would reach the Summit House where he would find comfortable shelter from the storm.

Walking as fast as his weary limbs would carry him, he climbed piles of craggy rocks until he found himself on more regular rising ground. It was at this point that he finally noticed his feet, hands, and face ached from a cold air that he estimated to be not less than ten degrees below zero. Despite his discomfort he pressed on, going first in one direction and then another as he was buffeted about by the ferocity of the storm.

Adding to the Lizzie Bourne tragedy on the summit of Mount Washington was the fact that she was only one hundred yards from the shelter of the Tip Top House at the time of her death. Taking this experience, and his own into consideration, Dr. Ball later wrote, "I am convinced that the only safe way to visit Mount Washington is to take a guide, and the unsafe way is to go without one."

As the day wore on he found it necessary to stop, face away from the wind, and thrash his arms around himself in order to restore some warmth to his body. Because his hands were now swollen, he sought to protect them by alternately placing them in his pockets. And because he was more and more being thrown to the ground by the force of the wind, in order to have the use of his hands he tied the umbrella to a button on his coat.

As he secured the umbrella, he concluded that this was the toughest storm that he had ever encountered, and that the cold was the most severe he had yet endured.

As he toiled on he experienced an unusual pain in the bones of his face. Placing a hand to his face, he found that it was totally encased in ice. On further inspection he also discovered that a row of icicles two inches in length had formed around the visor of his cap. His eyelashes were also riddled with ice, and he frequently had to remove it in order to see.

To fortify his flagging spirit he told himself, "The summit must be near. I will not turn back yet. At the Summit House I can make myself comfortable. The storm is too violent to continue long, especially so early in the season as October."

Facing into the wind, he shouted, "I will still try for the Summit House!"

Struggling on with the hope that he was on some part of the fourth peak, he found that with each step forward often there were several steps lost backward. Also, the intensity of the storm appeared to increase. Sheets of snow now descended on him in hard crystallized grains that struck his eyes with painful intensity.

At length he suddenly came upon comparatively level ground. With his whole frame shaking from the debilitating cold he cried out, "Mount Washington at last! And here is the summit!"

His feeling of victory was shortlived. The storm grew more violent than ever.

Continuing on with the rise of the land as his only guide, at length he saw a dark shape ahead of him. Thinking it was the Summit House, after suffering several falls he succeeded in reaching it. He was disappointed to learn that it was nothing more than a large rock.

As he groped in different directions, the cold grew even more intense and his breathing became extremely labored. He finally concluded that he had to descend. When he attempted to follow his tracks back, though, he discovered that they were nowhere to be found. By chance he happened upon one of the stakes which marked the route of the Carriage Road. When he attempted to follow succeeding stakes downward, in time he lost them altogether in a thick patch of stunted brushwood.

While searching for others in the deep snow, he was soon startled by the realization that night was coming on. Forced to face the fact that he was hopelessly lost, he was now determined to continue downward even though he did not know which side of the mountain he was on.

While hurrying over and around the rocks, the violent wind at

(Photo courtesy of Jean Palm, Randolph librarian)

A modest wooden marker and a track-side cairn of weathered stones still mark the spot today where 23-year-old Elizabeth Greene Bourne of Kennebunk, Maine, tragically died during her climb to the summit of Mount Washington on September 13, 1885, just one month prior to Dr. Ball's horrendous experience there. Today she is remembered as the first person to perish on the summit.

times drove him forward. When he stopped for a moment of reflection, he cried, "My God! Am I to pass the night here?"

Exhausted and trembling from the cold, he began to wonder if he was going to survive. Then a sudden gust of wind threw him to the ground. Springing back up, he looked around for anything that would give him shelter. Stepping onto a flat rock, he saw a small recess between it and a patch of low firs. Detaching his umbrella, he opened it and then thrust a hand into the snow looking for something that he could attach it to. He came in contact with a strong upturned root. Resting the handle of the umbrella against it, he fastened it to the root with the cord tied to his coat button.

Following a brief rest, he set to work pulling up bushes. He piled them on the umbrella to protect it from the wind. Next he battened in the sides of his little camp with crusts of snow, and with the tops of small firs that he struggled to twist off. The work was slow and painful, but was somewhat successful despite the fact that he could not use his penknife because of the condition of his fingers.

Then he next attempted to build a fire using paper from his wallet. He knew that ten-dollar bills were among the papers he burned. When his matches were nearly exhausted he quit because the wood would not kindle.

Having done all he could, he dragged himself under the umbrella. He was now prepared to spend the night shivering and chattering five thousand feet above any human habitation.

During the long night the storm continued to howl down the mountain with such violence that he often clutched the handle of the umbrella for fear that his only form of shelter would be blown away. And, to prevent sleep, he took strained positions that would force him to stay awake. First he leaned on one elbow, and then on another. Next he changed from side to side, and then he would bend forward and then backward.

To keep his mind active and alert, he thought of the Summit House, the comforts of the Camp House, his room at the Glen House and the accommodations available at the Alpine House where other beds awaited him. Then he thought of each member of his family, and of all his friends and acquaintances. He knew that each of them would offer him a place to stay could they but be made aware of his exposed situation.

In this manner he survived into the second day, which was Friday, October 26.

As the first rays of the morning light found their way beneath his umbrella, he was surprised that the night had passed as quickly as it did. When he attempted to move out from under the umbrella, he found that both his feet and hands were "more or less frozen." This forced him to creep out into the open on his hands and knees.

Supporting himself by placing his hands on the flat rock, for a long period of time he remained there stamping his feet in order to get the circulation restored so that he could walk. Once this was accomplished, he ascended the slope a short distance to try and determine the direction he wanted to take.

Though the snowstorm had stopped for the moment, the cold wind still blew hard against him and low clouds limited his view. Finding himself standing near the brush patch where he had lost the road stakes, he hoped that he could find where they led and to be able to follow them. Toward that end he once again fastened the umbrella to his coat, and with the aid of his cane he began a lengthy search.

Failing to find any other stakes, throughout that day he wandered aimlessly looking for an outlet that would lead him in the right direction. At nearly every step his frozen feet broke through the hard crust that had formed over the new snow. Periodically he cracked the ice off rocks desperately seeking water that would quench the burning thirst he had developed.

Toward noon he found himself staring down into a great ravine which became lost to view in a sea of low clouds. Turning around, he retraced his steps and headed back in the same direction that he had traveled for the past four hours. As he stumbled along, he became more aware of his hunger, weakened body, and frozen limbs. The lumps of snow and ice that he consumed from time to time afforded him only a temporary relief. Finally, at one spot, when he broke the ice he found a small trickling of water. This became his only luxury that day.

As he approached the area where he had spent the night, he heard a strange clinking sound coming from above him. Looking toward the top of a high bluff, he could see two men outlined against the sky. Again hearing the noise he concluded they were doing some type of work. Though he shouted repeatedly to them against the howling wind, they failed to hear him. Soon they disappeared from view. In his weakened condition he knew it would be futile to make any attempts to reach them. Later he learned that they were two guides whom Colonel Thompson of the Glen House had sent out to search for him.

Cruelly disappointed by this strange experience, he returned to where he had encamped. Upon reaching the flat rock, he observed that the sun would soon disappear from sight and that darkness would once again be upon him.

While he sat on the rock and pondered his next move, thick clouds gathered overhead which indicated that another snowstorm was brewing. Looking at them, he shuddered to think that he had to lie on the cold ground through another long night.

Thinking that he might find a better place where he would suffer less than he had the previous night, he went searching for it. During this time he once again found himself engulfed by heavy swirling snow as the fury of the next snowstorm intensified. It was only with some difficulty that he descended the short distance back to the flat rock that was necessary to his survival.

Fastening his umbrella to the same upturned root, he tried to enclose it better than he had previously. However, because of his swollen and almost useless hands he accomplished very little. Also, before he could crawl in for the night he knew that he had to get some form of water to ease the intolerable thirst that made his throat and stomach feel as though they were on fire.

Gathering up large crusts of snow, he placed them in front of him on the ground and pushed them under the umbrella. He then crawled in and passed the second night much as he had the first.

In the hours ahead he suffered a great deal for a want of water. Every few minutes he bit off a piece of the crust, but it only alleviated his distress while he was swallowing it. He quickly learned that it would not melt fast enough to quench his thirst.

He was also now distressed by being unable to take a full breath. His breathing came in short gasps, and his lungs appeared to only inflate to about half of their natural capacity. He attributed this weakness to the contracting action of the extreme cold on his chest.

In addition to this problem, he experienced a severe pain in his left side which felt as if there was a heavy weight resting there. Due to his deteriorating physical condition, he busied himself periodically by taking his pulse. He accomplished this by pressing his left hand against his right wrist. He found it to be nearly a third less than was natural for him. Despite his circumstances, this told him that if he did not fall asleep he would live to see another day.

As before, he fought off sleep by a constant variation in strained positions and by a multiplicity of thoughts. First he thought of the many agreeable acquaintances he had made in various parts of the world. This was followed by thoughts of friends at home and abroad from whom he had received favors, kindnesses, and many different types of hospitality. Then, as his frail covering quivered and bent from the strength of the wind that was screeching just over his head, he thought of the important part his umbrella had played in his preservation. He then realized how different everything would have been had the rain ceased before he began his climb, and if he had left it behind.

As the night wore on he also came to realize that his body had become so numb that he was no longer subject to the tremblings he had suffered from earlier. In fact, the sensation of cold was now succeeded by a kind of soothing glow which was working its way through every nerve and fibre of his being. Recognizing the danger this posed, he fought off his desire to sleep by making extra exertions.

The long night once again passed, and with the coming of daylight he at first resisted leaving his shelter in order to rest a little longer on his cold hard bed. Before long he gave up that idea, and crawled out from under the umbrella. As he emerged out in the open, he was amazed to see a building off in the distance below him.

Crawling to the front of the rock, he sat on it to ponder what house could be seen on this side of the mountain. Without realizing it, he was actually looking down on the Glen House where his painful journey had begun three days earlier.

Next, as he had done the day before, he supported himself against the rock and began to stamp his feet to restore the circulation. However, because his weakness was now much greater, he had to stop every few minutes to rest. Finally, after two draining hours, he was finally able to walk.

Tottering and slipping, he climbed a short distance looking for a clear view that would help to determine the direction he would take on this day. He knew that there was no longer any room for further error.

Since the house he was seeing was several miles off and on the far end of a large forest, he decided to go in the opposite direction to avoid getting lost in the woods. Starting off, he walked slowly and

The Short Adventurous Life of Dr. Benjamin Ball

unsteadily while bracing himself against nearby rocks until he could gain better use of his frozen feet and hands. He frequently stopped to break off pieces of ice from the rocks to ease the pain of his unending thirst.

As he stumbled along he found that it was difficult to hold his body erect, and that he was inclined to stoop forward like a man who was bowed down by age. Though he often raised himself upright, soon he was back in the same bent posture. He then thought of how long he had been without food, drink, or sleep, and the fact that he had constantly been exposed to extreme cold.

Due to the ferocity of the winter storms and sub-zero temperatures on Mount Washington, the buildings become encased in thick coats of snow and ice. Following his exposure to the elements there in October of 1855, Dr. Ball wrote: "It ought to be known to all that the two summit houses are closed by the middle of September each year, when the proprietors leave, and do not again return until the next June."

With the aid of the cane, and by placing his left hand on the rocks, he hobbled on hoping that each step was bringing him to the outlet.

Toward the middle of the day he rested upon a large flat rock to plot his next direction. He had just decided to move up a hundred feet higher in order to keep the house below in view, when to his joy and astonishment he saw a party of men coming into sight around the angle of a nearby bluff.

As six of them came into view he could see that they were carrying long poles. They appeared to be looking for something. Not realizing that they were searching for his body, Dr. Ball shouted to them. They stopped and stared at him in amazement and disbelief.

This scene of a winter storm on the summit of Mount Washington by engraver R. Schelling, which was published in 1882, dramatically illustrated what the two terrible nights must have been like for Dr. Benjamin Ball who had no more than his umbrella for a shelter during his ordeal. When found, he was famished, exhausted, and almost delirious.

Joseph S. Hall, who only a month earlier had helped to carry Lizzie Bourne's body to the Glen House, was the first to approach him. In a tone of doubt he asked, "Is this Dr. Ball?"

When Dr. Ball answered that he was, Hall further asked, "Are you the person who left the Glen House Wednesday afternoon to walk up on the new road?"

Dr. Ball again answered him in the affirmative.

Realizing that the whole situation was incredible, Hall also asked him, "And have you been out on the Mountain since that time?"

Dr. Ball assured him that he had.

Hall then exclaimed, "It is very wonderful! Why, how could you preserve yourself all this time? You had nothing to eat and nothing

This small one-story building, known as the Camp House at the time of Dr. Ball's ordeal, was located halfway to the summit of Mount Washington. During his initial ascent, Dr. Ball was forced to spend the night here after his clothes became encased in ice. It was also here that Mr. Myers welcomed him "back from the dead" three days later.

to drink! And you can stand!"

Dr. Ball was then told that men had been out looking for him since the day before. Hall informed him that the men with him were all experienced guides who were now out in search of him, and that they were Francis Smith, J.J. Davis, Thomas Culhane, Patrick Culhane and an Irishman named Thomas.

Dr. Ball inquired if anyone had been looking for him on the high bluff the previous afternoon. Francis Smith told him that he and another man had been there, and that the wind had been blowing very hard. This confirmed Dr. Ball's belief that this was why they did not respond to his shouts.

Unable to endure his thirst any longer, he then asked them for a drink. He was distressed to learn that they were not carrying liquid in any form. With the best of intentions, one man handed him a piece of gingerbread. However, it was impossible for him to swallow it. Besides, he had little desire for food.

After wretching from what little gingerbread he had placed in his dry mouth, Dr. Ball threw his arms around the necks of two of the men and he was helped along the path toward the Camp House. When they came to a rock that had a small hollow in the top, he got some relief from the two swallows of water that it provided.

Since the party was able to work its way down the mountain at a good pace, they soon arrived at the Camp House. After Mr. Myers welcomed Dr. Ball "back from the dead," he told him, "I know that you have had a severe trial. During your first night out, the water in a bowl here was frozen thick in a room adjoining one which had a fire going."

He also told him, "Towards night of that first day I went up on the Ledge, and while standing and looking to see if you were not yet coming I froze both of my heels. And such a night of anxiety I never wish to pass again! All night long the storm beat down upon the house. Since I could not sleep I spent the night walking to and fro and looking out the door. And how, thought I, must it be for you on the mountain, and during the whole of that long night?"

A short time later, when Dr. Ball's boots were removed, both feet were found to be frozen. They were immediately plunged into cold water until the frost was removed. At this time he also attempted to drink a cup of warm tea, but his stomach rejected it. Cold water, which he craved, was the only liquid that he could retain.

After his feet and badly swollen hands were wrapped in flannel, he was placed on a gentle horse named Tom. With a man walking on each side, he was brought down the Carriage Road to Colonel Thompson who was waiting for him with horses and a carriage. Thompson had been notified by means of signal flags that Dr. Ball had been found. He watched the descent by telescope.

Welcoming Dr. Ball back, he said, "You have been through what no other person has, or probably will again in a thousand years."

After the party arrived at the Glen House at about five o'clock that afternoon, Dr. Ball was made as comfortable as possible. When asked what he would like first for nourishment, he asked for a little hot cordial. Next he drank a small quantity of gruel to which milk was added. This was fed to him at intervals of an hour along with occasional swallows of water.

This is the Glen House in Green's Grant where Dr. Ball spent the first week of his recovery following his harrowing ordeal on Mount Washington. Originally a public house owned by John Bellow, this is the way it looked after Colonel Joseph M. Thompson purchased it and made substantial additions.

(Photo courtesy of Dick Hamilton)

A short time later, when Colonel Thompson was about to send an errand boy to Gorham for the mail, he asked Dr. Ball if he had any communication he would like to make. Dr. Ball requested that a few lines be sent to his brothers in Boston informing them of his accident and of his improving condition.

Through the first few hours following his return, though he was strengthened by the care he was receiving, his hands and feet remained greatly swollen and turned a sickly black. Their appearance led his caregivers to conclude that all vitality in them was lost. The sense of feeling was also gone, and they seemed to be no more than cold clay attached to his limbs. Both his right foot and right hand were also found to be more severely frozen than their opposite counterpart.

Dr. Ball suggested that his hosts apply a poultice of flaxseed meal along with oil and charcoal, but Joseph Hall, who had experience with frozen limbs, recommended a poultice of charred hickory leaves that were pulverized and simmered with fresh lard. Since Dr. Ball had no objection to this treatment, once the poultice was cooled it was laid on his hands and feet and enclosed with large cloths.

Since Dr. Ball had now been without sleep for close to eighty hours, toward nine o'clock that evening he began to experience a strong desire to do just that. Hall remained in the room with him, and during the night he aroused him from an extremely deep slumber several times as a precautionary measure.

For the first few days following his rescue, Dr. Ball's sufferings were comparatively light. Dr. Wardwell of Gorham attended him, as did his brother, Dr. A. Ball of Boston. At this time he ran a slight fever, and his severe dehydration required that he be given water often during the day and every half hour at night. Then, beginning at his feet, slight chills frequently ran through his body causing his whole nervous system to vibrate. His feet, still without feeling, remained distorted by swelling and became covered with water blisters. About the ankles, and just above his injuries, the pain grew quite severe. When cramps finally set in, for the first few minutes he found the pain quite excruciating. Though his hands ached and burned day and night, under the circumstances he still felt that he was comfortably well off.

After remaining at the Glen House for a week, he then made preparations to return home. By means of a sofa placed in the carriage, on the day of his departure he was able to ride comfortably to Gorham. Once aboard the train he reclined all the way to Boston. Arriving there that evening, he was met by his brothers and conveyed to the American House.

Four months after his ordeal he was remarkably recovered from it. His hands were nearly well, with no loss except for a single nail from one finger. As for his feet, he was able to use them in moderation. With the coming of cold weather, however, he found them to be much more sensitive to the cold than they had been previously.

Tragically, having survived this ordeal, he died four years later on December 11, 1859, at the age of 39 in the Chiriquy region of Panama. According to the news account detailing his death, he had not enjoyed vigorous health following his dramatic exposure to the elements on Mount Washington. In this respect, the account stated, "In order to avoid the rigors of our New England climate this past winter, he made a visit to Central America. He intended to return early next spring, and to establish a medical practice in Brooklyn, New York."

The account further noted, "While in Central America he made explorations amid the striking volcanic scenery of the Chiriquy Province. During the temporary absence of his traveling companions he started from Bocas del Toro in a canoe with a Spanish sailor. He wanted to examine a stream that was rich with fish. Unfortunately they were exposed all night to a sudden rain which induced a severe bilious fever in Dr. Ball. Faithfully attended in a neighboring village by the sailor, he was in full possession of his faculties almost to the hour of his death which occurred some ten days after the attack began."

A sad irony, to say the least, this is how the short adventurous life of Dr. Benjamin Lincoln Ball ended. And, as Joseph Hall once wrote to Dr. Ball's brother in Boston following his rescue on Mount Washington, "There is nothing in the history of the White Mountains to compare with this case of your brother; and I am sure its parallel will not be known in time to come."

To this day it remains a truly unique experience.